Counselling

Aileen Milne

TEACH YOURSELF BOOKS

For UK orders: please contact Bookpoint Ltd, 130 Milton Park, Abingdon, Oxon OX14 4SB. Telephone: (44) 01235 400414, Fax: (44) 01235 400454. Lines are open from 9.00–6.00, Monday to Saturday, with a 24 hour message answering service. Email address: orders@bookpoint.co.uk

For USA & Canada orders: please contact NTC/Contemporary Publishing, 4255 West Touhy Avenue, Lincolnwood, Illinois 60646–1975, USA. Telephone: (847) 679 5500, Fax: (847) 679 2494.

Long renowned as the authoritative source for self-guided learning – with more than 30 million copies sold worldwide – the *Teach Yourself* series includes over 200 titles in the fields of languages, crafts, hobbies, business and education.

A catalogue entry for this title is available from The British Library.

Library of Congress Catalog Card Number: On file

First published in UK 1999 by Hodder Headline Plc, 338 Euston Road, London NW1 3BH.

First published in US 1999 by NTC/Contemporary Publishing, 4255 West Touhy Avenue, Lincolnwood (Chicago), Illinois 60646–1975, USA.

Typeset by Transet Limited, Coventry, England.
Printed in Great Britain for Hodder & Stoughton Educational, a division of Hodder Headline Plc, 338 Euston Road, London NW1 3BH by Cox & Wyman Ltd, Reading, Berkshire.

Impression number   10 9 8 7 6 5 4
Year   2005 2004 2003 2002 2001

CONTENTS

Introduction _____ **vii**

Acknowledgements _____ **x**

Part One – The Fundamentals _____ **1**

1 | The Counselling Role _____ **1**

Psychotherapy and counselling: where they
   differ and where they converge _____ 2
The counselling role _____ 5
Those who seek out counselling _____ 7
The active listener _____ 9
The counsellor–client relationship _____ 9
Ways in which a counsellor's role differs from
   that of a friend _____ 12
Acquiring skills for personal use _____ 15

2 | The Counsellor's Role _____ **16**

Qualities of a counsellor _____ 16
Creating core conditions _____ 19
Acceptance and self-development _____ 20
Life experience _____ 21
What do you want to get out of counselling? ____ 22
The emotional demands and rewards of personal
   growth _____ 24

3 | The Benefits of Acquiring Counselling Skills _ **27**

The use of communication skills in personal
   relationships _____ 27
Self-indulgence or a developmental stage? _____ 29
Uses of counselling skills in work settings _____ 32

4 | Skills Used in Counselling _____ **43**
Sharpening our awareness _____ 43
Use of questions _____ 44
Use of empathy _____ 49
Awareness of body language _____ 51
Reflecting skills _____ 54
More advanced skills _____ 60
How skills can be applied to personal and work
  situations _____ 70

5 | Practice Makes You Competent _____ **72**
Forms of practice _____ 72
Singular exercises _____ 72
Practising with others _____ 75
Role play _____ 78
The role of observer _____ 79

6 | Enjoying the Exploration _____ **86**
Attending workshops _____ 86
Visualization _____ 87
Assertiveness training _____ 92
Stress management _____ 94
Meditation _____ 97
Dreams _____ 99

**Part Two – A Deeper Understanding –
Training to a Professional Level** _____ **103**

7 | Course Components _____ **103**
Background _____ 103
Choosing a course _____ 104
Key course components _____ 105
Developing self-awareness _____ 108
Supervision _____ 111
Theory and practice _____ 115
Personal therapy _____ 116
Exams and on-going assessment _____ 116
Integrationism _____ 119
Professional considerations _____ 122

8 │ The Three Major Approaches _____ **124**

Section 1: The Psychodynamic Approach _____ 124

The unconscious _____ 125

Developmental psychology _____ 128

Transference and countertransference _____ 137

Resistances and defences _____ 143

Aim of therapy _____ 145

Role of the counsellor: the therapeutic relationship _ 145

C.G. Jung _____ 147

Section 2: The Humanistic/Person-Centred Approach _ 151

The person-centred approach _____ 153

The Rogerian core conditions model _____ 153

The person-centred view of the person _____ 156

The therapeutic relationship _____ 159

Qualities of the counsellor _____ 162

Aims of therapy _____ 163

Process of change _____ 164

Section 3: The Behavioural/Cognitive-behavioural
  Model _____ 167

Origins _____ 167

Operant and classical conditioning _____ 168

Characteristics, techniques and applications _____ 170

Who and what problems behavioural therapy
  can help _____ 172

The therapist _____ 175

The therapeutic relationship _____ 179

Cognitive-behavioural approaches _____ 180

9 │ Demystifying the Jargon _____ **189**

The defences _____ 190

Other terms _____ 197

10 │ Dealing with Anger _____ **203**

Anger and the trainee counsellor _____ 203

A gestalt method _____ 207

Appropriate and inappropriate expression of anger _ 209

Working with a video _____ 212

The psychodynamic perspective _____ 214

11 | Underlying Issues _____ **218**
Grief _____ 218
Normalizing the grief _____ 221
Depression _____ 225
The letter and the empty chair technique _____ 226
The suicidal client _____ 228
Some of the reasons and situations of suicidal
   intention _____ 230
How can a counsellor help? _____ 233
Self-harm _____ 234
Issues of control _____ 234
Anger and depression _____ 235
Who self-harms? _____ 236
What can help the counsellor _____ 238
Abuse _____ 240
Confidentiality and client disclosure _____ 241
Trust _____ 243
Power issues _____ 244
An integrative approach _____ 245

12 | Cultural Issues _____ **248**
Background _____ 248
The concept of culture _____ 248
Family, community and gender roles _____ 251
Skills _____ 252
The therapeutic relationship _____ 253
A creative integrative approach _____ 259
Concept of self _____ 259
Institutionalized racism _____ 262
Summary _____ 265

Resources _____ **266**
Contact details _____ 266
Visual aids resources _____ 268

Suggested Further Reading _____ **269**

INTRODUCTION

Teach Yourself Counselling introduces various aspects of counselling with the aim of presenting the reader with an overview of the main themes, theories, skills and applications of one-to-one counselling. There is a large amount of literature available on the subject of counselling and it can be intimidating to the person who is interested but not sure where to start. People have asked me what kind of counselling I do. In the early days I would launch into an explanation about psychodynamic or integrative, only to realize that the person was more puzzled than ever. It became apparent that information like this was meaningless unless a person had a basic understanding of counselling skills and the role of a counsellor. Contrary to the beliefs of some, counselling does not solely consist of being listened to by a benevolent figure who is passively sympathetic. The counsellor is a skilled, active listener who relates to others with a view to helping them with what they find unsatisfactory about their lives and what they want to change and are willing to work at changing.

The material covered may interest those who think they might like to have counselling but wonder what it involves or if it would be of any use to them. Many people turn to counselling at times of difficulty in their lives when they feel overwhelmed by problems or situations. They feel unhappy and vulnerable and it follows that an enormous amount of trust, hope and expectations may be placed on the counsellor and on the healing capabilities of counselling, yet most of us enter into the counsellor–client relationship without knowing anything much about counselling on any level.

This book also informs the individual who would like to learn about counselling skills with a view to communicating with others more effectively, both in the workplace and in their private lives.

While writing the book I also had in mind the person who has already begun training or is interested in training as a counsellor.

The book covers a broad spectrum and is comprised of two parts. It begins simply, by focusing on the roles of counselling and on the counsellor. Skills and the core conditions of the person-centred approach are introduced and discussed in relation to their use in other areas of life outside counselling. Simple skills exercises are suggested as a means of developing powers of observation and attentiveness. The first part concludes with Chapter 6, 'Enjoying the Exploration', which suggests methods of self-development and reflection which complement the aims and beliefs of counselling and prepare the individual for helping others.

The second part of the book takes the reader a stage further into the theories, concepts and techniques of counselling. It addresses the person who has embarked on training or who is interested in becoming a counsellor in a voluntary or a professional capacity and begins by looking at course components. Material in this section includes an outline of the three main approaches to counselling; that is, the psychodynamic approach which originates from the psychoanalytic model; the person-centred approach which represents the humanistic model and the behavioural/cognitive-behavioural approach. Therapeutic jargon is highlighted and explained. Other technical terms are explained in context throughout the text. Where topics are touched on rather than gone into in any depth, then further reading is suggested (see page 269) to enable the reader to follow up their interest and build a deeper understanding. It has been my intention to write as clearly and simply as the subject that I am writing about allows.

I am a practising counsellor. I have a professional diploma in counselling. My own training began at an agency within the voluntary sector. The training I received there was intensive and personally demanding. It concentrated on the psychodynamic way of working with unconscious processes and transference. I read books on counselling and psychotherapy and embarked on personal therapy which gave me the experience of being a client. However, as good as the relatively short training was, I believe that the true learning of how to be a counsellor with a client began, for me, with my first session with a client. At that point I moved from learning about counselling to actually doing it; that is, being with a person who came to me for help in dealing with their life problems.

Sometimes newly trained counsellors are thrown in at the deep end and find themselves working with issues that they are unprepared for: the angry client, the client who discloses that they have suffered abuse, the client who feels suicidal, the grieving client or the person who self-harms. Chapters 10 and 11 deal with these subjects and Chapter 12 looks at the particular concerns of working with cultural difference.

The intention is that these chapters will go some way towards demonstrating that we learn fundamentally how to be with our clients (or those whom we hope to help) from the clients themselves – if we listen, attend and respond appropriately. These subjects are introduced to provide insight into the challenges which are inherent to the work. Self-responsibility and the development of personal resources are central themes and goals of counselling which apply equally to the counsellor. The later chapters refer to how experienced counsellors may work with their clients, offering guidelines. As we shall explore in the book, many counsellors work integratively – blending two or more approaches. Counselling is a continual learning process about ourselves, about other individuals and – in the larger picture – about human psychology. Each encounter between two people is unique and what a counsellor brings to counselling as an individual is also unique.

Finally, where case studies have been included, care has been taken to protect the anonymity of the client.

This book is dedicated to my mother Georgina May.

Acknowledgements

Thanks to the following publishers for granting the permission to use material for which they hold copyright: Constable & Co. Ltd (UK and Commonwealth rights), for extracts from text by Carl Rogers: *On Becoming a Person* and *The Carl Rogers Reader*, edited by Howard Kirschenbaum and Valerie Land Henderson; for copyright permission for US material see Sterling Lord Literistic Inc.;

Blandford Press for material used from *Wake Up to Your Dreams* by Linda Sheppard; Butterworths for permission to use extracts from *Individual Psychotherapy and the Science of Psychodynamics* by David H. Malan; Penguin UK (UK and Commonwealth rights) and Harper Collins Publishers (US rights) for permission to include material from *Carl Rogers on Encounter Groups* by Carl Rogers; Hodder and Stoughton for the use of material from *Teach Yourself Visualisation* by Pauline Wills and *Teach Yourself Meditation* by Naomi Ozaniec; The British Association for Counselling Publications for material used from *Counselling*, the Journal of the BAC; Sage Publications Ltd for material used from *Transcultural Counselling in Action* by Patricia d'Ardenne and Aruna Mahtani (1989) and from Dr Patricia d'Ardenne for same; Ubaldini Editore for permission to reproduce material from *Transpersonal Development: The Dimension Beyond Psychosynthesis* by Roberto Assagioli MD; The Random House Group Ltd (UK and Commonwealth rights) and W.W. Norton, New York (US rights) for permission for material used from *Childhood and Society* by Erik Erikson; Brooks/Cole Publications Co. a division of Wadsworth Inc. for an extract from *The Skilled Helper* by Gerard Egan; The University of California Press for material from *The Johari Window: A Graphic Model of Interpersonal Relations* by Jo Luft and Harry Ingham; Houghton Mifflin & Co. for permisison to use an extract from *A Way of Being* by Carl Rogers; Open University Press for material from *An Introduction to Counselling* by John McLeod.

Every effort has been made to trace the correct copyright holder, but if any have been inadvertently overlooked the publisher will be pleased to make the necessary arrangements at the first opportunity.

Thanks also to Morowa Selassie, Roy Radcliffe and Diana Harrison for their contributions. Also a special thanks to Trisha Ledeboer for word-processing the manuscript and to Jill Birch and Jenny Knight for editing and preparing the manuscript for publication.

1 | THE COUNSELLING ROLE

Counselling is a diverse activity which takes many forms: people may receive counselling individually, or have couple counselling or family counselling – in which the dynamics between family members will be the focus of the work. The capacity and setting in which counsellors work also varies, ranging from a few hours a week doing voluntary work with an agency or organization to working privately in a professional practice. Some counselling involves working with particular client groups – examples are student counselling and marriage counselling; and some focus on particular problems – for example, medical conditions like cancer or AIDS or social problems like alcohol or drug abuse. To add to the complexity, there are many 'schools' of counselling which are informed by their own particular theoretical frameworks. These can, however, be identified and understood by the three core approaches of **behavioural**, **analytical** and **humanistic** perspectives which will be explored in subsequent chapters.

Given that there has been a proliferation of counselling activity in the past twenty years or so in Western societies, it seems likely that counselling is fulfilling a need which was in the past met by other means. People in the community – family members, neighbours, friends, local doctors and clergy – formed emotional and social support systems for individuals.

Many of us no longer live in supportive communities bound together by religious faith and beliefs; we live in fragmented societies alienated from our surroundings and each other. Our world horizons have expanded; the cities where many of us live are large and impersonal. Perhaps in seeking counselling we attempt to repersonalize our lives. We take our problems to a place where we feel we will be listened to and where our thoughts and feelings are regarded as important. The meaning and role of counselling is ever evolving to meet the challenges of modern social pressures and demands which we often attempt to deal with at cost to our inner world. The role of counselling has been defined by its aims and values. Aims include providing an environment that enables the client to work towards living in a more resourceful and personally fulfilling way. Integrity, respect and impartiality are basic values which are demonstrated throughout the counselling process.

We enter into a counselling relationship when we engage the help of a counsellor in mutual agreement. No one can be forced into a counselling–client relationship; a person chooses to have counselling, otherwise it is not counselling at all. The activity of counselling has been defined in many ways. The following are some of the ways in which it is believed to help people resolve problems or help people live their lives in a more insightful, fulfilling way. Counselling can help people:

- to clarify what is important to them in their lives;
- to get in touch with their inner resources;
- in the exploration of feelings, thoughts and meanings particular to them;
- by offering support at times of crisis;
- by offering support during developmental and transitional periods;
- to work through 'stuck' issues – this may involve integrating childhood experiences;
- to reach a resolution of problems.

Psychotherapy and counselling: where they differ and where they converge

The terms **counselling**, **psychotherapy** and **therapy** often seem to be used in an interchangeable way, their differences unclear to the uninitiated. In particular, the use of the term 'therapy' is widespread. A dictionary of psychology definition of therapy would include the words: 'treatment of disease or disorder' and 'to make better'. If we look at the word in two parts, *dis* and *ease*, we see that it refers to the state of a person who is no longer at ease with themselves in their physical and/or psychological state. Therapy when applied to counselling is a process which hopefully 'makes better' by helping the person it relates to to identify and work on the areas of disorder and dis-ease in their lives that cause problems or distress.

The word 'therapy' has come to be a generic term used to describe something that is helpful or nurturing in some way or that gives relief from the strains of everyday life, hence such terms as 'retail therapy'. It is also used as an abbreviated form of 'psychotherapy'. The word 'therapist' is used likewise as an abbreviated form of 'psychotherapist', but many counsellors also refer to themselves as therapists.

Similarities between psychotherapy and counselling

Psychotherapy and counselling are regarded as separate professions. They have their own professional associations which safeguard the interests of both clients and practitioners. Among the functions that these professional associations serve is the accreditation of training courses and the accreditation of individual practitioners.

Although they have separate identities in the field of therapy, it is a widely held view that there is a lot of overlap between the two. Both use a similar theoretical framework of reference; the same training materials, books and resources are used on courses. This is particularly true when courses are based around the same theoretical 'school' or approach; for example, person centred or psychodynamic. A person may reach professional status as either a person-centred counsellor or a psychotherapist, yet their fundamental differences are unclear. The humanistic psychologist Carl Rogers, for example, made no clear distinction between the two titles, sometimes referring to himself as a counsellor and at other times as a psychotherapist. Members of both professions work in similar settings in medical and health centres, doctors' surgeries and clinics, which can add to the confusion. The therapist and writer Wyndy Dryden, discussing the difference between the two titles in *Self and Society*, a humanistic psychology journal, jokes that the main difference is: 'About £8,000 a year.' He states that he finds difficulty in making clear distinctions between the two activities.

In *Ordinary Ecstasy*, John Rowan states, 'Every technique which is used in personal growth and in counselling is also used in psychotherapy and vice versa.'

Differences between psychotherapy and counselling

Length and depth of training

There are a few differences which can be identified at training level. Psychotherapy usually involves longer training. It is possible to obtain a certificate in counselling within a few months and a diploma in a year. There is a lack of regularity in awarding such titles; many courses demand three years' part-time study to reach diploma level. This variance in length, and presumably depth of training to reach the same status of qualification, brings up ethical issues of standards. It is obviously important for the consumer – the client – to check out what the counsellor's qualifications and experience are when embarking on therapy.

Whereas to obtain professional level a counsellor would most likely be expected to train for a period of two to three years part-time, a psychotherapist would have spent a minimum of three years and often longer in training. Psychotherapy training often incorporates a year of working in a health care setting or private practice towards the end of the course, providing case study material for assessment.

Origins

Psychotherapy originates from Freudian psychoanalysis, and because of this some psychotherapists hold the view that it is only appropriate to use the term in relation to its Freudian roots, distinguishing it from counselling. It is difficult, however, to make clear-cut distinctions because the psychodynamic approach to counselling is also steeped in Freudian concepts and theory, its central theoretical focus being the unconscious and transference. Counselling has emerged in the context of marriage guidance, pastoral care, educational settings and voluntary organizations, and has subsequently developed into private practice.

Length of treatment

It is generally thought that psychotherapists work long term with clients while counsellors tend to work short term, or in crisis situations. There are no hard and fast rules. Counselling can incorporate both short- and long-term ways of working; it at times begins with a short-term focus and for various reasons results in long-term therapy. Long-term counselling is common and, conversely, it is not uncommon for psychotherapists to offer 'brief psychotherapy'. Often the two activities are indistinguishable from each other, especially when the practitioners are very experienced. In some situations practitioners are restricted by the limited resources of their workplace; it may be deemed more satisfactory to offer six to eight weeks' therapy to a number of people rather than long-term therapy to only a few.

Depth of work

The extended training of the psychotherapist is designed to equip them to work in more depth with clients. However, although this is used as a focus of training, it is not always the case that psychotherapists exclusively cater for the client with more difficulties. It does seem true to say, as a general rule, that while the counsellor sees a client once a week for a single session, the psychotherapist may see a client two or more times in a week.

Personal therapy for trainees

Both professions require trainees to have personal therapy for the duration of the course. A psychotherapist in training, who is expecting to see individual clients two or more times a week, is usually required by the conditions of their course to have the corresponding amount of personal therapy throughout the training. The same applies to the counsellor who is training with a view to seeing individuals once a week; they too will require personal therapy once a week for the duration of the course, although this requirement does not necessarily apply to courses of short duration.

The counselling role

Counselling can take many forms:

- doctors refer patients to counsellors who practise alongside them in their surgeries;

- teachers and youth workers will often direct young people to counselling agencies for help;
- counsellors are called to accidents and disaster areas to counsel the victims and their families;
- individuals seek counselling for themselves for all kinds of reasons;
- counselling is used in a variety of settings in education, in pastoral care and, increasingly, in industry too.

The role counselling plays in society is increasingly multifaceted and always supportive. As we go into the twenty-first century counselling seems to be very much a part of our lives, no longer regarded as a luxury or indulgence. Therapy is seen for the most part as a sensible move towards self-care and healing. The majority of us have an open mind about it, taking the view that anything that is nurturing, supportive and self-enlightening is bound to be useful.

Roles within roles

In order that we can make informed choices about in what capacity we would like to get involved in counselling, it is important to make distinctions between the different roles of counselling. What has been described previously, in relation to psychotherapy, was the counsellor who is trained to a professional level. This is the counsellor who works with a doctor, and the counsellor who counsels students in an educational establishment or a social services setting. These counsellors are most likely to be accredited by a national professional counselling association; for example, the British Association for Counselling, the American Counseling Association or the Australian Institute of Professional Counsellors. Accreditation acts as a guarantee to an employer or a client of the qualifications and experience of the practitioner.

Other counsellors, who are not working at a professional level but nevertheless provide a very valuable service, are trained by agencies to offer help in specialized areas such as bereavement, alcohol abuse, drug abuse and race issues. The initial training before the helpers begin to counsel clients is likely to be of comparatively short duration. This is not to say that they are less competent, taking into account the specifics of their work; specialist agencies usually provide their counsellors with excellent on-going training and supervision. These counsellors are likely to be working in the voluntary sector, usually offering one or two days' help to the agency per week. Many people whose interest in counselling began in this way go on to further training to a professional level. Social workers, teachers, youth workers, managers and probation officers who want to be more attuned to the needs of the people they work with are among those who learn counselling skills as an enhancement to the work they already do.

Ways to participate in counselling

To recap, there are three different ways to work in counselling:

1 As a professional, which will require years of study to acquire knowledge of skills, theory and practical experience.
2 By working in the voluntary sector within an organization which will offer training, sometimes in a specialist area.
3 As part of a job, probably using basic skills to enhance communication and listening/responding abilities.

Other uses for acquired counselling skills are personal development and learning how to be an effective supporter of colleagues, family and friends.

Those who seek out counselling

Who goes to counselling?

■ From a counsellor's perspective, are they different from you or me?
■ Are they a certain type of person who is unable to cope as the rest of us do?

The answer to both these questions is usually a simple 'No'. Often the presenting problems clients bring to session are not outside our own life experiences. When they are, the counsellor would be wise to find out as much as possible about the subject or to admit that the client would do better to find a counsellor with expertise in the particular problem – for example, sexual abuse, a serious case of self-harming or a drug habit. There are often underlying problems and issues that are not obvious at first, which will not arise until some time into the therapy when trust and support have been established between counsellor and client. Sometimes an ethical judgement has to be made about whether or not we as counsellors are equipped, through our training and experience, to work at the level required by the severity of the client's problems or the state of their mental health.

The counsellor enters the counselling role as a professional or skilled helper, sufficiently trained, sufficiently self-aware and experienced in the job at hand. It is this efficiency which will allow the client to accept their role and trust the therapeutic counselling relationship.

Problems people take to counselling

As a counsellor I am often asked: 'What kind of problems do people who want counselling have?' I have sometimes wondered if those posing the question do so because they would like to have counselling for some reason but feel that their problem is not somehow 'big enough' to warrant the attention.

People go to counselling for all kinds of reasons, which may be: following a bereavement or a divorce, stress at work or school, depression or low self-esteem. There are many other factors which may leave them feeling alone and overwhelmed with hopelessness.

Some people find they want help with a life transition – for example, both men and women may find moving into the second part of their lives very difficult. We are often told 'Life begins at 40', but many people in their forties reach a crisis of identity or purpose. They feel panic stricken that the dreams of their youth may never be fulfilled. This can be a time, like other times of transition, to take stock, examine and re-evaluate ourselves and aspects of our lives. Another difficult time is the teenage years when we make the transition from childhood proper into the grown-up realms of decision making and responsibility. When an individual seeks counselling it is because they have internal conflicts and pent-up feelings of some form that are spoiling their enjoyment of life.

The active listener

Counsellors are commonly thought of as sympathetic professional 'listening ears'. As I hope will become apparent in the topics we explore in this book, there are many skills involved. A trained and experienced counsellor is adept at active listening. The skills this requires will be covered in a later chapter, but suffice it to say at the moment that the counsellor is far from passive or merely receptive. They are actively involved in giving the client full attention and appropriate responses. This is a lot more complex than it first sounds. Basically, effective counselling employs active listening and empathic responding.

The counsellor–client relationship

Increasingly it is the relationship between the counsellor and client which is seen as crucial to a successful therapeutic process, more so than the counsellor's choice of theoretical background. Therapists like Petrushka Clarkson and Michael Khan see this working relationship as a fundamental determining factor as to how much a client is able to benefit from therapy. In *Between Therapist and Client: The New Relationship*, Khan promotes the integration of the psychodynamic and humanistic models; and Clarkson's *The Therapeutic Relationship* explores 'five modalities' of relationship. The counsellor–client relationship is both complex and simple, like humans themselves. Generally speaking, whatever theories the counsellor is familiar with – many favour an integrated or eclectic approach, working with a few or many theoretical models (see Chapter 8) – the basic requisites are the same. These are that the counsellor provides an environment of privacy, safety and assured confidentiality, is non-defensive and shows respect for the client at all times.

A non-judgemental stance encourages an openness and an understanding to develop. A position of acceptance of the client means that the counsellor can help the client get in touch with their innermost feelings, facilitating the gradual trust in their own inner resources. No therapist can ever take away painful experiences which have happened in a person's life but they can help another to acknowledge and understand what they have gone through, helping them to work through complex feelings they have experienced in the past, or are presently feeling, so that hopefully in time the client can move forward. By their warm, accepting attitude towards clients, counsellors are conveying: 'I accept you; given what has happened to you in your life it is understandable that you should feel the way you do or that you have behaved the way you have behaved.' This is not token blanket approval of everything a client has felt or done, but rather an empathic response, as if having walked in their shoes and felt what they have felt. The 'as if' stance is necessary to sustain because the counsellor would be of no use at all in the client's self-understanding and growth if the helper could not maintain a separate self from the client in the professional 'holding' role.

Non-directive counselling

Most counsellors will not offer advice or tell the client what they should do, or take advantage in any way of the client who is, after all, in a vulnerable position. Some forms of counselling are more directive or goal orientated than others but none the less the counsellor would never tell the client what to do, rather they would help clients to identify and clarify areas in their lives that they want to change and also help clients to tap into their own resources regarding solutions. This is a different stance from that of giving advice or setting an agenda designed by the counsellor. The non-directive position respects the autonomy of the individual and their innate ability to find their own solutions.

The working alliance

The working alliance is, as it sounds, the agreement and established framework of the work that is mutually undertaken. In order that the client can place trust in their chosen counsellor, a framework needs to be established at the onset in which both client and counsellor are in agreement about the ways in which they will work together. This helps the client, to a certain degree, to know what to expect and helps establish continuity and trust. When the counsellor and the client agree to enter into a working relationship, they enter into a contract (which can be either verbal or written). The client is asked at the onset what they may be hoping for from the counselling, what their expectations may be. The counsellor will inform the prospective client of the service they can offer and give details of their training and way of working. The initial meeting is very important; both the client and counsellor are assessing whether or not they think they could work together.

The fifty-minute therapy hour

Usually a counsellor will agree to see a client for fifty minutes once a week in the same room, in the premises they are working from. Why, you may ask, fifty minutes, as opposed to an hour? It has been my experience that not all counsellors work to fifty minutes per session, some prefer to have hourly sessions. The fifty-minute session is common to agencies where a counsellor may be seeing quite a few clients in a day. It has become a tradition, allowing fifty minutes of undivided attention for the client followed by a minimum of ten minutes' break for the counsellor when they may make a few confidential notes about what went on in the session or to have a few minutes to relax between seeing clients.

Confidentiality

A confidential setting provides the client with safety and privacy. Any limitation of these requirements may affect the counselling relationship adversely.

In some senses the term 'confidentiality' is a misnomer since the term means 'entrusted with secrets'. Some secrets may be dangerous to the client or others and it would be irresponsible for the counsellor to hold on to these. A practising counsellor needs to be aware of legal obligations and agency policies regarding, for example, cases of physical or sexual abuse when legal requirements may demand that confidential information is made available. Counsellors may be required by laws, regulations or institution procedures to create and maintain records, and they need to be aware of the inherent responsibilities, whether records are written, computerized or stored in any other form. The client needs to be informed of any conditions and limitations of confidentiality at the onset of counselling. It is also advisable to inform a client of the procedures in effect to ensure their anonymity. Generally the practice of agencies is that when a client ceases to have counselling, then any notes the counsellor may have made during the therapy are destroyed, but records may be stored for a specified period of time. To ensure the privacy of the client, they are often given a number or their initials are used on forms rather than the full name. The same procedures can be agreed to in the initial intake sessions when working within a private practice.

Ways in which a counsellor's role differs from that of a friend

A friend by the very nature of the relationship has a vested interest. Something told to a friend may be embarrassing, shocking or hurtful to them. It may be something they feel ill equipped to deal with, or involve mixed loyalties. Also, with friends we sometimes assume a certain kind of persona which we feel is acceptable to them; for example, a mask that says: 'I am a person who can cope with anything life throws at me' when we wish others to believe that nothing fazes us; or another – which can be the most detrimental of all to our self-awareness and development, 'I am always a helpful and kind person.' How can we then confide in a friend that we are not coping at all, or tell them that we are feeling pretty murderous towards some people at the moment, including them?

Confidentiality and a friend

A friend may agree not to tell anyone else something that is said in confidence but later, in a moment of weakness, or because they think it may be best to tell another for whatever reason, may go ahead and divulge a sacred secret. The feelings of betrayal can be damaging to both individuals and their friendship.

To be in a position to help, a friend or family member needs to be aware of these and other possible pitfalls. The danger is that as an unskilled helper we leap in at times where angels would fear to tread, realizing too late that we are ill equipped and unable to cope with such a responsible position. The fact that we are emotionally involved with the person need not, however, be a drawback, as we will be exploring in a later chapter.

But first in order that we can appreciate:

- ■ what can go wrong when unskilled helpers take on the task of helping;
- ■ what a counsellor can offer someone who can't confide in those close to them

let's look at a couple of hypothetical case studies.

Case study 1 – Telling a friend

A young woman who I will call Donna has recently discovered that she is pregnant. She is 17; her relationship with her boyfriend, the father of her unborn child, is not stable. He has been violent towards her on more than one occasion and although he is very young himself he is a married man. Donna is beside herself with worry and confides in a close friend one night when she has had a drink. Donna has not told anyone else. Her parents do not know about her relationship with this man. The friend promises not to tell anyone, but tells Donna she should have an abortion or her life will be ruined, and that she should ditch the man as soon as possible. These comments, although said out of genuine concern and affection for the girl, have the effect of panicking her even more. Donna's friend, seeing her increasingly upset, confides in another friend, who tells her own mother, who then tells Donna's mother. All those concerned are well meaning but such snowballing effects can limit a person's choices. When she is confronted by her mother, Donna feels embarrassed, guilty and shameful. She wants to end her parents' anguish and therefore is in the position that she is likely to do anything those close to her are in favour of, including having an abortion, rather than thinking and feeling what the best plan of action is for herself.

This is not suggesting that all parents would automatically be dictatorial and insist on their daughter having an abortion in this situation or that they would necessarily skim over what the girl needs. This example is chosen to differentiate between confiding in someone close to us and the associated pitfalls, and taking our problems to a counsellor.

Working with a counsellor

The counsellor may be emotionally attuned to the client within the therapeutic relationship but not emotionally involved in the sense that their emotions interfere with the process. They are not there to offer advice in the sense of telling someone what to do but rather to help the client find out what they want to do; what will work for them. In Donna's situation, the issues that the counsellor might help her focus on are: her feelings about being pregnant, how she feels about the possibility of becoming a mother, the impact this may have on her life, what she feels towards her boyfriend and the sense of loneliness and other emotions she may presently be experiencing, as well as looking at the various options open to her. Obviously in this case some information and guidance may be appropriate as Donna has only a few weeks in which to decide which is the best outcome for her.

Case study 2

A middle-aged man, who I will call Colin, has come for counselling because he feels that he is not coping at the moment. He hasn't told anyone that he has sought help for himself in the form of counselling because it is a source of shame for him to admit that he doesn't feel in control of his life and he feels he needs help. Colin was made redundant six months ago and although he has been trying to establish himself as a freelance worker, prospective clients are prejudiced towards his age. At 52 years of age Colin is feeling a failure – a 'has been' with no useful future. Exacerbating the situation, his wife's mother has died recently and because Colin had been feeling depressed himself he has felt unable to be of comfort to his wife. Consequently, she has become increasingly withdrawn. His son too has his own problems with his marriage and, besides, Colin has never been one to confide in others, friends or family. He has always been the stoic provider, the reliable father and husband, and he is now feeling without a role in life. As a person who has rarely shown his emotions, he is now feeling 'all at sea'. In this frame of mind there really isn't anyone Colin feels he can share his feelings of inadequacy with. The image he thought others perceived him as having was virtually all he had left to bolster his sinking self-esteem.

Taking these presenting problems to counselling

Colin felt that he had nothing to lose by going to counselling. He had no image to live up to there. He could explore his feelings of inadequacy, shame and depression and growing sense of hopelessness. With the help of his counsellor he was able to talk about his fears: of ageing, of feeling that he was of no use to anyone, of perhaps in future being unable to look after himself even. Many issues came to the fore for Colin as he thought about his childhood and his overbearing father's expectations of him. He began to be aware of patterns in his life. He began to understand why he had always felt compelled to be an achiever and why he could not express or even access his emotions readily.

Acquiring skills for personal use

An understanding of basic counselling skills can be useful to any relationship. This doesn't mean that by acquiring a few skills you will be able to eradicate totally any problems you have with those you care about or be equipped to work at the same depth as an experienced counsellor. What I suggest is that by learning simple listening and responding techniques you can extend your repertoire of how you communicate with others. The probable outcome of this is that relationships will be improved.

Had Colin's wife, for example, had a usable knowledge of basic counselling skills, of Rogerian core conditions, which are explored in Chapter 8, she would have had the ability to sit back from the situation and be less overwhelmed by her own fear. She would have been able to understand her own feelings and her requirements of him. She would have been able to listen more actively, entering into an exploration of his thoughts and feelings.

The success of this kind of activity to a certain extent depends on our having the ability to put our own needs aside, but this can be viewed as a temporary situation. When we are able to listen to the distress of another human being and not heavily identify with, resist or take offence in relation to that distress in some way, we open channels of greater communication which in time can benefit everybody.

2 | THE COUNSELLOR'S ROLE

Perhaps you are interested in getting involved with counselling in some capacity but are not sure what it may involve. You may not be convinced that you have the right qualities, or perhaps you are unsure how much you would be able to commit in terms of training and counselling hours and how demanding this kind of work can be.

Qualities of a counsellor

Kahlil Gibran wrote in *The Prophet*: 'No man can reveal to you aught but that which already lies half asleep in the dawning of your knowledge.' These words speak to the would-be counsellor and client alike. We are all potentially our own healers and problem solvers. Counsellors are not super-beings who have a monopoly on emotional strength and wisdom. Nor are they omnipotent, or all seeing, or all knowing. Although people often have the expectation that counsellors will 'sort out' their problems, it is the clients themselves, guided and encouraged by their relationship with the counsellor, who ultimately have to do the work.

Like other professionals, counsellors have knowledge of their work that has come through training and experience. While a practising counsellor will retain theoretical knowledge as a backdrop, the most important factor in what they achieve is likely to be the time and attention they give to a client. Carl Jung advised the therapist: 'Learn your theories as well as you can, but put them aside when you touch the miracle of the living soul.' This reminds us of the uniqueness of each one of us and suggests to us that no encounter with one person will be quite the same as that with another. Clients, as individuals with individual problems, are the counsellor's primary concern.

While brainstorming in a training session qualities we might expect in a counsellor, the following words and phrases were suggested by participants. Some of the suggestions demonstrate the high expectations that the prospective counsellors had of themselves. They included:

> Integrity, an ability to look at oneself, knowledge of theory, humility, empathy, a liking of others, an interest in people, kindness, non-judgemental attitude, respect for others, a good memory for detail, being a good listener, patience, sensitivity, in control of own emotions, professionalism, ethical behaviour.

To have all of these attributes is a tall order. These are ideals which most probably we feel we may fall short of at times. As an afterthought, someone added: 'being courageous'. That seemed to resonate with the trainer, who smiled in agreement and commented that a counsellor does need courage to face the problems a client brings and to be in the experience with them.

A view of the 'skilled helper'

In his book *The Skilled Helper* (1975; 2nd ed. 1982), Gerard Egan suggests an effective 'skilled helper' is committed to their own growth – intellectual, social, emotional and spiritual, and that such helpers need to become 'potent human beings', which corresponds with Carl Rogers' term 'authentic self'. Egan sees potent human beings as 'people with both the resources and the will to act'. Rogers regarded the ability to express ourselves freely and spontaneously as important to our well-being and Freud, expressing it differently but with similar meaning, talked of having the 'freedom to love and work'. The skilled helper does not necessarily work as a professional counsellor but is familiar with and competent at using counselling skills.

According to Egan, the following factors will contribute to the effectiveness of a skilled helper, who ideally:

Has basic intelligence, with respect for ideas.

Reads, learns, is familiar with theory and is adept at making good use of it.

Has skills of evaluation.

Has common sense and social adeptness/intelligence.

Has a certain easiness with others.

Is at home in the social emotional world, their own and that of others.

Is able to respond effectively to a wide range of human needs.

Is not afraid of deep human emotions, their own and others, and is willing to work at the level of distress.

Is willing to explore their own feelings and behaviour and work at recognizing and integrating all aspects of self.

Can read non-verbal messages. (pp. 26–8)

Can these personal qualities be acquired?

Do you recognize yourself in the above descriptions? While most of these qualities named can be developed as skills, others are definite aspects of character which some people have more leaning towards than others; for example, not everyone is comfortable at working with strong emotions or high levels of distress or has an easiness around the majority of people. A widely held view among therapists is that to a large extent qualities which are beneficial to the counsellor can be developed through training and personal therapy.

Not everyone will be considered to be suitable counsellor material by those who select for organizations or training courses. Selection procedures are usually thorough at all levels. Selection may take place over one or a number of days. Within this time various assessment techniques are used by the selectors. The qualities they will be looking for include:

1 An ability to mix with others in an assessment situation (self-esteem and boundary issues).
2 An adaptability/spontaneity – able to respond to various set 'tasks'.
3 An ability to self-assess.
4 Observational qualities – insightfulness.
5 An ability to be themselves; e.g. what Carl Rogers called being 'real', genuine and congruent.

6 Evidence of warmth of character; e.g. empathic responding.

7 The nominee being in a position in their life that is not at odds with the demands of training, which involves embarking on a self-growth programme and working with others in various levels of intimacy. (If a person is in the middle of divorce proceedings, or has been recently bereaved, it may not be a good time to begin a new and demanding enterprise.)

The methods usually used to assess the above factors include exercises, role plays and games. Sometimes painting or drawing or elements of psychodrama are used. Individuals also have interviews with staff members or experienced counsellors from the organization, agency or educational establishment.

Individuals assess their own suitability – some drop out of counselling at selection stage, deciding that it is not for them. Others leave at various stages of training. Still others choose to train in gradual stages in correlation with their own personal development.

Creating core conditions

Of all the positive qualities already mentioned, the most important are generally considered to be encapsulated in the core conditions or values which originated from Carl Rogers' ideas of client-centred therapy, now more commonly referred to as person-centred therapy. These are **congruence**, **unconditional positive regard** and **empathy**; they can be abbreviated to CUE – a form that is easily remembered. (These and other details of person-centred therapy are the subject of a later chapter.) Other terms that are sometimes used in connection with the core conditions are: **non-possessive warmth**, **acceptance** and a **non-judgemental attitude**. **Genuineness** is sometimes used instead of 'congruence'.

Being non-judgemental

What does it mean to be non-judgemental towards another? Is that possible, considering that we make decisions all the time about what we like, dislike, tolerate or enjoy about other people? To judge a person can mean to have a opinion about whether they are a good or bad person or whether we approve or disapprove of their behaviour. The stance we take towards others is often strongly related to our own conditioning and life experiences. We may consider a person 'right' in their thoughts, emotions and behaviour because those are similar to our own. We can identify with their experiences. We may despise and reject in others aspects of character which we reject in ourselves.

How then can a counsellor be any different? This may be more easily understood if we view the non-judgemental approach as a position taken outside ordinary social interaction. Rather than rigidly classifying someone's behaviour or opinions as 'good' or 'bad', we need to consider the whole person. We then may understand the privilege of our position and adopt a receptive, supportive attitude. An empathic response to the client would be for the counsellor to understand that, given the circumstances and the experiences of the client's life, it is little wonder that they think, feel or behave in a certain way.

It is debatable whether we can ever truly sustain a non-judgemental approach with our clients. I personally see it as an ideal. When I find I am judging a client on some level I ask myself what I am feeling, what is going on for both myself and the client at the time, and I make sure I address the issues in supervision. A counsellor would have grounds for concern when a client's behaviour is in danger of seriously harming either the client or anyone associated with them. Some kind of judgement as to what immediately needs addressing may be necessary. That judgement would be based on the client's behaviour and how the situation can be made safe, rather than on dismissing the whole human being.

Acceptance and self-development

It is considered important for counsellors to have personal therapy or counselling in order that they can explore their own prejudices and unresolved emotional issues, which might otherwise get in the way of constructive work with a client. The often quoted words over the Temple of Delphi, 'Know Thyself', have great significance for anyone wishing to become a counsellor of others.

None of us is without human foibles. We are all flawed and the counsellor should get to know themselves and acknowledge what Jung termed our 'Shadow Side' (see Chapter 8). Only then can would-be counsellors, who bear witness to the human splendours and weaknesses in others, be compassionate to the flaws of their clients.

Personal therapy gradually helps us to become more comfortable around distress and strong emotions. How can we expect ourselves to, for example, be capable of 'holding' a client through their angry feelings if we haven't to some extent come to terms with our own anger?

Life experience

The most useful experience of all for preparation as a counsellor is to have lived and learned. Our own life experience obviously gives us insight into the situations of others, although there is a dichotomy in this. It would be a mistake to assume that because we have had a similar experience – for example, a divorce or the death of a loved one – our responses would be exactly the same as another's.

Example

I witnessed a relevant incident on a selection day at a counselling agency, at an early stage of my interest in therapy. As one of the exercises the nominees were given a piece of paper with a brief outline of a case study written on it. They were asked to think for a few minutes about how they might respond to their particular case. One example read: 'A 16-year-old girl has come for counselling. She has recently discovered that she was adopted as a baby. Although she wants to find out about her biological parents and possibly at some stage meet her mother she is extremely anxious about this prospect.'

The nominee who received these details had by coincidence also been adopted. She responded by saying that she would tell the girl that she also had been adopted, tell her not to worry and say that her biological mother would most certainly be delighted to hear from her as her own mother had been and assure her that

---

everything would be all right. This answer obviously reflected her particular experiences.

While this response was well meaning and no doubt in the spirit of 'openness', it was misguided. No two people will have exactly the same experience and this amount of self-disclosure on the part of the counsellor would take the focus away from the girl's underlying feelings. The counsellor appears to want to solve any problems before they arise and make the girl optimistic. On realizing that she is not being listened to, and is being required by the counsellor to adopt a positive attitude, she would be likely to feel unable to express her fears and anxieties, let alone explore them.

When we give people our subjective views, we sometimes assume an authority and we become no longer attentive to a different viewpoint. As counsellors we may try to salve a situation by reassurance. I felt I had witnessed an incident that was a very valuable lesson, that the therapist's role is not to reassure and thereby avoid difficult feelings, but rather to help the client get in touch with feelings and stay with them.

Counselling is one of the few vocations where age is not a problem. To come to counselling in our thirties, forties or at a greater age means we come with an abundance of life experience. Hopefully we have learned from experiences, good and bad. We have gone through times which stretched our emotional and psychological resources and survived the trauma. Tutors and trainers in counselling look for evidence of these experiences in prospective trainees. Generally speaking the amount of life experience in the young is much less than in those who are older. That is why the majority of counselling and psychotherapy courses require the trainee counsellor to be a specified age, usually 25 years or over.

What do you want to get out of counselling?

Teaching, social work and nursing are examples of the more obvious types of occupations that benefit from the acquisition of counselling skills, but they would be a benefit in any work that involves skilful interactional communication.

You may be interested in changing your career direction. People who become counsellors come from diverse backgrounds. I have met counsellors who have been businessmen and women, teachers, housewives, nurses and social workers. Some have initially taken up counselling on a voluntary basis or as an enhancement to their work but have been so inspired by what they have learned and experienced that they have changed track altogether and gone on to become professional counsellors or psychotherapists. Many people who become interested in counselling have had intensive therapy themselves. They have first-hand experience as a client. They feel that therapy has been a positive experience and are consequently interested in pursuing counselling as a career. Others choose to work in areas where they themselves have suffered trauma; for example, a woman who has been physically abused by her husband may choose to counsel in a woman's refuge, and a former drug user may train to work in an agency as a drugs counsellor.

Commitments

Training as a professional counsellor can be a lengthy business. The more thoroughly we train the more commitment is involved in terms of time, finance and energy. Many people receive an initial training through a counselling agency, which may offer training over a relatively short period of ten to twelve weeks, after which the trainees begin to counsel clients in a voluntary capacity. Before embarking on the training, which is usually free, the trainees may be required to commit themselves to working a minimum of a few hours per week for a year or more. This is a good way to start counselling training as it gives a grounding in both theory and practice. Agencies and organizations that enlist volunteer counsellors usually provide on-going training and supervision for their helpers. Good supervision is essential in any form of counselling.

It may be useful to ask yourself a few questions:

- Why do I want to counsel other people?
- What do I want to get out of counselling?
- How much time can I give on a voluntary basis?

■ Am I hoping to make a career out of counselling?
■ Have I the financial resources to embark on a lengthy
   programme of learning?
■ Am I willing to be personally challenged?

Counselling or using counselling skills?

When visiting a holistic clinic, I asked the receptionist if any counsellors practised there. She replied that most of the practitioners at the clinic 'did a bit of counselling along with the treatment'. As a counsellor I instantly felt my role had been rendered defunct. Think about the tables being turned – imagine a counsellor who, within the counselling session, gives neck manipulation as a sideline.

The humour in this imagined situation and the casualness of the receptionist's remark led me to wonder how people view counselling. On closer enquiry I found that one practitioner, a reflexologist, had attended a short counselling skills course. She was an empathic, warm person but she had no counselling qualifications. I felt she wasn't a counsellor, or in fact counselling, but she was employing counselling skills, possibly to very good effect. In her capacity as an alternative therapist she was working with the healing model, which acknowledges the triad connection of mind, body and spirit. She talked to her clients about their upsets and tensions in relation to their state of health. That is a valid, insightful way to work and forms the basis of holistic medicine and treatment; that is, treating the whole person, each part related to the other, linking cause and effect. If, for example, a person holds tension in their stomach, in time they are likely to develop physical problems in that area. This is a simple example but it illustrates the connection between our emotional states and thought processes and the effect they have on our bodies.

The emotional demands and rewards of personal growth

Training for the role of counsellor to other people requires a willingness to self-examine and an acceptance of our self in its entirety. Even on the shortest of courses, the trainee who is hoping to be in the responsible role of counselling others will be focusing on personal attitudes and feelings towards their self and others.

How can we have understanding of and empathy for others if we have little understanding or tolerance of ourselves? In person-centred therapy the counsellor is required to adopt a stance of 'unconditional positive regard' towards the client. This, as we have already seen, is to be non-judgemental, accepting, warm and supportive. To judge another person negatively is to take a superior position for ourselves, to elevate ourselves. To take the role of empathic listener and supporter of another person necessitates a dropping of these attitudes and a recognition that we are all in the same position, we are all human. This requires a willingness to self-scrutinize and self-assess.

It is impossible to become a counsellor without entering into personal development, awareness, growth – call it what you will. It has frequently been referred to as a journey taken inwardly and, like most journeys, it has its high and low points, with marvellous landscapes to enjoy at times and bumpy rides to endure at others. Be prepared to be challenged, to meet difficulties while you unravel and try to understand yourself before you are let loose on others. The experience can be life changing.

Through personal therapy you may hope to understand yourself, how you think, feel and behave, in more depth. Some of the following issues are likely to present themselves: your expectations of others, personal motivations, problem areas (i.e. conflicts, difficulties, unresolved material), how you relate to another person in intimacy, aspects of your childhood, your values, prejudices and self-esteem.

It is not difficult to see why self-exploration is challenging and demanding. It can also at times be frustrating, but sticking with it – what therapists call 'going with the process' – does yield rewards. Self-exploration through participating in therapy offers unique opportunities. These include being able to explore our individuality and discovering our potential and inner resources. It is a wonderful opportunity to be open and non-defensive with someone who calls on us to challenge some of our perceptions and it is a chance to release 'stuck' feelings and reintroduce spontaneity into our lives.

Trainees and fellow explorers

While training you will be working with others and, when you choose to, sharing intimate details of yourself. This calls for a great deal of honesty and courage. You may well be surprised at aspects of your character that surface when you feel trust for people you are working with in mutual exploration. For example, you may perceive yourself to be a serious person and be shocked to find others perceive you as often being flippant, or vice versa. Feedback is a valuable source of material for self-enquiry, giving us insight into both positive and negative aspects of our personalities. It lets us know how we react towards others and how they in turn react towards us. Working together in one-to-one practice, triad practice or groupwork demands that we take responsibility for ourselves; this includes looking after ourselves within the group dynamic. People frequently form close bonds through taking part in each other's development, considering it to be an enriching and stimulating experience.

3 THE BENEFITS OF ACQUIRING COUNSELLING SKILLS

The use of communication skills in personal relationships

Essentially, counselling is concerned with communication, yet clearly it is different from other interpersonal exchanges. Other than when we are in exceptional circumstances we use communication skills or interpersonal skills every day of our lives. In our work and in our leisure time we listen to each other, notice what others are doing and how they appear to be feeling, and we talk to each other on various levels. The use of counselling skills differs from other relationship skills in that there is emphasis on attention to one person only (the client), who is communicating their life details, their thoughts and feelings both past and present, to the other (the counsellor). The counsellor puts aside their own preoccupations and self-concerns in order to give full attention to the client.

It is not a reciprocal relationship primarily based on conversation; the focus is always on the client. In ordinary everyday social intercourse we expect people to share thoughts and feelings to varying degrees. People give advice and help each other by relating to and identifying similarities in emotions or events that they have experienced. Their intention is to say: 'I understand where you are coming from, you are not alone.' They aim to comfort, to lessen the other person's pain and feelings of alienation. Whilst valuable in establishing social bonding and integration, this kind of interactional discourse has its limits as it remains reciprocal to a large extent.

Subjective support

As unskilled helpers we tend to evaluate the suffering of others by comparing it to our own experiences and how we deal with them.

When we are in a close relationship with another it may be harder to be objective. If we experience someone else's problems from a subjective viewpoint we may hear something they say as a criticism and become defensive. Without extra skills to inform us we may continue to relate to and appeal to the part of their persona which we find most acceptable and comfortable for us. Changes in other people often call for changes in ourselves and in the way that we relate to each other.

Using the example of Colin from Chapter 1, imagine what the response would be if he told a friend or a member of his family about his feelings of hopelessness. A subjective way of responding might be one of the following.

1. A friend's possible response

Let's suppose that Colin's friend responded to his depression by saying: 'I felt like that when I lost my job but something will turn up, you'll see', or 'Come on, it's not as bad as it seems. Have a drink, that'll cheer you up. This isn't like you.'

Colin's friend is trying to do what comes automatically to most people; he aims to cheer Colin up, take him out of his problems. Going into his problems and staying with them at Colin's pace could prove more fruitful. While the friend's responses may intend to reassure, they are likely to have the opposite effect. The solutions offered represent his inability and unwillingness to investigate Colin's predicament any further. He thinks that Colin is just 'down in the dumps' and that he is not behaving like the Colin he knows – he will soon 'snap out of it' (notice how many clichés we use to explain troubling emotions!). Each time he sees Colin, which becomes less and less frequently, he attempts to bolster him up by being cheerful himself.

2. His wife's possible response

Colin's wife may say: 'Pull yourself together; look at the effect you are having on your family. I don't know what's got into you, you're just feeling sorry for yourself. You have responsibilities to face up to – you're being pathetic. I've got problems too, but I have to get on with things.'

This response is more condemnatory than the last example. Living with Colin, she is more involved on a daily basis than his friend is. She is becoming increasingly critical of him because he appears to be rejecting her and the life they have led, which leaves her feeling criticized. Her way of dealing with Colin's depression is to withdraw her affection from him, which leaves him feeling more desolate and unlovable in his present emotional state.

Her response suggests that she thinks he is being self-indulgent and that the only way she can accept him is when he is 'strong' and supportive. In her view, he has duties towards his family that he is not fulfilling.

These two responses reveal the individual's requirements of Colin, as a friend and as a husband. In both cases there is a reluctance to face the depth of his anguish. This kind of reaction could actually make him feel more alienated from his friends and family and result in further depression.

Neither of these responses addresses the emotional devastation Colin is experiencing. Friends and family may find it hard to be anything but subjective in the views they offer. It can be frightening when someone close to us appears to radically change in character. In both cases, Colin's suffering is possibly being noted by the listener but he is neither permitted nor encouraged to explore it. To ameliorate the distress of others who are close to him he is indirectly asked to bury (as he may have been many times before) his deeply felt emotions and to 'just get on with it'.

Self-indulgence or a developmental stage?

The Scottish psychiatrist R.D. Laing suggested that a psychological breakdown is better regarded as a breakthrough. What Colin was experiencing can be regarded as a developmental challenge. Nothing in life is for ever or guaranteed. We change, our circumstances change, sometimes cruelly. Within our lifetime we have many adjustments to make, physically, psychologically and spiritually. We are likely to encounter failure, rejection, death of those we love, divorce of ourselves or someone close to us, ageing and depression – to name but a few. It is often said that when one door closes another opens. This is a reassuring view which hopefully is true, but it has to be acknowledged that sometimes we find ourselves in the middle of a cold, stark place with only the closed door in view. We may, like Colin, feel helpless and shut off from those around us. At such times we need someone to have the courage to really hear us and accept this desperate part of us. Many of the responses we get from friends and family, who basically wish us well, focus on how we will feel in the future, such as 'Things will get better, you're just going through a difficult time', and do not deal with how we feel in the present. It is crucial that the present feelings are acknowledged and accepted. When one person adopts the use of counselling skills it frees the other in the sense that they, the person who is focusing on the problems, do not have to be relating to how the listener is feeling too.

Applying the core conditions to Colin's situation

The telling question is: Were Colin's friend and wife showing signs of really listening to him? Let's look at how the core conditions of Rogerian person-centred therapy might be applied.

Unconditional positive regard

What can this mean in relation to Colin, his family and friends, and their largely subjective responses to his anguish? Do they respect him? They would probably argue that they both love and respect him. But the key point is whether they are able to demonstrate that they fully accept him when he needs their understanding. Using the short description of their responses as representing their general attitude to Colin's problems, would you consider that they, for example:

- Respect his right to express his emotions?
- Accept different aspects of his personality – some positive, some negative?
- Respect his right to have different values from theirs?
- Respect his right to self-exploration and self-discovery?
- Respect his right to change?

Are they able to be objective, accepting what Colin is saying and demonstrating without blocking out or censuring the painful truth of the situation? To put this another way:

- Are they adopting a non-judgemental stance?
- Are they accepting his vulnerability?
- Are they able to see beyond their own requirements of him?

Genuineness or congruence

Would you say that Colin's wife and friend are being honest and open with him? For example:

- Are they sharing their real feelings with him? – fear, inadequacy, anger, pity etc.
- Are they affirming that they hear what he is saying?
- Are they able to admit that they don't have the solutions?
- Are they willing to enter the struggle with him – rather than retreating into the safety of 'quick fix' answers?

Empathy

Would you say that Colin's wife and friend are empathic in their responses? Are they showing him that they are willing to enter into his experience with him as if they were experiencing the same, effectively walking in his shoes? (See Chapter 4.) For example:

- Are they really listening?
- Are they focusing on Colin's thoughts and feelings?
- Are they able to put their own requirements and problems aside?
- Are they able to be involved in what he is going through without getting totally lost in the process?
- Are they able to differentiate between Colin's and their own feelings; fear, pain, loss etc.?

By acquiring counselling skills you will not become a counsellor *per se*. However, by learning how to use some of the skills and by familiarizing yourself with core conditions you can enhance your relationship with others, helping you to acknowledge and understand both other people's feelings and your own.

Had Colin's wife and friend had knowledge of certain skills, they could have responded differently. They could have listened actively and adopted the values of respect, genuineness, empathy and acceptance, and answered in the affirmative to most of the questions set out above. They would have been able to own their feelings and been aware of their need to project their anxieties back on to Colin.

Disentangling the web

Familiarity with the basic skills and core conditions can in time act as useful 'antennae', giving us a keener awareness of what we and others express through our behaviour. Most of us do not possess the skills to listen actively. We need to learn skills such as summing up, checking that what we have heard is correct, reflecting back the other person's thoughts and feelings and asking open questions.

Ironically, it has been my experience that by adopting valuing qualities such as positive regard, acceptance and empathy I can be both closer to and at the same time more detached from the person I want to help. Saying to ourselves that the other person deserves our time, respect and warmth allows us to concentrate on them in depth. By adopting the use of the skills we can become more aware of our own reactions, our feelings and how we generally relate to people.

The acquisition of these skills is empowering. It can help us gain insight into other people's behaviour as well as our own. Shakespeare described features of human relationships as a 'tangled web'. They are not always easy and yet they are the main source of human fulfilment – in marriage, partnership, family life, community life and work. Lack of communication is often cited as the reason why relationships break down. Without the tools of good communication we are apt to respond defensively when, for example, others are angry with us. We feel blamed and rush to our own defence without finding out the associated reasons and feelings of the other person. We take offence at each other's moods and actions if they are at odds with, or in some way exclude, our own. Also we may lose a sense of ourselves in relation to other people.

Uses of counselling skills in work settings

Many people benefit from the use of counselling skills in their jobs. Those who work in the caring profession – like nurses and social workers – may have had relevant skills included in their training. Those in any job which involves interaction with other people could benefit, including those working in large corporate companies in personnel departments and managerial roles. With this in mind, let's look briefly at a few examples of how people can and do use skills and adopt core values at work. In the main example I draw on my own experiences of working in groups with young people in the school environment.

Teachers and counselling skills

It is widely recognized that teachers play an enormously important role in a young person's life. Between the ages of 5 and 16 years or older, children spend more weekday hours in the school environment with teachers than they do with their parents. Any educational system has high requirements of its pupils. The smooth running of schools depends on pupils' collective and individual ability to conform to these requirements. To a large extent individuality is subjugated to the needs of the collective identity and of the school as a whole. Both teachers and pupils are required to conform to certain modes of behaviour. This is necessary for the safe and effective management of establishments that sometimes contain a thousand or more people.

For a large part of the day, five days a week, children sit at their tables. Although modern teaching methods employ groupwork and open discussion there is still an emphasis on passive learning during which the pupil takes in information mechanically. Sometimes there is little rapport between teachers and pupils and there are pressures on both to maintain high academic performance and achieve good results. There may be few opportunities to self-express or let off steam other than in sporting and playground activities. A number of children have problems slotting into the school system. All these factors make for a potentially eruptive atmosphere.

A child or young person in trouble

Teachers realize that a happy, well-adjusted child tends to work more productively, both separately and with others. I use 'well-adjusted' here to mean a child who has self-esteem and a strong enough sense of self (what Freud termed 'Ego strength') to engage with others within the school environment. At a counselling agency where I initially trained there was a high proportion of teachers among the trainees. They recognized that at times their pupils needed emotional support which they would try to give but felt unable to do this satisfactorily. One of these teachers commented that it was a fine balancing act trying to be sympathetic to pupils' problems while also maintaining boundaries. He felt that acquiring some counselling skills would help him cope with testing situations where he was acting as confidant to a child. He realized that his main role was that of a teacher, not a counsellor, and appreciated that he was deficient in the skills he needed in order to give the children confidence to seek out further help. He recognized that in his role as a middle man, he would benefit from learning additional skills.

Communication problems between teacher and pupil

A child may be quiet, withdrawn or sullen, increasingly miss school, and never get homework or projects in on time. Often this child feels the wrath of the teacher when clearly they need help. The teacher too may be stressed, overworked and exasperated by the individual needs of this troublesome child. The child is 'acting out' – their behaviour is saying that there is something drastically wrong in their life right now.

In this type of situation communication can break down rapidly. The child is in deep water. Punitive measures only serve to alienate them further. It becomes a pupil versus teacher and school situation, and the problem may escalate. Sometimes the child is eventually excluded from school. The resources needed to educate rejected children can be enormous, and these resources could have been placed within the original school setting at the onset of problems. Ideally, schools would have a resident counsellor who would provide the troubled pupil with individual support, support that says: 'We appreciate that something is wrong in your world, we want to understand and help you. To do this we will set time aside to spend with you, to look at your needs one to one – you are worth that attention.' Unfortunately having a counsellor as a member of staff is not usually regarded as a necessity and lack of funds is often cited as the reason.

Example – Listening to pupils

During a group session I once facilitated in a school, it became apparent to me that the pupils, who were between the ages of 13 and 14, were feeling aggrieved. They told me that they had not been informed that their timetable had been changed. They had come to school that morning expecting to have a double session of PE, which they enjoyed, and found instead that they were to have a double session of science. This meant that they would be carrying their PE kits around all day. They were annoyed because this was not the first time this had happened. I asked if there were any procedures in place at the school by which they could air grievances, and they said, 'Nobody would listen.'

I suggested a role play as a way of helping them express what they were feeling. Two boys volunteered, one to act as teacher, the other as a representative pupil. The group then made a list of things they would like to say. The 'teacher' sat in the room in the middle of the group circle, and the 'pupil' went outside the room and knocked on the door. The exchange went like this.

Teacher   'Come in.'

Pupil   *[looking hesitant as he comes in]* 'Please, sir, I'd like to talk to you about what happened today. We are really fed up that you didn't let us know that we would be having Science instead of PE.'

          [The teacher looks impatient and keeps checking his watch]

Teacher   'I haven't got time at the moment; see me about it tomorrow.'

Pupil   'I thought you would say that.'

Teacher   'You'll have a new timetable by the end of the week.'

          [The teacher continues to look busy and the communication ends. The pupil goes off grumbling to himself.]

The brevity of the exchange left me feeling quite frustrated, a feeling that I guessed mirrored the pupils' feelings. We all returned to the group circle and discussed what had happened. The following facts were acknowledged by the pupils, some of whom were surprisingly empathic:

- The young people in the group did not feel on the whole that the teachers listened to their grievances.
- They acknowledged that the teachers were very busy.
- They said that the teachers were often preoccupied.
- They realized that the teachers were answerable to other teachers and that they had to check things out.
- There were some teachers (no names were ever used) whom they didn't like.
- They said that the teachers they did not like treated them unfairly in some way.

When I asked the pupils their feelings in relation to grievances, they made the following comments:

- They felt upset when teachers ignored them.
- They felt angry.
- They felt that their views were not respected.
- In school they felt disempowered – they had no voice and were treated like little children and their feelings were disregarded and didn't matter.

I asked the pupils how they expressed these feelings. In answer there were a lot of shrugs, 'don't knows' and a 'What's the point, you'd only end up getting detention or something.' It didn't occur to any of them that they could express their dissatisfaction and frustration because they associated strong feelings with not being heard and with possible punishment.

When I asked them how frustration and dissatisfaction expressed itself in their behaviour, they suggested the following:

- They sometimes hated the teachers.
- They might sometimes take it out on each other.
- They didn't feel like doing any work.
- They sometimes felt alienated from teachers and school.
- They didn't want to do homework.
- They were grumpier at home.
- They didn't want to go to school.

This example serves to demonstrate the undercurrent of largely unexpressed strong feelings that young people may harbour when they feel no one is listening to them. Clearly it is in the interests of both pupils and teachers that pupils are able to address their feelings within the school environment. This necessitates clear boundaries. It would not be in the interest of the smooth running of a school to have a riot of unleashed emotions. If dissatisfactions and problems are to be held and contained there needs to be a place to register them before they escalate into something less manageable – this could be the school counsellor or it could be a skilled, empathic teacher who is capable of putting counselling skills to use.

The school given as an example was by no means atypical. My guess is that many schools have communication problems between teachers and pupils as well as between teachers themselves. In fact, some of the teachers I spoke to at this particular school prided themselves on the improved communication they felt they had with the pupils.

Skills that could have been used

The teacher in the role play would have responded better if he had applied the basics of counselling skills and the core conditions. He would have stopped, listened and asked interested open questions, taking the opportunity to develop a relationship with the pupil. When he told the pupil that he was too busy, that could have been interpreted as dismissive and uncaring (they and their grievances are not at all important to him – as if they don't exist). The comment about the new timetable has a subtext that could be understood to mean that he considers himself to be beyond mistakes. In both these responses he fails to acknowledge his humanness and seems to regard himself as above criticism from pupils. Because of this he loses a valuable opportunity to make contact with the pupil and repair the damage.

I'm sure that by now you have an understanding of the core conditions and how they can be applied. Without wishing to labour the point, we'll briefly look at how the teacher might have put these and listening skills to good use.

Empathy

If the teacher had demonstrated that he was able to understand that the pupils were missing something they enjoyed doing, and that they had been given no prior notice to allow them to acclimatize to the change, this would have conveyed empathic understanding of their situation. He would also have shown appreciation of the fact that to enable them to let go of the grievance it was important for them to be able to register a complaint and receive an apology and an explanation.

Respect or positive regard

It is a well-accepted fact, backed by social learning theories, that a child learns from example – what behavioural psychology calls 'vicarious' means. If we assume this to be true, then it follows that if a teacher consistently treats pupils with respect, then this will be reciprocated by pupils in their attitude towards the teacher. He could have demonstrated positive regard by thanking the pupils for informing him of their grievances and commending the representative for taking on the task of approaching him.

Genuineness

The Rogerian meaning of 'genuineness' applied to teaching would involve the teacher's engagement with the pupils as individuals. In any profession it is easy to take refuge in a role which distances ourselves from situations that challenge us, especially if our energies and resources are already stretched. This teacher would have been 'real' with his pupils if he had acknowledged, both to himself and his pupils, that he could get things wrong at times, and then apologized and taken steps to rectify his mistakes. When authority figures appear infallible that can engender fear in others about their own imperfections.

Acceptance

Good teaching or 'facilitation of learning' (a term favoured by Carl Rogers) instils a sense of self-worth in a child, not only by encouraging academic achievement but also by fostering awareness that they can be valued for themselves and for what they have to offer. For a child to value themselves they need to feel that they are (most of the time at least) acceptable to others and that as individuals they have a part to play.

Rogers, an innovative educationist, felt strongly that the teacher was a facilitator of learning. He believed that a teacher's role was to enable and empower a child to learn by supplying a supportive, responsive and non-judgemental environment. The facilitator values the individual as unique in their abilities and contributions. In his paper 'The Politics of Education' (1977), he observes the following:

> The teacher is the possessor of knowledge, the student the expected recipient.
> The teacher is the possessor of power, the student the one who obeys.
> Rule by authority is the accepted policy in the classroom.
> Trust is at a minimum.
> Democracy and its values are ignored and scorned in practice.

(Source: The Carl Rogers Reader, pp. 323–5)

Although Rogers wrote about these matters over twenty years ago, the issues he raised are still relevant today. If a teacher is able to use the core conditions and is familiar with various counselling skills, then he can put these to use in various contexts, in one-to-one relationship with a child or young person who is demonstrating antisocial behaviour and also in relation to the class as a whole, in the understanding and management of group dynamics.

The following account is by Roy Radcliffe, a teacher who trained and worked as a volunteer counsellor of young people. He relates how counselling skills continue to enhance his teaching role.

> If one considers counselling to be a specialized or more insightful form of communication then it is an essential skill of all teachers. Most young people are not natural subscribers to education within its institutional form, especially when they may be taking ten subjects, a number of which they will believe to be irrelevant. A significant proportion of students are gently coerced into learning by parents, teachers, various societal institutions and the fears that they may have about their futures. This leads to conflict of interests between the

students' reluctance and the demands placed upon teachers from school management and national government to get better and better results regardless. This conflict of interest will often lead to potential confrontation (especially given the natural rebelliousness of teenagers struggling with the developmental stages of separation and identity development).

It is in the minimization of conflict, confrontation and the creation of a partnership for learning that counselling skills are so necessary. Counselling skills such as:

> Being able to hear what is not being said
> Hearing the general tone of the communication
> The reading of body language
> The creation of a body language that does not enflame situations
> Being able to surmise what emotions may be behind a specific response
> Being able to ask open questions that broaden discussions rather than narrow them
> Being able to listen to strong emotions being articulated
> To hear and see the transference
> To allow an individual to feel heard
> Empathising with young people

The most important factor has been that I can step outside the confines of my role as a teacher and see the broader picture. It is the knowledge that any student is a part of a broader picture (even if I don't know the details of that picture) that enables me to deal in a more empathic way with them.

An uncomfortably high proportion of the students that sit in front of us are damaged in psychological ways. The wound they carry can be from divorce, bereavement, abuse, poor parenting and many that we can't imagine. Some will be the traumas that are associated with development and the teenage years, which can seem unimportant to adults but earth shattering to them. Because these students are not blank slates and school is not treated in isolation I can end up with a child who may be sullen, explosive, resentful, depressed or just simply unhappy. It is easier to deal with the angry, resentful and rebellious student; the problem is being made visible. The worrying ones are the unhappy and depressive; it's not visible. The problem is that most young people of this age have not learned to be reflective about where the feelings and moods come from. They simply act out.

This is where counselling skills are worth their weight in gold. Firstly in the recognition that this is acting out and not just a troublesome individual. It will often be that some action on my part will have mirrored a raw spot in their life, and it is safer to react against me than the real source. It is no different from the transference that happens in counselling sessions. Counselling skills allow you to question in a supportive, non-threatening and empathic way that can bring the background issue into focus. They allow you to hold the anger or resentment in a safe way. To confront in a gentle fashion. Most importantly they can allow you to help a child see where the current emotions are coming from and to build in mechanisms that can allow that child to express them safely and build more productive behaviour patterns.

Roy Radcliffe

A doctor

A doctor told me that he had undertaken brief counselling training because he was increasingly dissatisfied with his lack of ability to be fully attentive of his patients. He realized that many of his patients needed to feel that they were being listened to and responded to as if they were important. He appreciated that his manner was not conveying his genuine concern. He joked that at the time he had more of a relationship with his prescription pad than with his patients.

He considers that the counselling skills he has acquired have helped him to look more deeply at the patient as an individual. Subsequently he is more inclined to suggest that a patient who is suffering from depression has counselling or psychotherapy than to prescribe antidepressants automatically – he now prescribes these less frequently. He told me that he is more likely than before to ask depressed patients, and patients who have persistent symptoms that resist medication, questions about what is going on in their lives and their relationships with significant others as a means of assessing appropriate treatment.

A probation officer

I asked an ex-colleague of mine who had trained and worked on a voluntary basis as a counsellor how she uses her skills in her new career as a probation officer. She said that the skills she learned are of great value to her. She can engage with her clients (young offenders) on an empathic level, appreciating the whole person. She is more likely to make links between the offender's crimes and their childhood past, which helps her to write pre-sentencing reports. In these she may comment on events in the offender's childhood which she considers to have had a traumatic effect, resulting in poor self-esteem and an inability to handle difficulties. She stressed that this in no way made her a 'soft touch'. She had become able, because of her counselling skills, to challenge effectively, in an unthreatening manner. This might, for instance, include challenging the offender's attitude towards issues of power and control. Having the skills also helped her to recognize certain patterns of behaviour. She commented:

> Sometimes a persistent offender enjoys having a problem in the sense that it in some way defines him. He becomes caught up in a cycle of repetition of events. By tentative challenging I can bring issues into the open. In this way he can choose to own his behaviour and make some sense of it.

The knowledge and practice of listening and responding skills can give us more choice about how to deal with some stresses in the work environment. It is important when we use counselling skills for us to be aware of our limitations as helpers, recognizing when we are out of our depth and when it is time to refer a person who needs help to someone with appropriate training and experience – otherwise there can be a conflict of roles. The objective is not, after all, to overload ourselves with responsibilities but rather to lighten our load by improving our relationships with those around us.

4 SKILLS USED IN COUNSELLING

This chapter considers the basic skills of counselling that you would expect to learn in theory and experience in practice if you attended any beginners' counselling training.

Sharpening our awareness

Speaking, hearing, seeing, feeling and thinking are all ways in which we respond and give attention to each other. At times of emergency we often have a heightened response to another who is in need; both head and heart go into operative mode. In our concern for the person we examine the most effective way to help them find relief from their predicament and we are highly focused. At other times, especially when strong emotions are involved, we are often at a loss about how to be of any help to the distressed person. By identifying and developing simple skills we can enhance our ability to be more fully present for another person when they are distressed or experiencing difficulties in their lives. Although I am aware that some readers may be interested in acquiring skills as would-be helpers rather than counsellors, for the sake of clarity I use the terms 'counsellor' and 'client' to denote the different roles. It would be equally appropriate to use the terms 'helper' and colleague, friend, or family member.

The basic skills that counsellors use involve listening, observing, attending and responding. Active listening requires full attention, an alertness to every nuance, to what is both implicitly and openly said, thereby helping the client to clarify confused feelings and thoughts. The ground skills which help us respond effectively include reflecting: paraphrasing and summarizing, appropriate questioning and empathy. Responding on an empathic level involves responding to content – to what is being verbally conveyed – and to feelings, by tentatively reflecting back your understanding of the feelings your client is expressing.

Use of questions

Think about how you respond when others come to you for help, advice or general succour. Do you fire a lot of questions at them, questions like: 'What's wrong?', 'Why are you so upset?', 'Is it something she or he has said to you?' Asking questions may seem the most natural thing to do on these occasions, but questioning can be off-putting if overdone. Questions can be intrusive and too forceful, and may be used to satisfy our own curiosity, none of which is beneficial to the helping process. Yet questions, used tentatively and sensitively, are necessary for the exploration and clarification of facts and feelings.

In counselling, questions tend to be used sparingly because clients are generally encouraged to tackle problems at their own pace. During therapy painful material inevitably surfaces and insensitive questioning from the therapist is destructive to building trust. One of the tenets of therapy is the belief that people can self-heal, that they possess an innate ability to recognize what they need and, given the right set of circumstances, they can re-orientate themselves to what is meaningful in their lives. In other words, most of us do not want other people telling us what to do, nor do we want others delving nosily into our business. We do appreciate someone being with us in our troubles and listening attentively with sensitivity while we make sense of our situation.

Closed questions

When we ask a closed question, it is usually met with a closed response – that is, a response which doesn't allow any further exploration. Closed questions are useful for information gathering when we need to know specific facts or specific information; for example, in an intake session with a new client when a counsellor notes marriage status, number of children, medical details, work details and so on; or in the case of a younger person details of school, college and whom they live with.

The answer to a closed question is often 'yes', 'no' or 'don't know'. The closed question begins: 'Do you', 'Can you', 'Have you', 'Is it', 'Would you say', 'Could it', 'Don't you think' and so on. The problem with questioning which invites a 'yes' or 'no' type of reply is that it can leave both parties facing a blank wall and lead to more questioning. While you are bombarding someone with questions, their feelings are subdued. In contrast, open questions allow further exploration of meanings, thoughts and feelings and encourage clients to impart additional material.

It is a good idea when using questions to ask yourself what the purpose is, and if it is assisting or hindering the helping process. You may be information gathering when it would be more appropriate to wait, giving the client time to get in touch with feelings associated with what they are telling you. The excessive use of questioning by an inexperienced counsellor can be a ploy adopted to distance the counsellor from the client – for example, when the counsellor is uncomfortable with their own feelings with regard to what the client is expressing or with silences during the session. A golden rule when counselling is to use your ears and eyes more than your mouth!

Why? Why not?

'Why' is best used sparingly. Think of a question like: 'Why did you do that?' and how loaded it is. The word 'Why' implies that the answer is instantly accessible. It may involve validation or denial of the client's actions which can result in a defensive response. 'Why' can sound accusatory – it may be seen as expressing displeasure or disapproval and may have associations with past feelings of getting things wrong. 'Why' is also difficult to answer in relation to feelings. It can take the client into thinking mode as part of an intellectual rationalizing exercise which avoids the world of emotions. Not surprisingly a question like 'Why do you feel this?' or 'Why do you think that?' is more likely than not to be met with a shrug and 'I don't know', and may result in the client losing track of what they are thinking and feeling.

Open questions

Open questions are valuable because they enable the expression of thoughts, feelings and personal meanings. They invite the other person to talk, to communicate and self-explore. They allow time to explore situations. Open questions begin with 'How', 'Where', 'When', 'What', 'In what way' and so forth. The answers given to them allow the counsellor to have a clearer understanding of the difficulties and thereby help the client to be more specific.

An example of an open question is: 'I'm not clear what you mean when you say that you feel easily hurt. Could you give me an example?' Clarifying non-direct questions can be useful; for example: 'Can you say a bit more about that?', encouraging elaboration of points. This type of questioning also requires the client to be reflective. Open questions have no 'right' answer.

Multiple and frequent questions

Don't ask too many questions – be sparing. It is important to respect the client's right to privacy. Some issues may be delicate and too intimate to rush into. Allow time for trust to develop. The client, especially in the first few sessions when it is crucial to establish trust, may feel interrogated rather than supported. This will impede the building of rapport. The frequent use of questions does not allow time for the exploration of thoughts and feelings as and when they arise; therapy can then be experienced as confusing as the counsellor's interest appears to be initiated on a superficial level only. Beware of using multiple questions, with one question superseding another in a string of enquiry. This can be experienced as annoying and distracting as well as confusing and gives little indication of the counsellor's competence. Ask one question at a time and listen with full attention to the response.

When you come to practise your skills (e.g. in role play), use questions appropriately rather than bombarding the 'client' with one question after another. It helps to instil the habit of placing questioning in context with other skills at training level. Questions form a small part of skills use. Skills like paraphrasing and reflecting feelings and content and other methods of attentive responding motivate the client to talk openly.

Leading questions

Leading questions imply answers that the questioner would find acceptable. Leading – or biased – questions can effectively stop clients expressing their thoughts and feelings for fear of ridicule. For example:

'You're not thinking of leaving your children, are you?'
'You're not going to cry, are you?'

These questions consist of an instructive statement: 'You wouldn't give up your job', followed by a question, 'Would you?' The first part indirectly tells the other person what to do, then the second appears to give an option. This is not empathic sensitive questioning, it is judgemental and restrictive, and will do nothing to enhance the relationship.

Questions to ask about your questions

■ Are you trying to clear up a point? (clarifying)
■ Are you information gathering?
■ Does the question help your client to explore self and situation?
■ Does the question have any therapeutic value – i.e. helping in some way?
■ Are you avoiding anything by asking a question? You may be filling a space, trying to put a client whom you perceive as uncomfortable with silences at ease, or perhaps you as counsellor find it difficult to manage silences.

Asking too many questions can be an attempt to force change or to control the direction of the sessions; both can cause the client to deflect from issues rather than going into them. Let the client move at their own pace; the point after all is to lessen distress, not to add to it. There is a role for challenging when an experienced counsellor feels that the client will benefit from it, but a less experienced person with counselling skills would be advised to challenge extremely tentatively, respecting the other person's right to reach new perspectives in their own time.

Some general rules for questioning

■ Use open questions when possible.
■ Avoid closed questions which invite 'yes' or 'no' replies, except when requiring the client to be more precise or when seeking specific information.

- Use indirect questions as a softer approach.
- Use questions sparingly.
- Be aware that some forms of questioning may suggest disapproval or criticism.
- Use one appropriate question at a time.
- Check the purpose of your question before you go ahead.
- Be aware of the tone of your voice, the speed of the question, how it is generally delivered and the message it may convey.

To recap, the purpose of a question is:

- To clarify – to help the client be more concrete and specific.
- To help identify problems and the factors which have created them.
- To gain useful information.
- To help the counsellor to have a clear understanding of the client's situation.
- To help the client get in touch with unexpressed emotions.
- To check reality – i.e. did I get that right? – or specific meanings – e.g. 'You said ... I wonder what that means for you?'
- To explore underlying thoughts, feelings and meanings.
- To enable or encourage further insight into what has been expressed, leading to unexplored material.

The following are examples of open and closed questions; note in each pair how (a) invites a yes/no/don't know answer, while (b) invites expression of feelings.

1 (a) *Closed question*: Were you upset when that happened?

   (b) *Open question*: How did you feel when that happened?

2 (a) *Closed question*: Could you quit smoking if you really wanted to?

   (b) *Open question*: What sorts of problems do you think you might have if you tried to give up smoking?

3 (a) *Closed question*: Do you still love your partner?

   (b) *Open question*: Tell me how you feel about your partner.

4 (a) *Closed question*: Could it be that you start arguments with your wife?

   (b) *Open question*: What happens when you and your wife argue?

5 (a) *Closed question*: Were you sad when your grandmother died?

   (b) *Open question*: How did you feel when your grandmother died?

No. 4 is an example of how a closed question can also be challenging. Open questions focus on feelings and content.

Unlike the (a) questions, the (b) questions address associated feelings – inviting the client to talk about feelings such as fear, hurt or dependency. No. 2(a) could be experienced as a challenge – as a judgemental remark relating to strength or weakness of character. In contrast no. 2(b) is a more empathic form of questioning, acknowledging the possible difficulty of the task.

Notice the language that you use when questioning. The word 'quit' in no. 2(a) may be appropriate to use, depending on the language your client uses, but it could add to the sense of being challenged. The words 'if you really wanted to' could also be loaded with implication if out of context with what your client has been saying. It could seem that you are suggesting that they don't really want to give up and be received as a criticism.

Use of empathy

Empathy has been described in a number of ways: as if walking in another's shoes, entering into another person's frame of reference, or having the ability to experience life as the other person does by temporarily entering into the client's world of thoughts, meanings and feelings. Empathy is an expression of the regard and respect the counsellor holds for the client whose frame of reference (the inner world including aspects of self: values, thoughts, meanings, feelings, cultural influences, experiences and perceptions) may be quite different from that of the counsellor. Counsellors do not lose themselves in their clients' material. It is important that counsellors retain their own sense of self. They would be of little use if they began sobbing uncontrollably when a client was attempting to express grief. This is a caricature of a situation, but serves to make the point. The client needs to feel 'held' as well as understood. True empathic responding does both. To be held therapeutically means to feel that the counsellor is capable of accepting and supporting us through anything that we, as clients, bring. The counsellor conveys to the client that they are unjudgemental, unshockable and strong enough not to have to be protected from what we may envisage to be our unacceptable or even hateful side. It can be a marvellous relief to admit all and let go of what we envisage as inappropriate thoughts and feelings and to meet with an accepting, empathic response.

Empathic responding circumnavigates all the other skills. The ability to empathize with another is enhanced by an ever-alert attentiveness to facial expressions, body language, gestures and so on, and not only to what is being openly conveyed but also to the underlying implications. Intuition or 'hunches' have a part to play in empathic responding.

On the subject of trusting his intuition – the feelings, words, impulses and fantasies that emerged when he was facilitating in groupwork – Rogers wrote (*Carl Rogers on Encounter Groups*, p. 53):

> While a responsible business executive is speaking, I may suddenly have the fantasy of the small boy he is carrying around within himself – the small boy that he was, shy, inadequate, fearful – a child he endeavours to deny; of whom he is ashamed. And I am wishing that he would love and cherish this youngster. So I may voice this fantasy – not as something true, but as a fantasy in me. Often this brings a surprising depth of reaction and profound insights.

Empathy and sympathy

Empathy is sometimes confused with sympathy. When we feel sympathy for someone we view them with pity: 'Poor Jennifer – she really can't cope now Harry has left her.' Pity is often linked with victimhood. While pity makes a victim of the sufferer, empathy empowers them; it says: 'I have a sense of your world – you do not stand alone, we will go through this together.' The other person becomes an important subject rather than a specimen object whose problems are far removed from ourselves. We can tell we are objectifying someone when in our minds we slot them into a sociological category or stereotype like 'the abandoned wife', 'the single parent' or the adolescent 'delinquent'. These classifications stifle empathic understanding which relates to each individual and views their experiences as unique.

Carl Rogers, who is sometimes referred to as the father of humanistic psychology, talked about his own initial experiences of being counselled. He relates in *A Way of Being* (p. 12) how he felt he was being rescued from the chaos of his feelings:

> These persons have heard me without judging me, diagnosing me, appraising me, or evaluating me. They have just listened and clarified and responded to me at all the levels at which I was communicating. I can testify that when you are in psychological distress and someone really hears you without judgement on you, without trying to take responsibility for you, without trying to mold you, it feels damn good!

Awareness of body language

Our inner emotional state is communicated through our bodies. We give each other messages through body movement, the intonation of our voice, facial expressions, posture, gestures and eye contact. Some of these movements may be slight or fleeting but in the heightened atmosphere of one-to-one counselling they are more often than not registered. When we counsel others we need to be aware of two sets of body language, our own and that of our client. As a helper our body needs to demonstrate behaviour that is facilitative. In psychological terminology, non-facilitative behaviour is called 'adverse stimulus'. This occurs when we display an attitude which is off-putting to the client. We may display signs of non-attention; for example, looking bored, yawning, fidgeting or showing distractive behaviour. Another example of adverse stimulus is punitive attention – when the helper looks stern, perhaps tight lipped, raising their eyebrows or staring fixedly at the speaker. It is not difficult to appreciate how this type of response acts as a deterrent to accessing any material which the client senses the helper may disapprove of.

Other mannerisms like picking at your fingers, shrugging or sniffing could be distracting to the client. This all seems so obvious and we may think we avoid all these, but it can be a revelation to watch ourselves in the act of counselling on video. What we think of as giving occasional assuring nods during a session may look exaggerated when we view ourselves on video, giving us a 'nodding dog' appearance. It is not uncommon for trainee counsellors to be shocked to see themselves smiling inanely throughout a session or to see themselves constantly shifting around in their chairs.

Posture

Our posture reveals the degree of interest we have in the client. When we sit back, away from the other, we display an attitude of distancing ourselves; and when we lean towards them we engage and show interest. Similarly, when we cross our arms and legs we convey the message that we are less open to the other person. We are in some way protecting ourselves by closing off. In contrast, a relaxed and attentive posture tells the client that we are comfortable with ourselves and with them in the helping process. Although it would be unnatural to sit totally still throughout, too much shifting around can be distracting and fits into the category of 'fidgeting'.

As with everything in life, there are always exceptions to the rules and sometimes what seems a mistake often proves to be useful. I personally think it's good to learn the skills and also retain as much of ourselves as possible so that we respond in both a spontaneous and an appropriate way. An example is that if we find ourselves crossing our arms and legs during the session, rather than thinking

'Oh no, I shouldn't be doing this', it is more useful to observe yourself and note, 'I have my legs and arms crossed. I wonder why? Perhaps I am uncomfortable with what is being expressed, or it may be that in some way I am reflecting what my client is feeling.'

A counsellor working in the person-centred mode who finds themselves yawning at times throughout a session, in the spirit of being genuine and congruent might say to a client something to the effect, 'I'm yawning again and I can see it's off-putting to you. I do feel a bit bored ... I don't want to be bored and it makes me uncomfortable that I'm yawning when you're talking to me. I think maybe I am reacting to what you're saying because you have repeated it many times.' Although Carl Rogers is perhaps more widely known for his 'unconditional positive regard' (from the Core Conditions Model), in the interest of being 'real' (genuine, congruent) with a client he would be direct and honest about his feelings and reactions towards the client.

The tone of voice

The tone of our voice also acts as an indicator of our thoughts and attitudes. If we speak too quietly or hesitantly the other person may find it hard to have confidence in us as a helper. It would be counterproductive to be too forceful or bombastic in the way we interact. If, as counsellors, we talk clearly at a fairly steady level rather than sounding rushed or excited, and without mumbling or stumbling over our words, then we are probably getting it right. Sometimes it is appropriate to mirror the tone of the client's voice to help them hear the emotion conveyed.

Although humour can be useful at times, when used sparingly, it is not a good idea to adopt a jocular manner with your clients. It can inhibit their expression of deeper feelings. It is neither the counsellor nor the client's obligation to entertain or cheer up the other. In fact this approach would totally defeat the potential benefits of having counselling.

Words and body language

Words can be either congruent or incongruent with what our body is demonstrating. For example, we may say 'I understand' while looking perplexed, or say 'No, that doesn't shock me' having raised our eyebrows and crossed our arms and legs. What the body is doing is an indicator of deeper, sometimes unconscious feelings. A common display of incongruence is when a client says that they are angry while smiling, or that they are deeply sad with no emotion whatsoever. This tells us that the client is not comfortable in expressing their true emotions. What the client and counsellor hear is reinforced or contradicted by what they see demonstrated by the body language of the other.

The client's body language

While we as counsellor or helper need to be aware of our body language, it is also our work to decode, understand and interpret the body language of our client. What might their body language tell us? Body and facial expression can inform us about hidden feelings. For example:

- She is angry – her mouth is tensed. Her eyes are narrowed and she is leaning back in her chair and is avoiding eye contact.
- He is very upset and near to tears – he has placed his hand up to his forehead and his mouth is twitching. He is leaning slightly forward and his head is down.
- He is eager to be understood – he is leaning towards me, with his feet placed firmly on the floor; he gesticulates freely with his hands, he is talking intently and his eyes are fixed on mine.

Reflecting skills

Paraphrasing, summarizing and mirroring are ways of reflecting back the client's thoughts and feelings. They are methods of reiterating client expression in order that:

- The client can (re)hear what they are saying.
- The client gets a sense of themselves, i.e. how they are expressing themselves – as if a mirror were being held up to them.
- The counsellor checks what they are understanding (meanings, thoughts and feelings) is correct.

- There is clarification of certain points (without asking intrusive questions).
- The material is made more 'manageable' for both counsellor and client.
- There is on-going communication between counsellor and client.
- Threads may be joined together to make a more coherent whole.

Paraphrasing

Paraphrasing involves reflecting back the content and feelings of what the client is saying by drawing out the salient parts. Usually the content is repeated in the counsellor's own words, which gives a slightly different perspective on the material. Paraphrasing is best used at natural intervals or when it seems appropriate to reiterate what is being conveyed. It lets the client know that you are following what they say, that you are attentive to their personal details and understanding of their feelings and meanings. It isn't the case that because the client has spoken then the counsellor is immediately required to paraphrase the details back; it is instead a matter of sensitively gauging when it is appropriate to use the skill.

As individuals, counsellors will paraphrase differently – as with all the skills there is no absolute set formula. How wooden and unspontaneous the act of counselling would be if there were. Counsellors develop their own style. Some talk more than others, some may put emphasis on one or two skills in preference to others.

Examples of paraphrasing

1 (a) The client's statement

When I was a teenager I used to wish that my dad was dead – because he was cruel to me at times – and when he did die, a few years later, I felt a mixture of relief and sadness but the relief made me feel guilty, and now fifteen years on I still feel guilty when I think of some of the things I said and did to him.

(b) The counsellor's response

For a long time now you have felt guilty about your negative feelings and actions towards your father when he was alive.

He could be very harsh with you at times and when he died you felt a sense of freedom as well as sadness.

Comment: In these examples the responses reflect back, in the counsellor's own language, the content of what the client has related and also the client's feelings.

Feeling words from the counsellor's response: guilty, negative, harsh, freedom, sadness.

2 (a) The client's statement

My teenage daughter lives with her father in another town and when she comes to stay with me I get irritated with how demanding she seems to be. She is always asking questions in great detail about how I spend my time and who I go out with … and everything else, and she won't entertain herself either and expects me to be a constant source of amusement.

(b) The counsellor's response

When your daughter comes to stay with you, you feel overwhelmed by her need for your love and attention. You feel irritated by her enquiries into your personal life and you wish she could be more self-sufficient while she is with you.

Feeling words and phrases: overwhelmed, love and attention, irritated, personal life, self-sufficient.

3 (a) The client's statement

I have broken up with my partner, although it was my doing – because I was feeling claustrophobic, restless, and felt I was losing my own identity. I have found living on my own a difficult experience. It seems like I am caught between the old adage of 'I can't live with them, and I can't live without them.'

(b) The counsellor's response

You left a relationship because you felt stifled by it and unable to express yourself while you were in it, but you find it hard living alone and sometimes you miss your ex-partner.

Feeling words and phrases: stifled, express yourself, hard living alone, miss.

4 (a) The client's statement

When it gets dark I feel a sense of hollowness. A void emerges and I don't know how to fill it. Sometimes I end up drinking my way through it, which in a sense seems to keep me occupied, and although I know I have a drink problem I don't feel I have the energy or imagination to fill the void more creatively.

(b) The counsellor's response

You drink in the evening because you feel an emptiness inside, you're low at the moment and feel unable to tackle the problem in a self-nurturing way.

Feeling words and phrases: emptiness inside, low, unable to tackle, self-nurturing.

To recap, paraphrasing has the following aspects. It:

- gives the client an opportunity to hear what they are saying, in a slightly different format which can lead to new insight;
- is a way of reflecting the content and feelings of what the client is saying;
- entails content and feelings being reflected back in the counsellor's own words;
- demonstrates the counsellor's attentiveness;
- gives the client an opportunity to clarify anything the counsellor is misunderstanding and the counsellor an opportunity to check that they are getting it right;
- is a way of keeping contact with the client.

Mirroring

Mirroring, which bears a resemblance to parroting, has to be used with sensitivity to be well received by and useful to the client. The counsellor mirrors by, for example, repeating a line a client has said or mirroring an expression (take care that this is not straight mimicking – it should be subtle). A client might say: 'I am enjoying my new job, it's a big challenge but I like challenges most of the time', with a grimace at the end of the statement. You may have noticed that he has mixed feelings about his new job and may be wondering if he has made the right decision in accepting it or doubting that he is up to it. To check this out you may choose to subtly mirror the grimace and pick up on his words: 'Most of the time ...' This could be useful to him, leading him into examining what it is he is not enjoying, perhaps a challenge in his life that he has not yet mentioned.

Summarizing

Summarizing is similar to paraphrasing, but it requires the putting together of larger chunks of information when a client has talked for a length of time. While paraphrasing is relevant to one statement of whatever length, summarizing puts together a few or many statements. It is a way of keeping contact with a client, showing that you are following what they are saying and that you have an understanding of their underlying feelings. Another purpose of summarizing is that it brings together different threads in what has been expressed, providing an overview which enables the client to make connections.

There may be an overall theme which can be brought together by summarizing. For example, a client may spend a lot of the session saying how low he feels about different relationships he has with others, and although the story differs each time, a unifying theme emerges. He has said that his father is undemonstrative and critical of him, no matter how much he tries to please him; his wife is sexually unresponsive to him although he is tender and affectionate with her; and a friend he recently supported through a divorce seems now to have no time for him.

You, as counsellor, could join these themes together by giving a summary of the different things that have been said, and by then adding an interpretative summary like: 'I think what you are saying is that you feel although you try your best to get close to those who matter to you, you feel that they do not respond to you or appreciate you in the way that you would like.' An underlying theme may be repeated throughout a session or even over a number of sessions and accurate summarizing can sharpen the client's perception as to what lies behind repetitive thoughts, feelings and behaviour.

The point of both paraphrasing and summarizing is to assist in further exploration of troubling issues, to help the client reach new insights into their problems. It is especially important when summarizing a lot of received information to conclude with an enquiry about the accuracy of your understanding. You can check this out by saying, 'Is that what you feel?', or 'Does that sum it up?' or simply 'Am I getting this right?' Otherwise you may be going off on an agenda of your own. Use your own language to reflect back and try not to use stock phrases as these can sound stiff and may be experienced by the client as insincere. The idea is to learn skills, not set formulas. When you become familiar with the skills you can trust in yourself to use your positive qualities to ascertain what is needed at the time.

To recap the uses of summarizing:

1 It is useful at intervals in the session to give a sense of connection between threads or themes of what the client has been saying.
2 It gives the client an overview of their situation or experiences and moves the session along.
3 It is useful towards the end of a counselling session, to highlight the central concerns.

Minimal responses

Minimal responses are made to demonstrate the counsellor's attentiveness and understanding of what is said and also to encourage the client to continue. Minimal encouragements convey interest. Minimal responses include:

- Mm, Uh-huh.
- Nodding.
- Using one word such as 'so', 'and', 'then'.
- Repeating one or a few key words the client has used.
- Restating the exact words of the client's statement apart from placing it in the second person, e.g. The client says: 'I feel so stupid', the counsellor says: 'You feel so stupid.' This is particularly useful when the comment is uttered as a throw-away line that may be covering a deeper hurt.
- Silence is another form of minimal response that allows the client time to think, feel and find expression – 'Silence is golden.'

Words

People use specific words to communicate inner emotions. It is more difficult to say to another, 'I completely lost control and I was destructive in my behaviour' than 'I was in a rage.' The word 'rage' says a lot more than 'angry'; the word 'joy' is more revealing than 'happy'; the word 'morose' more specific than 'sad' or 'depressed'; the word 'devastated' more emotionally packed than 'hurt' and so on. Refer to the evocative/feelings word list and see what feelings particular words evoke in you.

Here is a word of caution. Inevitably we as counsellors may have at times a different understanding of a particular word or phrase from that of the client, so check that your understanding corresponds with the client's meaning. Clients whose culture or background differs from the counsellor may use a word in an unfamiliar way. In paraphrasing and summarizing the counsellor uses their own words to reflect back their understanding; the words which are used need to reflect accurately the client's meaning but they may put emphasis on a feeling, offering the client more insight. For example, a client might say 'I am very tired', and in paraphrasing the counsellor might say, 'You are exhausted'. This may lead the client to say 'Yes, I am exhausted – I really don't think I can go on like this', leading to a cathartic release of emotion.

More advanced skills

Silences

Managing silence means having the ability to recognize a constructive silence. It may take some time to feel comfortable with silences. Ask yourself the following questions:

- How comfortable am I with silences?
- How often do I spend time by myself in silence?
- What associations do I have with silence?

Allowing silences gives the client space to reflect. You may experience awkwardness at handling a silence as a new counsellor but your threshold of silence will increase with experience and you will be able to discern between different types. Sometimes clients

List of evocative/feeling words
I feel ...
I am ...

accepted
acknowledged
affectionate
aggravated
aggressive
alone
angry
anxious
appreciated
assertive
attractive
attuned
awful
awkward

bashful
belittled
best
betrayed
bitter
bored
burdened

carefree
careless
caught out
cautious
cheerful
confused
content
cosseted
criticized

daring
dehumanized
delighted
dependent
depressed
devalued

devastated
dirty
discontented
disgusting
disheartened
disloyal
distant
distressed

embarrassed
empowered
empty
enthusiastic
evil
exhausted

feckless
free
friendly
frightened
furious

great
grief stricken
guilty
gutted

happy
heartbroken
heartened
heavy
heavy-hearted
humiliated
hurt

ignored
interested
irresponsible
irritated

jealous
jittery
joyful
jumpy

keen
kindly

light-hearted
listless
lonely
loved
loving

mad
manic
miserable
moany
morose
mournful

naughty
needy
neglected
nervous

obliged
optimistic
ordinary
outcast
overcome

passionate
pessimistic
petrified
powerful
powerless

raging
rejected
respected

respectful
responsible

sad
secure
shy
silly
strong
supported

tense
torn
troubled
trusting

ugly
unappreciated
unattractive
uneasy
unloved
unsupported
uptight
useless

valued
vulnerable

wanted
weak
weary
willing
worn out
worried

are nervous, especially in the first or second session, and a protracted silence may be experienced as excruciatingly uncomfortable. In this case it would be advisable to acknowledge what you understand to be a rising discomfort on their behalf by saying something like 'I imagine it is difficult for you to be here.' This will serve two purposes. Firstly, it breaks an uncomfortable silence and, secondly, it is likely to lead to disclosure of feelings. Clients can get lost in their own thoughts and feelings or feel overawed by them, and a silence may then occur. A summary of what you have understood would be useful at such a time. Sometimes a silence begins because the client is hoping for something from the counsellor; this might be reassurance or confirmation that the counsellor has been listening, or has understood what has been said.

Emotions experienced during a silence – for example, feelings of awkwardness or anger – may help the client access material they are avoiding or are unaware of. Transferential material may come to the surface. (Transference is outlined in Chapter 8.) You, as counsellor or helper, may become a punitive parent whose mode of punishing is to distance themselves emotionally from the 'offender' by means of silence. At a time like this you might say, 'I sense that you are feeling uncomfortable with this silence and I remember you saying that your mother used to get angry then refuse to speak to anyone in the family for days.' The client may make connections, realizing how deeply this has affected them, both in their childhood responses and in their adult reactions towards others who appear to 'switch off' from them. Silences are more often than not constructive, even if a little awkward. A protracted silence often has an air of expectancy about it. My experience has been that silences lead to new ground. It would be a mistake to presume always to 'know' what a particular silence was about.

In *On Learning from the Patient*, psychotherapist Patrick Casement writes: 'The therapist's openness to the unknown in the patient leaves more room for the patient to contribute to any subsequent knowing, and what is thus jointly discovered has a freshness which belongs to both.' Silences can give us an opportunity to be open to the, as yet, unknown.

Immediacy

Immediacy involves working in the 'here and now', within the dynamic of the counsellor–client relationship. The skill of immediacy can be used to:

1 Bring the client's feelings back into the relationship.

2 Enable the relationship to reach greater depths of intimacy.

3 Challenge the client–counsellor relationship by looking at what is going on between them in the 'here and now' (e.g. in the moment).

4 Help the client to see more clearly and own, both in positive and negative ways, how they relate to others and the effects of this.

5 Help the client to see and deal with their resistance, i.e. being late, missing appointments etc.

6 Look at how the counsellor–client relationship is developing.

7 Give the client an opportunity to air any anxieties, doubts or dissatisfactions, e.g. with regard to their expectations of counselling.

Appropriate times to use immediacy include:

■ When the session is directionless, seeming to be going in circles, yet you as counsellor feel that something is 'in the air' that needs clearing.

■ When there is tension in the room, e.g. resentment or anger.

■ When transference or countertransference (see Chapter 8) is interfering with the process.

■ When there is attraction in the relationship – e.g. a male counsellor may notice that a young female client has begun to dress provocatively and is coquettish in her behaviour.

■ When there is a dependency. The counsellor may wish to address the way in which a client is increasingly seeking approval or advice.

■ When something new and fresh has developed in the relationship, e.g. a deepening trust.

Examples of immediacy

1 Immediacy is a skill used by the counsellor to address directly issues that the client is expressing indirectly. For example, a client may say, 'I don't like my teacher/boss/partner – they are so critical of everything I do.' The counsellor sees this as an opportunity to help the client access negative thoughts and feelings that they may be harbouring towards the counsellor. The counsellor says, 'I wonder if you are talking about me too? Perhaps you feel criticized by me and would like to tell me that you don't like me.'

2 This example corresponds with the fourth point in the list immediately above. A young woman is expressing something indirectly through her dress and behaviour. A male counsellor may bring the subject into the relationship by saying something like 'I've noticed you are dressed in a way that reveals a great deal of your body [she is wearing a very short skirt and low top] and I am experiencing you as flirty – I wondered what's going on for you right now.'

This type of situation is not an unusual one. Sometimes when clients feel valued by a counsellor who is of the opposite sex, they confuse the attentive responding with other forms of intimacy, including sexuality. This applies particularly to clients who have experienced sexual abuse, who have internalized 'conditions of worth' with regard to their sexuality. By using immediacy the counsellor brings to the client's attention the pattern of behaviour and gives her the opportunity to explore and understand the issues.

3 Immediacy may be used at the onset of counselling; e.g. 'I am aware that this is a strange experience for you' or 'You may be feeling scared/embarrassed coming here and telling me this' or 'I imagine it is very difficult for you to be here in this session. I wondered what's going on for you right now.'

The counsellor conveys empathic understanding right at the beginning by using immediacy and also a willingness to engage in a therapeutic involvement.

4 An example of how immediacy is used to address issues of dependency is given by the situation in which a client wants the counsellor's approval all the time, asking what they should do. The counsellor might respond with 'I notice how often you are asking my opinion. I wonder what this is saying about how our relationship is developing ...' Another example is when a client appears upset because a holiday break is coming up when the counsellor won't be available for a few sessions. The counsellor's use of immediacy in this situation could be 'You have been very quiet since I reminded you of the holidays coming up. Perhaps you are feeling that I'm abandoning you.'

5 Immediacy is at times used to address the client's resistance (towards therapy) as it is happening. The client may have ambivalent feelings towards therapy and part of them does not want to assist in the counselling process; instead they offer resistance. Immediacy helps the process by enabling the counsellor and client to look at the ambivalent feelings.

Examples of resistance include lateness or missing sessions, and the use of passivity and silence when the client has previously talked openly. In the latter situation the counsellor can address what is happening in the 'here and now' by saying, 'You are very quiet when you normally talk quite freely. How are you feeling right now?'

The main benefits of immediacy are that it gives the client opportunities to experience difficulties in relating to other people in a new way; issues are aired and explored with interest within the client–counsellor context and are seen by the client not only to be non-damaging but to have a positive, constructive outcome.

Challenging

Challenging is used to help the client explore inconsistencies in their behaviour or how they express themselves. For example, 'You say you feel really angry when he does that, yet you laugh as you tell me.' Another example would be, 'You appear to be withdrawn today and I'm wondering if it is because I was not able to make it here for your session last week?' The behaviour is challenged rather than the person. In cognitive behavioural therapy a client's irrational thoughts might be challenged and the client encouraged to replace them with more realistic affirming beliefs. Challenging or confrontation work best when a good working relationship has been established. The client is less likely to hear the challenge as criticism or feel threatened and is therefore more likely to be able to make good use of it.

I would suggest that it can be a relief to be challenged in a therapeutic (i.e. helping) situation, as it gives an opportunity to look at areas where we are 'stuck'. Hopefully the client will perceive that they are with a person who can see the inconsistencies of their behaviour and the ways they have fashioned to protect themselves, and yet who demonstrates interest and is non-judgemental. Being challenged by another and feeling accepted and not harshly judged can help us accept ourselves. We have a received sense of 'It's OK to be imperfect.' When we are constructively challenged, that invites us to own our behaviour and accept responsibility for it. The counsellor may challenge the client to personalize their thoughts and feelings in the interest of self-awareness and self-acceptance. Instead of using a generalization like 'Anyone would have felt miserable if that had happened to them', the client is encouraged to claim (and thereby legitimize) their thoughts and feelings – for example 'I feel miserable because ...'

Challenging others necessitates honest assessment of our ability to challenge ourselves. For example:

- Do you deal effectively with your own problems?
- Are you open to being personally challenged?
- Do you challenge yourself?
- Are you willing to engage deeply with others?

Challenging or confrontation helps the client to self-challenge and is best used when there is a possibility of change. It is appropriate to use it in situations where something is either being avoided or remains unknown to the client. These include the following situations.

1 The client's non-verbal behaviour is incongruent with what they say.

2 The client ignores or fails to recognize self-defeating or self-destructive behaviour.

3 The client avoids talking about an issue that is obviously vexing them.

4 The client self-contradicts, distorts or uses rationalization or manipulative behaviour, or there are other discrepancies.

5 The client fails to recognize the consequences of their behaviour.

6 The client demonstrates signs of resistance – repeatedly missing sessions, being late or taking 'flight into health'.

7 The client has little sense of reality.

Examples of confrontation

Example 1

To confront incongruence between body and verbal language. The client says, 'I feel excited about going to college' in a flat, depressed tone of voice, sighing while changing position in the chair.

The counsellor's confrontation:

'When you said you felt excited about going to college I noticed that the tone of your voice was flat and you sighed heavily when you shifted around in your chair.'

Note: The counsellor reflects what they have observed and heard but gives no extra interpretation, which allows the client to offer their own understanding from the feedback.

Example 2

To confront when a client is continually deflecting from an important issue by changing the subject. The client has briefly referred to the hurtful actions of a friend several times during the session but then deflects from the subject by talking about seemingly unrelated (trivial) material.

The counsellor's confrontation:

'I'm confused – I've noticed that you have begun talking a few times about how hurt you feel about your friend's behaviour, but then you make a joke and change the subject altogether.'

Note: The counsellor began by expressing their feelings by saying, 'I'm confused', followed by a concrete statement of their observation without any interpretation. Because there is no judgement implied, a response like this is usually experienced as non-threatening.

Example 3

A confrontation that addresses repetition in client behaviour – for example, blaming and giving excuses. The client has come to session after session complaining of a situation that he is in – he blames others, says he is going to do something about the situation, then offers excuses when he doesn't.

The counsellor's confrontation:

'I hear what you are saying. There are difficulties in the situation you are presently in. You've been going through this for some time now and I wonder what concrete steps you are taking towards sorting it out.'

Note: Again this confrontation is factual but not accusatory or rejecting. It challenges the client to reassess his passive attitude.

Self-disclosure (sometimes called 'helper self-sharing')

The counsellor may, at times, feel that it is appropriate to share some personal experience or detail about themselves with the client. The purpose of self-disclosure on the part of the counsellor is to model non-defensive self-disclosure, to enter more fully into a reciprocal relationship (as in person-centred therapy) and to help the client perceive their own experience or problems more clearly. It is not to meet the needs of the counsellor.

An example taken from my own work was when a client felt she was 'going mad' after the death of her husband. She felt that he was in the room with her at times. I told her that I had had similar sensations when someone close to me had died. This appeared to help her.

Be clear about why you choose to self-disclose. It can be helpful to the client to 'normalize' their behaviour; that is, say that the behaviour is understandable under the circumstances. It would not be appropriate, for example, to say this to someone who was suffering from a delusional disorder or was displaying signs of mental illness.

Focusing, timing and pacing

It is important that no one is hurried along in line with a counsellor's agenda. Particularly if we are new to counselling or are desperate to help someone solve a problem, we may have a need to see 'results'. Individuals have differing needs and approach their own healing or reach a resolution of their problems in their own way and in their own time. It would not be helpful for the client to have information or feelings teased out of them. However, counsellors often work with clients within a time-limited framework which requires focusing on specific problems.

Since it is not uncommon for agencies to offer six to eight sessions to a client, the time needs to be fully utilized, the work highly focused, containing a structure which includes:

- A beginning – where client history and information is gathered.
- A middle – the active stage that includes identifying and working through a specific problem.
- An ending – that acknowledges work that has been achieved, issues that still need addressing and the way forward for the client.

The success of brief counselling work depends to a large extent on the counsellor's ability to keep the work focused and on the client's own motivation.

How skills can be applied to personal and work situations

- Listen carefully and attentively, without being defensive or attacking.
- Use your powers of observation – notice the person's body language, appearance, gestures, posture, eye contact and tone of voice.
- Don't bombard the person with questions.
- Use questions to open out what the person is trying to convey and to expand your understanding of the other person's thoughts, feelings and meanings.
- Paraphrase (repeating, not verbatim but in your own words) as a means of checking and clarifying the content of what is being said and the feelings behind it.
- Use minimal responses such as 'Yes', 'mm', 'uh-huh', nodding etc. to demonstrate attention, to show you are following the verbal communication and to encourage further exploration.
- Summarize when the person has talked for a while, in order to keep track of and to join together threads or themes of what they have said, and as a means of checking and helping the person see an overall picture.
- Use immediacy to address 'here and now' issues in the relationship.
- Use challenging and confrontation tentatively – examine your motives, they are not to be used to accuse or humiliate, or as an act of revenge; examine your own agenda and challenge the behaviour, not the person; your aim is to help the person in some way, perhaps to broaden their awareness of their behaviour and how it affects others.

An appropriate time to use confrontation skills is when a person has become rude or angry towards others or is repeatedly demonstrating destructive behaviour. At work it may be necessary to confront an employee who is continually late for work, and at school a pupil with late assignments and so on. Remember the aim of the confrontation. Is it intended to achieve a greater understanding of the problems? Be aware of whose needs are being met by the confrontation. Do you, for example, need to express your own frustration, irritability or stress? If so, it may be more productive to use immediacy skills of addressing what is happening between the two of you. Be 'real' yourself. Tell the other person about your feelings if they are in conflict with helping; for example, 'I would like to help but I am frightened/angry/upset', but convey this in a way that is not dismissive or rejecting of the other person.

5 | PRACTICE MAKES YOU COMPETENT

The aim of this chapter is to give you, the reader, a sense of what the first stages of counselling training entail with regard to skills practice. For this purpose we shall look at the function of role play, the role of observer and the giving and receiving of feedback, and we shall focus on some basic learning exercises.

We consider ourselves skilled when we have become competent or proficient at using a skill. The theory you have been acquainted with up to this point – that is, this is the skill and this is what happens when you use it – is not enough in itself. If you really want to learn how to use the various skills and adopt the core values, there is nothing like the trial and error of experiential learning in the form of practical application. I recommend joining a basic skills training course to gain the benefits of group interaction, ideas and feedback as well as a tutor to supervise and guide you in the early stages of practice.

Forms of practice

Ways of practising the use of skills are:

- by observing or listening to yourself in various singular activities,
- by working in pairs,
- by working in practice triads,
- groupwork.

Singular exercises

There are a number of 'getting to know yourself' exercises which you can begin with. These self-exploratory exercises involve writing ideas, thoughts and feelings down on paper, drawing and working with a tape recorder. Try the following.

Exercise 1

The purpose of this exercise is to help you identify stress relievers which will help you get in touch with a support system created by yourself.

List ten things that you enjoy doing, in order of importance to you. Write alongside each item on the list how often you manage to do each: most days/once a week/once a month? If the answer is that you hardly ever do the things that you enjoy, what stops you? Ask yourself if it is possible to do it more frequently. Some things that we find most enjoyable – like taking a holiday – may be possible only once a year, but there are ways of making little holidays for ourselves: by resting, going away for short breaks and having time to ourselves. Be adaptable. Self-challenge yourself to make time to do as many things on your list as are immediately possible and strive towards fulfilling the others.

Exercise 2

Write or make a drawing to represent where you are now, where you were five years ago and where you would like to be in five years' time. Can you see a pattern, a continuum? Do you consider yourself to have progressed? If so, in what ways? (e.g. spiritually, financially, in your position in life, in your understanding of self and others). What areas of yourself would you like to develop?

Exercise 3

This exercise builds your powers of self-listening, which will help you listen attentively to others.

Using an audio recorder, record yourself talking about something meaningful to you in your life, either in the present or from the past. This could be a childhood memory of an experience with your parents or at school, or something related to partnerships or your children or a specific problem you are experiencing in the present. Spend between ten and twenty minutes recording, deciding on the time limit before you begin as a discipline (when you later practise skills exercises with others you will be working within time constraints).

The second part of the exercise is listening to the recording. Try to do this as if you are listening to someone else, noticing the words you use; the intonation of your voice; pauses, silences and so on; what you were talking about before the silence and how you broke it; coughing, giggling and hesitations. Do you laugh things off? Do you self-censure? Is your tone of voice congruent with what you are saying?

Try to understand your feelings as you speak.

Topics you might like to address within this exercise in relation to yourself are: failure, successes, values, fears, anger, prejudices and unresolved problems. Make notes, compare how you respond to different topics.

Exercise 4

This exercise is designed to put you in touch with your inner self-talk and introjected 'shoulds', 'oughts' and 'musts'. Albert Ellis, the originator of rational emotive behaviour therapy, calls these 'musturbation' – tyrannical unrealistic inner rules.

Make a list as follows:

- I should …
- I ought …
- I must …

When you have completed the list, ask yourself the question, 'Why?' Ask where the different expectations and demands that you make of yourself come from. Think which ones are really you and which ones you could part with. You can extend this exercise by sharing it with a partner and discussing your lists with each other.

Exercise 5

The purpose of this exercise is to identify and develop the qualities of a helper. Think of a crucial time in your life when you needed emotional support and someone helped you.

■ How? What was it they said, did, or expressed that helped? What, if any, special qualities did the person have?

■ How did you feel about telling them about your problems?

■ How did you feel afterwards?

Practising with others

When you work with others – a partner or others in a practice triad – using role play or personal material, you will use feedback as a learning tool. The use of feedback requires a specific approach if it is not to become open to abuse or sycophantic appraisal. It requires honest appraisal, self-scrutiny and humility. It is not easy to look at our weak points and worse to have a magnifying glass placed on them. Alongside this threatening aspect is the affirming, positive side of giving and receiving feedback. Our strengths are also highlighted.

Feedback should never be offensive, we need to bear in mind that none of us is perfect and all of us can improve our own skills.

Feedback

The benefit of working with others is that you can give and receive feedback. Feedback is information given to us by others concerning how they perceive us and what effect we have on them. It is an invaluable source in helping us identify our strengths and weaknesses in the way we apply the various skills. Giving and receiving feedback can be difficult. It is not an opportunity to 'get at' someone. In order that receiving feedback can be helpful to an individual, the person needs to be able to do the following:

- understand the information being offered to them,
- consider the information,
- act on the information.

Both giving and receiving feedback can be a delicate procedure. It is necessary to take it as impersonally as you can, remembering that it is one person's view of your work or behaviour. If you receive critical feedback on the same subject matter from three or more people, then it is probably worth taking that viewpoint on board even if you don't like it. Giving feedback requires us to be candid in our opinion without being offensive; for example, it would be totally inappropriate to say: 'That was useless, I could do better than that', but appropriate to say, 'It seemed when you did ... that it had this effect ..., perhaps you could have done this ...' Be respectful and sensitive without pussyfooting; remember that feedback has a constructive purpose. Your intention is purely to help the other person in improving their application of skills.

Some general rules for giving feedback

1 Be clear in what you are trying to say.
2 Be non-judgemental. You are entitled to have your view of the other person or of their 'performance', but keep it in mind that your views are not facts but are coloured by your own perspective. The one receiving the feedback and other observers may have different perceptions.
3 Address the person you are talking about directly as 'you' and use 'I' statements first to own your thoughts, feelings and opinions. For example: 'I think that it was helpful when you summarized at that point', 'I feel that it might have been more helpful to your client if you had stayed with the silence.' Using terms like 'most people' (e.g., 'Most people think that you asked too many direct questions') makes it difficult to decide if you are repeating what you have heard from others.
4 Use neutral and objective words. Describe what you have observed or experienced rather than evaluating or interpreting. To say, 'I noticed that you interrupted quite often when she was talking' is more helpful and acceptable to receive than 'Your Ego gets in the way – you seem incapable of listening to material with an emotional content.'

5 Feedback is concerned with specific behaviour or effects, not the character of the recipient.

6 Try to be specific by identifying words or behaviour that you are basing your feedback on.

7 Verbal and non-verbal messages need to be congruent. If they are at odds with each other, then you will be sending conflicting messages resulting in confusion. For example, if you say, 'I think this information will help you' with a tight-lipped expression and avoiding eye contact, that will confuse the listener.

8 Feedback is concerned with specific behaviour that is under the individual's control, that is subject to change. It would be ludicrous to tell someone, 'You haven't got an empathic face', but it would be appropriate to say, 'As a counsellor, you look stern at times during your practice session.'

9 If the recipient of the feedback becomes defensive or emotional, it is advisable for the giver of the feedback to accept and deal with it rather than trying to reason with or convince the recipient.

10 The recipient deserves respect as a person and as a learner of new skills.

Both 'negative' and 'positive' feedback are useful – don't forget to comment on what was done well. Giving positive feedback before negative feedback is considered a more acceptable approach. An alternative is a feedback 'sandwich', consisting of first positive, then negative, then positive feedback.

Receiving feedback

■ Listen attentively, without commenting, until the person who is giving the feedback has finished.

■ Try not to be defensive or to overreact to feedback. It is an opinion and is worth considering but it is not gospel.

■ Resist any temptation to defend, deny, apologize and so on.

■ Check out anything you have heard which you are unsure of, repeat the comments and ask questions if you are unclear of the meaning.

■ Evaluate the accuracy and potential value of what you have been offered.

■ Take responsibility for deciding what is relevant and useful to your progress.

■ Obtain additional information from as many other sources as are available to you, noting your own thoughts and feelings and how other people react to you.

Giving and receiving feedback is part of working with others and is integral to the personal growth element of acquiring counselling abilities.

Role play

Role play is what happens when the person who is acting as client adopts a role and set of problematic circumstances to present to the person acting as the counsellor. The client has the script of the role they are adopting to work from. The person playing the role can develop the character, improvising details which will enhance understanding of the 'story'. The words 'acting', 'improvising' and 'script' give these instructions an air of constituting amateur dramatics, which might seem daunting to the person who is client. Don't worry, good acting ability is not necessary. Role play is more a matter of entering into the set of circumstances – rather like the practice of empathy. The brief script you will read prior to taking on a persona is a guideline or baseline story to which you will inevitably bring parts of your own life experience. The counsellor's knowledge is limited to a few brief facts, enough to give them the bones which the client adds meat to with the help of the counsellor's interventions.

Exercises for working in pairs and practice triads

If you want to test the skills in action, it will be necessary to practise with at least one other person as your partner so that you can experience taking the role of counsellor and of client. To have a sense of your own progression it helps to:

■ have on-going feedback from another person about how they experienced your use of the skills,

■ have the opportunity to observe the other person in action.

An ideal method of practising skills is to work in a triad of counsellor, client and observer. An observer can give an overall view of the interaction which neither of the other two can while immersed in their roles. The observer can also be the time keeper during exercises.

The role of observer

When you work with others in a practice triad, one person becomes a client, one a counsellor and one an observer whose role it is to oversee the activities of the others. The observer watches over the interaction between counsellor and client, either writing notes or making mental notes with regard to the exchange. The observer notes the whole content of the session: the process, what happens, how, why, when, silences, awkwardness and so on, and the body language of the two participants.

When an exercise is finished the observer comments – that is, gives feedback – on the ways the counsellor helped (or didn't help) the client to explore issues generally, and also on how they met the criteria of specific tasks set by the exercise; for example, did they paraphrase effectively and summarize at the end of the session? Were they able to reflect back feelings to the other person (client)?

The observer also gives feedback to the person who is in the position of the client, commenting on anything that they think may be helpful; for example (observer addressing the client), 'I noticed when Jack [the person in the counsellor's role] asked you to tell him more about what happened, you looked hesitant, as if there was a moment when you were deciding if you wanted to, and then you went ahead and explained and explored your feelings more, and it was as if a light had come on and you looked relieved.'

When the observer gives the client or counsellor feedback, they listen without interruption until the end; then they can comment on the accuracy of the observations.

Another role of the observer is that of time keeper, checking that the others keep within the time limits of the exercise: for example, twenty minutes each for a particular role. The observer's presence is discreet and they would not, for instance, shout out, 'Time's up!', but instead quietly remind the others that their part of the exercise is coming to an end by saying, 'You have two minutes left.'

The observer usually maintains a low profile while the other two are engaged in the exercise, sitting in an unobtrusive position in the room, out of direct eye contact with the others.

In some cases, when it is appropriate to the exercise, the observer assists the person who is in the counselling role. If the counsellor feels 'stuck', they can call 'Time out' and step outside the room with the observer in order to confer and decide upon a positive way forward.

Exercises – Working in pairs or triads

The following sample exercises are adapted from some I have had experience of in my own training. Others are of my own creation. It is difficult to be sure of the origins of particular exercises because they are widely adopted, modified and adapted. I have found the work of Michael Jacobs to be particularly informative and easy to read; some exercises are included in the appendix to his book, *Still Small Voice*. Another of his books, *Insight and Experience: A Manual of Training in the Technique and Theory of Psychodynamic Counselling and Therapy,* is a rich source of inspiration, although it promotes some of the more advanced skills. The books of Richard Nelson-Jones, *Practical Counselling and Helping Skills* and *Human Relationship Skills,* also contain many skills exercises.

With a partner try out the experiences of being a counsellor and a client. Use a room that is uncluttered, sparsely furnished and, if possible, not so large that it is impersonal and not too tiny so that you are close together. It is best if the room has as few visual distractions as possible (large, vibrant posters on the wall would draw the eye towards them) and is also in a quiet location. Your room may not fit all these criteria, but use this advice as a guideline to helping you make the most of the space that is available to you. You will need two similar comfortable chairs, of the same height and positioned at a slight angle to each other, and as little external distraction or interruption as possible.

Exercise 1 – to practise skills of observation

As A, take five minutes to tell B what you noticed about them when they arrived for your session. This may be things like, 'I noticed you were dressed more casually than I have seen you dressed before' or 'I noticed you were wearing your hair up', and may refer to feelings that you sensed about the other person's emotional state, such as, 'I sensed you as being nervous, excited, light spirited'. It is helpful to own the feeling with 'I' rather than stating, 'You were nervous' – which is opinionated. While A is talking, B refrains from making any comment. When this is completed B responds to A's observation for five minutes from their own frame of reference; for example, 'I am dressed more casually today than I was at last week's session because last week I came from work and this week I came from the gym', or 'I was nervous today when I first came in, I suppose because ...' or 'I wasn't feeling excited but I did feel quite mischievous.' Then reverse roles and repeat the exercise.

Exercise 2 – reading a person

This exercise, too, is ideal for pair work. It demonstrates how verbal and non-verbal language can be incongruent with each other and is designed to help you to develop an eye and ear for detail.

As A, talk about any topic as a backdrop, during which you say one thing while demonstrating another through body language. Try the following examples (five minutes each):

- Say you are feeling happy with a glum face.
- Say you are perfectly relaxed while demonstrating otherwise.
- Say you understand what is being said while looking puzzled.

Minimum response from B, mainly observing.

Add more subtle examples of your own. Discuss and write down the effects on the giver and receiver of incongruent verbal and body messages. What reasons lie behind such behaviour? What might the dangers be? Is there anything to be gained? What do we lose in relating to each other in this way? What place has collusion in such interaction? Swap roles.

Exercise 3

A variation on the above exercise is as follows. A (subtly) mimes a sequence of emotions based on a stated scenario. On completion (five minutes) B decodes what took place. For example, B is given the following guide: A young man is meeting a girlfriend whom he has not seen for nearly a year, at the time when she broke off their engagement. A is given the following prompt: You are a young man who is talking to a girlfriend whom you haven't seen for nearly a year. At your last meeting she broke off your engagement. You were heartbroken. You don't feel that you have fully emotionally recovered. You still care deeply for her but you are determined to show her that you are fine and to keep your dignity intact. However, at times during the encounter you feel that you would like to be close to her once more and want to put your arms around her.

A can mouth words if it helps in the role play, but says nothing out loud. B reads what is happening through the miming – in body language, facial gestures, sighs, movements and mannerisms. Debrief for a few moments, then discuss what was happening, then swap roles using a different scenario. Either the scenario is created by a trainer or A creates the scenario and gives B the skeletal facts only from which to build a picture.

Exercise 4 – listening/not listening

The purpose of this exercise is twofold:

- To highlight the differences between feeling listened to and not feeling listened to.
- To experience in an exaggerated form what it is like to be in a non-listening mode – whether through losing concentration or by being bored by a person we are supposed to be listening to.

Decide who will act as the talker (A) and who will be the listener (B). A talks for five minutes about something that is meaningful to them, perhaps something about their childhood, a place they have visited that they loved or some other person or event of significance in their lives. B actively demonstrates their total lack of interest in any way they choose: by body language, facial expression, posture, eye contact. They do not speak. At the end of five minutes each takes a further few minutes telling the other in turn what they felt like. As B, what did it feel like to ignore the other person? As A, what did it feel like to be talking about something of importance and be ignored?

Staying in the same roles, replay what has taken place. This time B tries to convey their genuine interest to A (for five minutes as before) in as many methods of body language as possible but without talking. This can include facial expression, posture, eye contact and so forth. As before, at the end of the five minutes tell each other what it felt like to listen attentively and be listened to attentively (a few minutes each). What was it like as A to be listened to? How did B convey that they were listening? What was it like to concentrate on what A was saying about something that obviously held meaning for them?

Swap roles and repeat the exercise as before. Compare and contrast the two experiences; that is, of listening/being listened to and not listening/not being listened to.

Exercise 5 – practice in paraphrasing (differentiating between content and feeling)

The following exercise works best of all in a practice triad of client, counsellor and observer. If the person acting as counsellor experiences difficulty, they can call for 'time out' assistance from the observer. They can then take a few minutes outside the room to discuss the way forward. The observer also acts as time keeper, as usual.

In this exercise the person who assumes the role of the client decides on a topic with emotional content (i.e. which has strong associated feelings) that they are happy to share with the other person. It is always wise to look after yourself and to go into personal details only at a depth that you feel comfortable with. The observer keeps check of the time and informs the counsellor when the first part of the exercise is about to finish and when it is time to begin the second part of the exercise, when both content and feelings are reflected. Sometimes in the instructions to exercises it says 'take a few moments to debrief' – this means take a little time to come out of role. Debriefing instructions are usually included when the exercise might contain emotional content; for example, in the following exercise, during which the client's feelings are purposely ignored.

Decide who is to begin as client and who will take the counselling role. The client talks about the subject of their choice for twenty minutes in all. During the first ten minutes the counsellor reflects back to the client by paraphrasing at appropriate times (i.e. at 'natural' breaks) the content of what is being said only, without reflecting the client's feelings. For example, the client might say, 'I went to her workplace to see her and I was so angry – I told her what I thought about what she had done … but afterwards I did feel embarrassed because the other people in the office were listening.' The counsellor, reporting back factual details only, might say something like, 'You went to where she works to see her and told her what you thought of her behaviour. The other people in the office heard what you said.' Note that the words 'angry' and 'felt' and 'embarrassed' are excluded from the reflected material. When you have completed the task, take a couple of minutes to debrief.

Continue in the second part of the exercise (10 minutes). The counsellor uses paraphrasing to reflect back to the client both the content of what they are saying and the feelings expressed, using the paraphrasing formula: 'You feel … because …' For example, 'You felt angry with her but you feel embarrassed that you expressed anger towards her in her workplace because other people were listening.'

On completion the participants take a couple of moments to debrief, then in turn each person talks about the experience for a few minutes, i.e. what it was like working with only content acknowledged then content and feeling. Swap roles and repeat the whole of the exercise so that each person has the opportunity to experience all three roles. This exercise takes approximately 90 minutes to complete.

Skills can be practised by focusing on one skill at a time. Working in role play or with material offered by the client, the counsellor can focus on the use of empathy, paraphrasing, questions, summarizing and so on. A typical structure for a skills practice session is as follows:

The client talks for twenty minutes, during which the counsellor may concentrate on using one or two skills. At the end of the twenty minutes the client gives feedback to the counsellor (a few minutes), at the end of which the counsellor talks about their experience in their role (a few minutes), and finally the observer gives feedback to both the client and counsellor in relation to the encounter, but mainly to the counsellor in relation to their adeptness in using the skills (a few minutes). Feedback time is approximately 10 minutes in all. Roles are swapped so that each person has the opportunity to be in each.

6 ENJOYING THE EXPLORATION

Preparing to become a counsellor begins with gaining insight into ourselves, how we think, what matters to us, our main life concerns and how we relate to others in various situations and levels of intimacy. How can we hope to 'walk inside another's shoes' when we don't fully walk in our own?

There are many avenues to self-understanding and development. This chapter introduces techniques and methods which not only increase our personal awareness but also complement and enhance the use of counselling skills. They are suggestions only, some may interest you while others may not hold much appeal.

Attending workshops

Participating in workshops or training sessions offered by trained and experienced therapists gives us opportunities to focus on various aspects of ourselves and our lives, past and present, including:

- how we behave in particular situations and towards others;
- particular life experiences;
- our self-image;
- our fears, our hopes;
- transition periods;
- our value systems;
- our goals;
- how we play – e.g. express spontaneity, exuberance, joy;
- issues of dependency;
- self-reliance – coping mechanisms/strategies.

A range of workshops offered by counsellors and therapists, or others with appropriate knowledge, is advertised on notice boards in libraries, holistic clinics, colleges and universities. Take advantage of these as they are usually good fun as well as informative. Periodicals and magazines concerned with mind, body and spirit issues, such as the quarterly *Caduceus*, offer a choice of stimulating and exploratory workshops which address such diverse subject-matter as gender issues, sexuality, 'the inner child', stress and tension reduction, laughter and many more. Some deal with specific emotions such as anger or grief.

Myths, legends and fairytales are media used by therapists to stimulate imagination and creativity and to access individual inner potential. This may involve role play, visualization or guided imagery using elements of myth, fairytale or legend. For example, in a guided imagery you may be taken on a 'magical mystery tour' of your own imagining and imaging, entering into mysterious labyrinths and being asked such questions by the therapist who guides you as:

- What do you find in the labyrinth?
- Someone or something comes to assist you. Who or what are they? What do they/it look like?
- They help you move forward. How?

The person leading the guided imagery/visualization will ask you to focus on your feelings at particular points (e.g. fear, hope, jubilation, expectation, apprehension, sense of achievement). Exercises such as these are designed to help you draw on your inner resources and integrate disparate elements of the self. Personal values and priorities are also explored. The labyrinth may, at some point, reveal a room full of treasure or a transformational character. It is the participant's own imagination, or elements of their unconscious, which supplies the content of the 'story' and therefore what is revealed is specific in meaning to the individual.

Visualization

Visualization is also a means of attaining a state of relaxation or meditative state. The following visualization exercise is based on an exercise from Roberto Assagioli's *Transpersonal Development: The Dimension beyond Psychosynthesis* (p. 104):

> Let us imagine a closed rose-bud. Visualize the stem, the leaves and, at the top, the bud itself. It is green in appearance because the sepals are closed; then at the topmost point there is a pink tip. Try to visualize this as vividly as possible, keeping the image at the centre of your conscious mind. As you watch you gradually become aware that movement is taking place: the sepals begin to pull apart as their points turn outwards, enabling you to see the closed pink petals. The sepals move further apart ... now see the bud-shaped petals of a beautiful, delicate rose. Then the petals also begin to unfold. The bud continues to expand slowly until the rose is revealed in all its beauty and you are able to admire it with delight.
>
> At this point try to breathe in the scent of the rose and smell its characteristic perfume – delicate, sweet and pleasing to the senses. Take in its scent with pleasure. The symbol of perfume has also been used frequently in religious and mystical language ('the smell of holiness'), as indeed perfumes have been used in rituals (incense, etc.).
>
> Next visualize the whole plant and imagine the force of life rising up from its roots to the flower, producing this development. Pause in awed contemplation of this miracle of nature.
>
> Now identify yourself with the rose, or to be more precise, 'introject' the rose into yourself. Symbolically become a flower, a rose. The same Life that animates the Universe, that has produced the rose, is producing in you that same, if not a greater, miracle: the development, opening up and irradiation of your spiritual being. And we have the choice of taking an active part in our own inner flowering.

The following is an exercise from *Teach Yourself Visualisation* (pp. 55–6) by Pauline Wills and should follow a simple relaxation exercise.

The sea

Imagine that it is a beautifully warm and sunny day and that you are lying on the beach in a small sandy cove, surrounded by grey cliffs that have small green rock plants growing out of their crevices. You feel the softness of the sand beneath you and its slight movement as some of the small grains trickle through your fingers. Look at the blue sky above and sense the warmth from the sun penetrating your body. Close your eyes and listen to the cry of the seagulls and the roar of the waves as they break on the shore.

Lying and listening to these sounds, you become aware of the waves breaking on the shore and the sea travelling across the beach until it very gently laps over your feet. Initially the water feels cold in comparison with the warmth of the sun. As the water recedes, you feel it draw out and take with it any tension that has accumulated in your feet. Your feet relax and feel heavy. The next wave breaks and gently rolls over the sand, covering your feet and your legs. The coldness of the water feels invigorating. It recedes and takes your tension with it. Your legs relax. Hearing the next wave coming and breaking on the shore, you wait for the water to touch your feet and then move over your legs, hands, lower part of your arms and abdomen. The muscles and organs in your abdomen contract slightly as they experience the coldness of the sea. The water recedes and you allow it to take your tensions with it. Listening, and waiting expectantly, you prepare yourself for the next wave. It comes and covers your body up to your neck. A slight shiver goes through your body as the water comes into contact with your chest. But this is compensated by the feeling of lightness and relaxation that you experience when the water has drawn out and takes with it all your tension.

You know that the next wave will cover your entire body, but you are not afraid. Your intuition tells you that you will be able to breathe normally under the water. Wait and listen. It is coming. You embrace the water as it covers you and you give to it all your tension, toxins and pain with gratitude and love. The water slowly recedes. It leaves you feeling completely relaxed and renewed, physically, mentally and spiritually. A feeling of joy pervades you as you once more become aware of the warmth of the sun revitalising and re-energising the whole of your being.

When coming out of relaxation, gently start to move your feet; then flex the muscles in your legs; gently move your fingers; breathing in, raise your arms up over your head, stretching the whole of your body. Breathing out, bring your arms back down to your sides. Repeat this twice more, then open your eyes and slowly roll over on to your left side and sit up.

Freud recognized that in playing a part we find out more about ourselves. Here is an example of a self-exploratory exercise using a fairytale:

- Think of a fairytale most appropriate to your life. Which particular character do you identify with?
- What associations have you with your chosen character?
- What happens to them?
- What aspects of the story disempower or empower the character you have chosen?
- What would you like to rewrite or change in the fairytale?
- How does that apply to your life story and present situation?

Counsellors sometimes refer to archetypal fairytale or mythical figures. Useful parallels can be drawn between the experience of the representing figure and the client. For example, I had a client who had incredibly long hair and was very insecure in her relationship with her boyfriend. She regarded him as a passport to an exciting life which she thought would be closed to her if he finished their relationship. She had mentioned more than once that she would like to cut her hair but that he loved her long hair (which was waist length and very thick). I commented that what she was saying reminded me of the fairytale story of Rapunzel – that her hair represented a means of escape into the world of her boyfriend. It was food for thought, and opened up exploration of her self-image and self-esteem.

The Johari window

The Johari window originally devised by Jo Luft and Harry Ingham is presented in *The Johari Window: A Graphic Model for*

Interpersonal Relations. This model challenges our self-awareness, our ability to share ourselves with others and our willingness to explore the unknown. The Johari window offers a four-part representation of ourselves (see diagram).

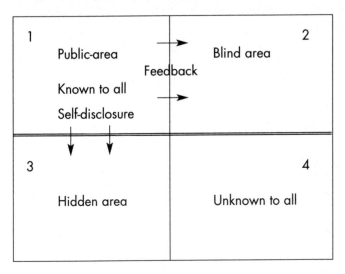

The Johari window

1 *Known to all*: The view from this is open; seen by everyone. This represents what we freely express for others to see, including our behaviour and attitudes. The view can be extended by self-disclosure.

2 *Blind area*: We cannot see this area of ourselves; it is unknown to us, but others are aware of it through aspects of our behaviour and body language. Our self-awareness can be extended by feedback from others.

3 *Hidden area*: This area represents the private part of ourselves, our secrets, shame, guilt feelings and so on. We are aware of it and choose not to share this part with others. We can choose to self-disclose, allowing others a view into our private world.

4 *Unknown to all*: This view of the individual is closed to everyone. It represents part of us that both we and

others are unaware of. It holds unconscious needs, impulses and anxieties and our untapped potential; we can gain insight into this part of ourselves through the counselling process.

Use the Johari window to assess yourself, as follows:

- What do you express freely – what are you comfortable with about yourself that you share with others?
- How do you feel about the blind areas – the aspects of you that others can see but you are unaware of?
- What feedback might upset you?
- What feedback might help you?
- What constitutes the private part of you?
- If the fourth part of the Johari window represents the unconscious part of you – closed to everyone, including yourself, how do you imagine you will access it?

Assertiveness training

Learning assertive behaviour has value for the would-be counsellor or helper, because assertiveness – contrary to widely held beliefs – is not about 'bolshiness', bulldozing the wishes of others or linked to any other form of aggression. Assertive behaviour is neither aggressive nor passive, but is concerned with clear, honest, direct communication.

Assertive skills encompass:

- taking responsibility for our own thoughts, emotions and behaviour;
- paying attention to human body language (sometimes called non-verbal communication);
- addressing the defensive behaviour of self and others;
- learning how to deal with criticism – giving and receiving;
- learning how to deal with compliments – giving and receiving;

- challenging and confronting – giving and receiving;
- specific techniques – e.g. being clear and concrete;
- prioritizing areas of our lives – asking clearly for what we want;
- examining values;
- self-esteem – valuing ourselves;
- decision making – choice awareness;
- accepting refusals, disappointments, rebukes – and surviving;
- 'unlearning' particular non-effective behaviour – e.g. covert manipulative interactions with others.

The assertiveness training model highlights four styles of behaviour commonly adopted by individuals in relation to others: Assertive, Passive, Aggressive and Passive/aggressive. For example, the Passive/aggressive person is covertly manipulative and 'others blaming' and although they aim to dominate or win, they present themselves as non-competitive.

On learning assertive behaviour, by reading relevant books or attending assertiveness training classes, we become aware of our fears and blocks – finding out how, for example, we live by what we think other people will think of us and by our internalized 'shoulds', 'musts' and 'oughts', which have most likely been absorbed in childhood. By becoming aware of our own irrational beliefs, and by developing the ability to replace these with alternative rational beliefs, we can help to challenge clients effectively to do likewise. Irrational beliefs are a focus of cognitive-behavioural approaches and in transactional analysis 'shoulds' and 'oughts' are examined within the framework of 'drivers' – such as 'be perfect', 'hurry up', 'be strong' (all of these are introjected parental rules).

Examples of irrational and rational beliefs

Irrational beliefs	*Rational beliefs*
I must always please others	It is unrealistic to expect that I can always please others
I must never be angry	It is OK to feel angry at times

| My happiness depends on other people's behaviour and attitudes | The source of my happiness is within me and is not dependent on other people |

Benefits

Assertiveness skills help you to get in touch with and deal with areas of weakness in communication with others; for example, many people find it difficult to challenge or confront others without becoming defensive, giving up or becoming aggressive. Assertiveness helps us to be concrete, with no hidden agendas.

Stress management

Counselling involves holding and containing the stress of others. Empathic responding requires an awareness of what the other is feeling and attempting to convey on various levels; as a counsellor you are aware of other people's stress, but what about your own? An understanding of stress management gives an awareness of how to identify stress in self and others.

1 *Physical effects*
   Palpitations, sweating, tenseness in muscles, loss of appetite, shaking, sleeplessness, 'butterflies' in the stomach

2 *Emotional effects*
   Depression, anger, resentment, distress, panic, fear, unhappiness, unrest, guilt, despair, impatience

3 *Effects on logical thinking*
   Inability to 'think straight' – analyse, make decisions, obsessional thoughts, forgetfulness, misjudgements, with flashes of intuition and of clear thought

4 *Effects on behaviour*
   Increased dependence/reliance on others; withdrawal from others, from responsibilities, work, etc.; agitation, little concentration, loss of temper, shouting, crying, aggressive drinking, 'road rage', no enthusiasm for life generally. Physical changes in the body (as opposed to manifestations): when we are stressed, adrenaline is released, causing a raised

level of tension in our muscles; we sweat to cool the body and our blood pressure goes up, preparing us for a 'flight or fight' response.

Through stress management we can also identify:

- Personal triggers, i.e. what brings stress on.
- Coping strategies/escape mechanisms, i.e. how we deal with stress, how to build on stress reduction.
- Support systems – personal support network, e.g. family, work, friends, church, organizations, community.

Methods of dealing with stress include:

- Changing behaviour/cognitions, i.e. what we tell ourselves ('I can't cope'), catastrophizing.
- Becoming more assertive.
- Using problem-solving models, goals, targets.
- Learning relaxation techniques: meditation, visualization and other ways of unwinding and enjoying ourselves (e.g. dancing, singing, yoga – which combines exercise and relaxation, painting).

Relaxation

Try a simple relaxation technique, which you may like to pass on to clients who suffer from high anxiety or stress levels. The basis of this relaxation technique was introduced, in the late 1930s, by Edmund Jacobson. It was later adopted by Joseph Wolpe (1961) in his *Systematic Desensitisation Treatment.*

The exercises involve tensing and relaxing in turn various groups of muscles throughout the body until a deep state of relaxation is reached. The following exercise would be initially therapist led. When it was learnt by the client it would be practised independently when needed.

The instructor begins:

'Lie on the floor on a thick large towel or mat with your legs straight and arms by your side. Let yourself get comfortable. Close your eyes and relax. Notice the sensations within your body and surrender yourself to the experience. Breathe naturally and easily.'

Notes for the instructor: The person leading the relaxation speaks in a slow, quiet, monotonous tone of voice. The instructions may vary slightly. Some individuals may feel too exposed lying down and may prefer to sit in a comfortable but upright chair while practising the exercise. The usual sequence is to work through the body, first tensing, then relaxing the various parts of the body. Begin with the toes and feet and work gradually upwards, finishing with the top of the head.

The instructor continues:

'Breathe in deeply, tensing the muscles in your feet. Hold your breath for a few moments while you tense the muscles in this area … Breathe out heavily, letting the tension go until your feet are completely relaxed. Tell yourself to relax on the out breath.'

Notes for the instructor: In this manner the instructor leads the client up through the body, addressing the main muscle groups: feet to calves, calves to thighs, thighs to buttocks, buttocks to abdomen, abdomen to chest and back, chest and back to fists, fists to arms, arms to shoulder and neck, shoulder and neck to muscles of the face, muscles of the face to scalp and top of head. Each instruction (e.g. tense the muscles in your abdomen as you breathe deeply) is followed by the instruction to hold the intake breath for a few seconds while the muscles are tense, then to relax and breathe normally. A sense of the travel of relaxation up through the body is given by summing up at certain points, when the instructor might say, 'Breathing normally, notice a feeling of relaxation and well-being flowing up from your feet through to your calves', and so on. The exercise is completed by focusing on the whole body state of relaxation.

The instructor concludes:

'Breathe naturally and place your awareness in the relaxed flow of energy freely moving around your body. Notice your breathing; on each exhalation feel yourself becoming more and more relaxed ... In a few minutes you will come back into your surroundings feeling relaxed and refreshed. Allow yourself to enjoy the feeling of well-being that permeates your body and mind ... When you are ready, open your eyes, roll over on your side and support yourself with your arm in a half-sitting position. Stay in this position until you are fully ready to sit up.

Notes for the instructor: Allow the participants or individual client some moments to relish the state of relaxation. This type of exercise may make people very relaxed and some even fall asleep. Yawning is common as tension is released from the body. It is therefore necessary to bring people back slowly into the surroundings.

Meditation

The object relations psychoanalyst D.W. Winnicott talked about the therapist's position of 'not knowing' – an open, receptive way of being, devoid of expectations and preconceptions, an emptying out. In *Playing and Reality*, he writes, 'If only we can wait, the patient arrives at understanding creatively and with immense joy, and I now enjoy this joy, more than I used to enjoy the sense of having been clever.'

Counselling work is stimulating, interesting and, at times, emotionally demanding. As a counsellor you are likely to spend quite a few hours a week with people who are troubled, unhappy or stressed out. You will hear sad, cruel and touching personal stories. You will be with others through their expression of strong emotions such as anger, fear, disappointment and grief. In the counsellor–client relationship you are likely, at times, to represent the client's mother or prime carer from the past. Although you will learn to work with this, rather than hook on to it, you will be aware of the 'neediness' of some clients and of the hopes and expectations they have of counselling.

Simple meditation techniques are an invaluable tool to a therapist as a means of unwinding, resting and recharging energy supplies and of developing non-attachment skills. If it attracts you, join a meditation class or learn a few simple meditation techniques that you can use in a spare moment. Begin with a simple ten-minute meditation exercise.

> Sit in a position you find comfortable which allows you to breathe freely, close your eyes and let everything drop away from you. Relax your body. Focus on your breath entering and leaving your body. Try not to interfere with the process – let it be. Calmly direct any wandering thoughts back to your breathing.

Naomi Ozaniec writes in *Teach Yourself Meditation* (p. 34–6):

Meditation enables us to develop a watching consciousness, it enables us to give birth to the watcher within. Buddhism names six root delusions and 20 secondary delusions. Looking at these takes us straight back to ourselves for there is no other place to be. The path to the Western mysteries is traditionally opened with the injunction, 'Know Thyself'. When you are ready to seek yourself, you are ready to begin meditation in earnest. But do not be mistaken – though your quest may undoubtedly take an outward form, the journey really takes place within. Perhaps it is time for a new injunction, the path may be opened in a thousand different ways. The phrase 'I am that I am' might serve as a new starting point for, in truth, you do not have to journey to find yourself, you merely have to open your eyes to who you, as you, are. This new injunction does not prevent change or growth, it merely affirms that you can own all that you are in each and every moment. Try meditating with the phrase and see if it brings you meaning.

The six root delusions are:

1. Attachment: our attachment to objects exaggerates and distorts.

2. Anger: anger destroys peace of mind and is harmful to the body.

3. Pride: through pride we exaggerate our own status.

4. Ignorance: this is considered to be the root of all delusions.

5. Negative doubt: this refers to aspects of the negative results of doubting the validity of Buddhist teaching.

6. Mistaken views: this refers to the way in which the philosophical views we take direct behaviour and action.

Exercise: looking within

Choose one of the root delusions as subjects for daily meditation. Try to see how this quality functions in your life. Become aware of the feelings and circumstances associated with it. Are you going to loosen the grip of this quality in your life? Stay with your chosen subject until you feel you have gained in understanding. You can always return to the same subject at a later date. When you are ready choose another subject and examine it in the same way.

Naomi Ozaniec, *Teach Yourself Meditation*

Psychosynthesis is a transpersonal or spiritual model of psychotherapy which incorporates many techniques embracing art, music, guided fantasy (visualization), and meditation. The Italian founder of psychosynthesis, Roberto Assagioli, was familiar with numerous fields of study, including the psychodynamic movement, anthropology and spiritual teachings. He believed meditation gave rise to a contemplative inner silence, leading to a receptive and pure consciousness of being.

Even short meditation sessions can create a sense of peace, improve concentration, attention and focusing; and act as a battery recharger. Some therapists say that through the regular practice of meditation they have increased their sense of intuition. Meditation instils an inner calm. It creates a familiarity with contemplative silence – a comfortableness with 'listening to the echo'.

Dreams

Dreams are focused on in the analytic, psychodynamic, Jungian and transpersonal approaches, all of which consider dreams to be a direct line to the unconscious mind. Barring the behavioural approach, all approaches acknowledge the importance of dreams in relation to the conscious. Freud regarded dreams to be the royal road (*via regia*) to the unconscious, and Jung believed dreams to contain messages from the pool of the collective unconscious (see Chapter 8).

In *Wake up to your Dreams* (p. 8), Linda Sheppard shares a Jungian view of the role of dreams as informative, instructive and healing:

> Dreams have been shared with other family or tribal members throughout time. As part of the process of initiation, dreams have been incubated in temples and related to shamans, priests and gurus. The products of these dreams have offered potent healing and problem-solving information, both for the dreamer and for the family, tribe, or community, of which the dreamer is a member.

In Gestalt therapy, which was founded by Fritz Perls, the 'empty chair' process helps the client to examine dream material – characters, symbols or objects from the dream are focused on and communicated within the therapy room. The client (dreamer) can actively imagine the dream or symbol, or person, into the chair and ask questions, or else sit in the chair and personify; that is, 'become' the character, symbol or motif. In this way fragments of dreams are reconstructed to form a deeper understanding as elements of the unconscious work with the conscious in the 'here and now'.

Anthropologist Van Gennep and religious historian Mircea Eliade attest to the respectful attention paid to dreams in primitive cultures; in ceremonies and rites of passage a dreamy, trance-like stage facilitated creative exploration and learning. The ancient Egyptians built dream temples, and the Bible refers to dreams as a source of instructive wisdom. Biblical stories allude to dreams as a medium through which God communicates with people – in both the Old and New Testaments. In Numbers 12: 6 we find 'Hear my words: If there is a prophet among you, I the Lord make myself known to him in a vision, I speak with him in a dream.' The future is revealed in a dream in Genesis 20: 3–7: 'But God came to Abimelech in a dream.' Mary's revelatory dream in Matthew 2: 12 gives instruction 'And being warned in a dream not to return to Herod, they departed to their own country by another way.'

Dreams have been traditionally regarded as practical, instructive and transformative, and to contain messages from the spiritual or transpersonal element of the human psyche. The dream world is a magical realm where time and space are transcended along with the limitations of the linear, logical mind. During dreams we experience a heightened awareness, an amazing capacity for detail, and we are alive to our creative self and our individual inner world of meaning. Dreams are rich in diverse imagery and symbolism, and although there are many books which aim to tell us the meanings of specific symbols, they do not take into account the idiosyncratic content of dream imagery.

Active imagination

Carl Jung introduced a technique he named **active imagination** to facilitate interaction between ego and the unconscious; he used the adjective 'active' to differentiate between the usual passive meaning of 'imagination'. Active imagination is a conscious activity entered into to engage the unconscious and the ego in dialogue.

There are variations on this technique, one of which is designed to assist dream analysis. The dream is re-entered by a process of relaxation in order that exploration of dream symbols, motifs and characters can take place. The dreamer becomes an actual participant in the dream scenario, entering into a dialogue with dream characters; questions can be addressed in respect of aspects of the dream and changes can be consciously made as a method of attaining insight into problem solving.

How to begin

Begin the inner journey of making contact with your unconscious mind by paying attention to your dreams. Keep a notebook and pencil by the side of your bed and write down as much as you can remember of the content of your dreams on awakening. Spend some time thinking about your dreams, and about what they mean to you. When you have familiarized yourself with the first two tasks, you may like to try to apply the technique of active imagination as a precursor to working in this way with clients.

Make yourself comfortable by sitting or lying down in a position that you feel relaxed in. Close your eyes and breathe slowly and deeply. By 'letting go' and relaxing, reallocate yourself back into your dream. You can ask for information by focusing on particular characters. Listen to the inner voice and let new insights unfold without asserting any conscious will on the proceedings.

Try out alternative courses of action or outcome.

Try out a new way of responding to situations; for example, facing a fearful image or confronting a task.

If you have written an account of the dream you can prepare yourself before re-entering it. Ask yourself what you would like to address. For example:

- Begin by identifying key characters.
- What questions do you have for them?
- What are you feeling, seeing, sensing at specific points in the dream?
- What remains hidden from you?
- What changes would you like to make? – e.g. Conclude an unfinished task or journey.

Again, on leaving the dream behind, make notes on new information, understanding and personal insights. By giving attention to the inner dream world, you will become familiar with the unconscious processes and begin to interact with them consciously.

Part Two A DEEPER UNDERSTANDING – TRAINING TO A PROFESSIONAL LEVEL

7 | COURSE COMPONENTS

Background

Counselling started becoming professionalized in countries like Australia, New Zealand and Great Britain in the late 1960s and early 1970s, when training courses in counselling were offered in universities for the first time. This followed a precedent set in the USA in the 1950s by the work of Rogers and his contemporaries. Originally a person training to become a psychoanalyst would undergo personal analysis for a considerable time. Receiving analysis from senior analysts was at the time the only method of becoming familiar with the workings of psychoanalysis. It was the responsibility of the training analyst to decide on whether or not the candidate was suitable material to become an analyst. Fritz Perls, for example, who founded the Gestalt approach to therapy, was analysed by Wilhelm Reich and Karen Horney. Gradually other methods of teaching and learning were added as the canon of analytical literature grew; case discussions were opened out to include analysts in training and theoretical seminars were introduced. It was the humanistic therapists, with their emphasis on the experiential, who introduced innovative ideas about therapy and with these new training methods evolved. In the 1940s and 1950s Carl Rogers and his associates experimented with different training techniques in client-centred therapy, some of which are still in use, notably students watching and commenting on films of counselling sessions, students as co-therapists in sessions, personal growth groups, peer and self-assessments. Skills training as a structured approach came later with the writings of the likes of Richard Carkhuff and Gerard Egan, who recognized the potential of counselling-based skills in terms of 'human resources' and 'helping skills' respectively. Counselling training has become highly structured and systematized, especially in an academic setting. Training courses are thriving and are today available in a variety of forms in universities, colleges, training institutes and agencies in many parts of the world.

Choosing a course

Professional associations offer accreditation to courses that meet their standards and this is worth keeping in mind when you select your course. We have looked at various ways in which those interested in becoming counsellors could sample a range of counselling techniques and associated theories and skills by attending workshops, undergoing skills training and selective reading. Participating in preparatory workshops or short skills-based training courses has the added advantage of extending self-awareness. Courses on offer range from non-certificated starter courses at basic skills level to Diplomas and MAs. Research at PhD level is also possible. Counselling has become highly professionalized, especially in the USA, where standards are particularly high. People do practise without professional credentials, considering themselves to be counsellors, but this is generally frowned upon by qualified practitioners and professional organizations alike as the ethical standards and the integrity of the unqualified practitioner are unknown.

Courses can be very expensive, and the cost of the personal therapy which is usually a condition of the professional course adds to the expense. Over a period of three years the total can seem extortionate and a criticism of counsellor training systems is that it is only the financially solvent, and that is usually middle-class people, who can afford to undertake training. However, financially disadvantaged people are usually eligible for help with fees, at the least. Some universities and colleges offer reduced fees for those on state benefits and can put prospective candidates in touch with charities and organizations that may offer funding.

A Diploma course in counselling, geared to a professional standard, usually comprises a foundation year, which may be certificated as a first stage, followed by a further two years. The complete training is likely to take three years part-time – possibly one day per week, although some courses entail weekend and week blocks of training. Choosing a course entails carrying out research, looking at various prospectuses to find out the conditions of entry, the format and content of the course, and the facilities and so on of universities, colleges and training institutions. You may remember from Chapter 1 that before being accepted on a reputable course that results in a professional qualification, you will be required to have training and/or experience relevant to the level you are hoping to enter. For example, a Diploma in Counselling course may require a candidate to have completed a certain number of hours' training through previous courses and/or to have had relevant experience working in a counselling capacity with an agency.

The candidate's work experience may be taken into consideration if it has involved understanding of and working with social or cultural diversity, or the use of counselling skills. You could find out about agencies offering counselling in your area, which will include work relating to specific groups and problems (i.e. family and couple relationships; sexual orientation; one-to-one counselling; telephone counselling; crisis counselling; drugs or alcohol abuse; physical, sexual or mental abuse; health-related counselling; age-related counselling (working with the elderly or young people). Yellow Pages contain details of many agencies. The agencies are usually very keen to have new recruits and will gladly send details of their training programmes, policies and practices.

Joining an agency that offers counselling is probably the best way to begin on a learning route to professionalism because of the training they offer, the availability of clients to work with and the back-up of close supervision. Established agencies or organizations usually work to ethical standards specified by a professional (overseeing) association, to which they have professional accountability through membership. At least some of the staff members will be accredited by a professional organization.

Key course components

- Theory
- Counselling skills
- Work on self-awareness

- Supervision of practice and 'outside' client work
- Written assignments
- Written exams or vivas
- On-going assessment (by tutor, peer and self)
- (in some cases) Research work – this is usually at MA or PhD level

Aims of training courses

- To develop an understanding of particular theoretical approaches – e.g. that of psychodynamic, person-centred, Gestalt, developmental psychology, interpersonal development, groupwork and dynamics.
- To further develop and acquire ease in the use of counselling skills, enabling discreet use.
- To deepen understanding of self in all areas – personal values, coping mechanisms, defences, expectations, prejudices, belief systems etc.
- To give insight, guidance and support and to check that the trainee is working ethically with clients.
- As a method of testing, deepening knowledge and understanding.
- To test summation of learning, knowledge and understanding of theory, integration and application, skills competency, professional issues, personal awareness, supervision and self-assessment.
- Feedback, monitoring progress, checking and encouraging development of weak spots, allowing movement to another stage of learning.
- To explore the contributions made by research, gain awareness of research methods, train in compiling and producing an original piece of work.

Skills

Skills practice forms part of the majority of counselling training courses. A basic skills course may contain mainly skills learning and practice, including a familiarization with Rogerian core conditions. The psychodynamic approaches are rich in theory and techniques which constitute the main skills (e.g. managing resistance, understanding defences, working with the transference and other unconscious processes). Integrative approaches which utilize the concepts, theories, techniques and applications of one or more approaches usually include a skills component, with Rogerian core conditions forming the baseline of skills use as proposed by Carkhuff in *The Art of Helping*. The human resources development model later added 'action skills', such as the use of immediacy and confrontation. The three-stage model of self-exploration, understanding and action, of Egan's *The Skilled Helper*, is another model that is widely used. Note the move from the specialist arena of 'therapist' to the lay person terminology of 'helper', which reflects that literature has become directed towards other workers who would benefit from helping skills; that is, doctors, nurses, business people and those in pastoral care. The micro-skills training approach, introduced by Ivey and Galvin (see **Suggested further reading**), sets out a programme of skills for therapists, business and medical interviews. Skills models tend to be adapted to suit the course; for example, a course might not include the 'influencing skills' or 'structuring a session' of the micro-counselling model in the repertoire of skills adopted, although structuring 'brief counselling' may be included in a skills programme. What is included largely depends on the orientation of the course. Skills can be adapted to fit into a particular cultural or social context.

Methods commonly used in the teaching/learning of skills

- Video demonstrations of 'expertise' of skill.
- Practice in triads of 'counsellor', 'client' and 'observer'.
- Brainstorming.
- Class handout examples of 'positive' and 'negative' use of skills.
- Video recordings, taken while practising the skills in practice triad, using role play or personal material.
- Performance feedback given by tutors and others.

The aim of familiarizing the trainee counsellor with such skills is to widen their repertoire of responses to client material and help them to discriminate between effective and ineffective ways of communicating or intervening. The minimum requirements for a competent counsellor are that they have a workable knowledge of theoretical models and a range of skills, and have developed self-awareness.

Developing self-awareness

Groupwork

Working in groups is commonly used as a method of developing self-awareness and interpersonal skills. As we have seen, the small group is utilized in the development of supervision skills, offering feedback and insight relating to each other's work with clients. Other groupwork is concerned with personal development and group processes. The key word to sum up the purpose of group-work is 'insight'. Experiencing oneself with and separate from others in a group is a learning process *par excellence*, likely to stir up complex, ambivalent, primary feelings such as rivalry between members, a need to merge with others, a need to assert one's own individuality, projections onto others (that which can't be personally owned) and fantasies about self and other participants.

The facilitator or conductor offers interpretations with regard to content and feelings of the group, addressing the following aspects:

1 Group regressions – infantile expression, e.g. experiencing sibling rivalry.
2 Repetitive conflict situations – often between two or three members of the group who 'act out' for others.
3 Sub-grouping – forming smaller groups to make the environment safer.
4 Scapegoating – one or two people represent 'bad' elements of the group (dangers) that cannot be individually acknowledged or divulged.
5 Repetitive long silences – withholding, withdrawing mechanisms, unwillingness to take risks.
6 Defence and coping mechanisms – e.g. shutting off, playing safe, intellectualizing.

7 Fantasies – about self and others related to early experiences; e.g. 'If I say what I think/feel then I'll be destroyed.' 'I am the leader of the group.' 'The facilitator is attracted to me / disapproves of me.'

The facilitators may intervene with an interpretation if they feel anxiety levels are becoming destructive, participants are missing the point or the process is in a 'stuck' mode, saying, 'I wonder if what is happening here is …' or 'Perhaps it's too painful for the group to acknowledge …'

Groupwork may comprise an integration of humanistic, psychoanalytic and cognitive-behaviour modes of relating, reflecting social/political patterns. For example, when the directive given by the facilitator is that the group is not therapeutic and is focusing in the 'here and now', strong defence mechanisms will come into play and may be interpreted by the facilitator in terms of Oedipal conflicts, rivalry, projections, denial, or an impulse to symbolically 'kill off', to integrate or oppress another in the group. Generally, interpretative comments are addressed to the group as a whole but they are addressed to individuals when the facilitator feels it will serve a positive purpose – perhaps to take the heat out of a situation or to challenge the person's behaviour or attitudes.

Positive experiences from groupwork

- Participants feel valued by others.
- Participants feel supported by others. They give and receive mirroring.
- Members engage in a process of identification and empathy as a means of resolving their own conflicts.
- Deeper levels of communication are reached – in a therapeutic context that which could not be communicated previously can be shared.
- Builds trust, confidence, affirmation of self.
- Helps individuals to re-own 'split off' parts of themselves.
- Stronger understanding of self in relation to others.
- Understanding of unconscious processes of groups and social situations.

The group matrix

The concept of the group matrix has evolved as a symbol of the way individual mental processes form a communication and interactional network with others.

The matrix represents a web of transpersonal, interpersonal and intrapsychical relationships.

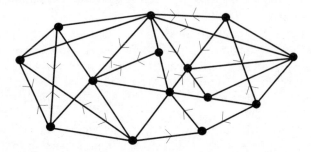

The individual can be seen as a nodal point in the group in relationship to, and in interaction with, all the other members of the group.

In the 1950s and 1960s S.H. Foulkes was a consultant in psychiatry, psychoanalysis and group analysis in Great Britain and the USA. In *Therapeutic Group Analysis*, he describes the group matrix as: 'The hypothetical web of communication and relationship in a given group ... the common shared ground which ultimately determines the meaning and significance of all events, and upon which all communications and interpretations, verbal and non-verbal, rest.'

The matrix has also been described in terms of an interpersonal, intrapsychical and transpersonal web – invisible channels of communication that hold both positive and negative potential for the group.

In *Practical Use of Dream Analysis*, Carl Jung described the matrix as a symbol of the mother: 'the mother as matrix, the hollow form, the vessel that carries and nourishes, and thus stands psychologically for the foundation of consciousness.'

The 'hypothetical web of communication and relationship' corresponds to the beliefs of ancient religions and traditions that what an individual thinks or feels affects others as individuals of the group and the group dynamic as a whole.

Each matrix pattern is unique to the particular group, fed as it is by each individual's experiencing and what they bring to the group from their past. The foundation matrix is what we bring from our own social network, including our belief systems, culture and ways of interacting.

Supervision

During training the trainee is given supervision by either a course tutor or an outside supervisor (i.e. one who comes in to carry out the task). Peer supervision is a feature of Diploma-level courses, in which the trainees learn the skills of supervision by observing the tutor at work and by practising under the watchful eye and listening ear of the tutor/supervisor.

Supervision always plays an important, supportive part of a counsellor's work. It is a 'sounding board', a safety net and a method of learning from a therapist who has more training and experience than the counsellors they are supervising.

The role of the supervisor

Proficient supervision gives the trainee counsellor room to 'move around' the client, helping them to understand the client from different angles. The following are ways in which supervisors assist:

- As a safety net for the counsellor – offering support and protection.
- As a third party who offers another perspective – a new insight, the 'aha' factor. The supervisor may, e.g., use symbolism or imagery to extend understanding.
- Help the counsellor explore transference and countertransference.
- Keep check on the counsellor's work – e.g. that they are working in an appropriate way with the client (that is, within ethical standards), including an exploration of theory and techniques being used.

- As 'outside' observers they can see blind spots and help the counsellor to explore 'stuckness'.
- Explore the client–counsellor relationship – the working alliance.
- Help planning structuring – questions like 'Where are you going with this?' assist clarification.

Safety net

The supervisor bears a lot of responsibility. They can be contacted by the counsellor if there are any major problems with a client that cannot wait until the next supervision session; for example, in the case of a disclosure concerning abuse which is either directly affecting the client or poses a danger to another person, or if a client talks about suicidal intention. A supervisor needs to be *au fait* with the legal obligations and requirements of certain situations and the policies and procedures of the agencies or institutions they work within. They are in a position to give advice and information to the counsellor if or when it is required. Supervision is highly skilled and those in supervisory roles are usually required to have specialist training to be accredited by a professional association. Supervisors have commonly had many years' experience as practising therapists.

As a third party the supervisor gets to know the client via the counsellor – that is, through the information that the client has given the counsellor, the content of the session and the counsellor's sense of the client's inner world. The supervisor seldom comes into direct contact with the client. Primarily the supervisor's work is to help the counsellor to focus, explore and reflect on client–counsellor issues. To do this the supervisor requires information about the following:

- The setting in which the counsellor works – contracts, number of sessions offered, frequency of sessions.
- The client – background details, history to help build a picture, e.g. medical problems, self-image.
- Presenting problems – the client's reasons for coming to counselling.
- Issues – what needs dealing with? What is happening? What is the most important issue at the moment?

■ Process – how is it moving forward? Any changes? New focus?

■ Theory – what theories/theoretical models are being referred to?

■ Issues for supervision – what does the counsellor want from supervision?

Effective, appropriate supervision

It is a requirement of professional associations that for accreditation a counsellor must have regular supervision from an appropriately qualified supervisor. The association will stipulate the ratio of hours of counselling to hours spent with a supervisor (e.g. four hours or four fifty-minute sessions of counselling require one hour of supervision). Professional associations are very helpful with enquiries and are often an excellent source of information and resources.

Group supervision

Group supervision is sometimes a practical option for small agencies and is a common component of training courses. Peer supervision entails a small group of counsellor trainees acting as supervisors of each other, usually with a tutor as the main supervisor and overseer of proceedings. Client casework is presented in the session and the trainee counsellor who is presenting client material to supervision gives the other members of the group written relevant details, including: agency setting, contract, client details (the client's real identity is protected by giving the initials only or a pseudonym), history, family relationships, presenting problems, current issues, what's happening in the counselling process and theory referred to. A genealogical chart is sometimes included in the notes for easy reference. The trainee also gives an informal oral presentation of the client's case. When they have finished talking through the case history of the client to the others, the other members then give their contribution, taking a supervisory role. This includes asking questions to help clarify details, challenging and offering observations with regard to relational elements, transference issues or incongruences in the presentation.

Transference and countertransference in supervision

The feelings of both client and counsellor are exposed through transferential material. The supervisor may observe, 'It sounds as if he is looking for mothering in you. How does that make you feel?' or may home in on the countertransference, using imagery to describe the counsellor: 'I see you flapping about like a mother hen, anxious about her little chick.' The purpose of making these sorts of observations is to offer the counsellor new insights; for example, into how the client is experiencing the counsellor in the transference, the client's feelings and behaviour and meanings, and the effects the client is having on the counsellor and the work.

Parallel process

An interesting dimension of transference is that a parallel process is likely to take place. What is happening in the client–counsellor relationship is likely at times to be echoed in the counsellor–supervisor relationship. For example, using the simple illustration above, the counsellor may feel exasperated, frustrated or angry with the supervisor and the supervisor, observing this development, may point this out: 'I sense that you're getting frustrated and angry with me as if I'm not giving you something. Maybe you would like reassurance and nurturing from me … a bit like your client?' The supervisor might withhold the words 'like your client', seeing if the counsellor makes the connection, or might be more explicit: 'You would like me to mother you.' (This could be said by a supervisor of either sex, since 'mothering' in therapeutic terms means 'nurturing and caring for'). The parallel process is an 'acting out' of the client or counsellor material and is a very useful tool of understanding what has been happening in the 'here and now' of a client session in relation to the 'here and now' of the counsellor–supervisor session.

There will be counsellor–supervisor transference and countertransference. For example, the counsellor may experience the supervisor as a critical parent (negative transference) or 'nurturing mother' (positive transference). The supervisor will be aware of the likelihood of corresponding countertransference-feeling reactions. Projection may also become an issue to work through. The counsellor who doubts their abilities as a counsellor may project dubious attributes of an 'authority figure' onto the supervisor, seeing the supervisor as tyrannical or a 'know it all'; or in the positive (but equally unreal) view see the supervisor as a 'guru', 'seer' or omnipotent.

It may be helpful at this point to recap on the difference between projection and transference.

■ Projection involves thoughts and feelings which cannot be acknowledged as the person's own, and which are therefore attributed 'safely' to someone else. The threatening aspect of self could be the 'authority figure' or the one who likes to think they 'know it all'.

■ Transference is when a person displaces or 'transfers' an emotion or affective attitude that belongs to a person and relationship from the past (usually a parent) onto a person in the present (e.g. the therapist).

Theory and practice

Part of the training will concentrate on the theoretical underpinnings, concepts, beliefs and aims of various approaches concerned with counselling. Developmental psychology, group theory and dynamics, mental health issues, ethics in counselling, bereavement, child abuse, aspects of sociology (class, race and cultural issues and gender issues) are all probable additional topics. The student needs not only to know and understand theory but also how to apply it. With this in mind, theory periods usually involve lectures given by tutors, followed by questions and forms of practice, such as small group discussion, brainstorming or exchanges of ideas and experiences (at times writing these down on flipchart paper). For example, following a lecture on gender issues a large group of twenty-plus trainees may be asked by a tutor to form smaller groups containing four each, providing a 'safer', more intimate environment to discuss awareness topics such as: 'Think back to when you first became aware of gender roles. Was it a positive or negative experience? What happened? How did you feel? How has that experience influenced your feelings and attitudes towards the opposite sex?' The members of the group talk to each other about their experiences and the effects for a period of time (possibly twenty minutes), at the end of which the large group reforms and a representative from each small group in turn relates the salient points of their discussion. The tutor may write these on a flipchart. Knowledge of theory and how the trainee is applying it is also explored within supervision sessions and in assignments.

Personal therapy

Personal therapy is also commonly a compulsory element of the training of a professional counsellor. Ways in which personal therapy enhances understanding:

1 Developing an ability to separate own material from that of the client – i.e. dealing with unresolved personal conflicts.

2 Learning from the counsellor/therapist subliminally, taking in how they are working/relating.

3 Being a client, building an understanding of what it feels like to be a client – e.g. vulnerable, apprehensive, dependent, trusting.

4 Gives experience of the processes, the stages of counselling – e.g. beginnings, endings, transference, resistance.

5 Deepens self-understanding of own personal issues, making links with childhood experiences and 'stuck' patterns of relating to others, through transference, exploring personal defences, resistances.

Exams and on-going assessment

It is worth considering what methods are used to assess learning on a course that interests you. Some people find exams a terrible pressure, while others prefer them to extensive on-going assessments. Written theory-based exams may be set at the end of each year. Some courses are more academic than others; some require the implementation of research methods, for example. Most commonly, testing procedures involve skills observation; written assignments; peer and tutor assessments and self-assessment, and written exams or vivas.

Vivas

A viva usually combines oral and written elements, an audio or video recording accompanied by a verbatim transcript of a section of the recorded session. Typically a viva will take the form of questions and discussion around the presented case material. Usually the counsellor in training makes, with the permission of the client – and when working with an agency the agency's approval – a few recordings of a counselling session from which one recording is chosen for the viva presentation. The recording chosen does not have to be technically perfect but is chosen to reflect use of theory, skills, awareness of the counselling process and so on. The following criteria are taken from a university professional diploma course in counselling.

Viva Case Study Presentation

To complete this assignment you must:

1. Provide a tape recording (audio or video) of one counselling session with a client.

2. Provide a verbatim transcript of a five-minute section of the same counselling interview.

3. Complete the attached case study pro forma making reference where possible to the transcript provided.

4. Submit two copies of each of the above for assessment by the date stated. These three elements will then form the basis of a discussion between yourself and two assessors. Each case discussion will last approximately 45 minutes and will take place in the supervision group slot.

Levels to Explore

1. An overview of the whole work with client to date

2. The work of the presented session

3. What is happening during the five-minute transcribe

4. General reflection on your own practice

Criteria for Assessment

1. Competency/skills: Evidence that the student has acted in a caring and skilled way in all dealings with clients. This will include indicators of core process skills (genuineness,

warmth, empathy), ability to manage boundaries of time and space, and evidence of maintaining a sound working alliance with the client.

2. Professional issues: Evidence that the student has maintained personal boundaries and professional standards. Demonstration of a clear awareness and practice in relation to ethical issues, including confidentiality.

3. Use of theory: Evidence that the student understands the relationship between theory and practice in their work.

4. Integration: Where differing approaches have been used, evidence that this integration (or eclecticism) has been thought through.

5. Personal awareness: Evidence that students are aware of and able to cope with their own process within the counselling relationship. Evidence that students make appropriate use of personal therapy where personal issues are raised in the counselling relationship.

6. Supervision: Evidence that students have made appropriate use of supervision to help them work more effectively with clients.

7. Self assessment: Evidence that the student has a realistic appraisal of their own involvement and effectiveness within the counselling relationship.

Other methods of assessment

An educational institution uses assessment to certify that an individual has reached the necessary standard in the work either to move on to the next stage or for the attainment of an award. Assessments are both summative, to assess the point a student has reached; and formative, helping in the development of an allotted task or goal. Assessment is an on-going process in that tutors, in a teaching role or as facilitators, are continually observing and noting the trainee's work in various learning situations; for example, via role playing or using personal issues in skills practice, in supervision groups, personal development groups or interpersonal groups, and in the contributions made in theory, learning and discussions. It is common practice to use a combination of tutor, peer and self-assessment at a culmination point of learning skills or theory. For example, year 1 of a counselling training course may concentrate on skills practice, at the end of which each student is assessed on their level of competence in using the skills. Feedback is usually given both orally and in written form. Peer assessments of an individual's ability to use various skills will be based on observation of the person counselling others and the personal experience of being counselled by the candidate in the triad format of skills practice. The individual student is also asked to assess their own abilities, highlighting strong and weaker aspects of what they have learned.

Written assignments are another criterion by which tutors/trainers can assess the learning of skills and theoretical perspectives. In academic settings and in training institutes alike students are usually asked to produce a minimum of two or three essays per year's training, of two to three thousand words, and a dissertation or project at the end of the last year of the course. The student is most likely to be asked to choose a topic for the dissertation that reflects the learning accumulated from the course and that has relevance for their client group. For people who haven't studied for quite some time and aren't used to planning and compiling a critical piece of written work, there are many self-help study books on the market that contain study tips, including various methods of structuring and planning essay assignments, and also exam strategies. Many colleges, universities and training institutes produce study starter packs or booklets to help the rusty student, with guidelines on how to organize study time, use libraries, plan work load, make lecture notes, read effectively, find relevant information, take notes from literature, write essays and reports and compile a bibliography.

Integrationism

Rather than describe themselves as counsellors who follow a single approach – humanistic, psychodynamic and so on – many practitioners describe the way they work as 'eclectic' or 'integrationist', meaning that they work with a combination of approaches. The term **eclecticism** is used to describe the selection of what the counsellor deems the most appropriate ideas and techniques from an array of theories or models, particular to the client's needs at the time. In **integrationism** a new model emerges by bringing elements of different theories and models together in a complementary fusion. In the 1950s, when humanistic views were coming to the fore, comparisons were made with other approaches, looking for meeting points and divergences. John McLeod concedes in *An Introduction to Counselling* that it would be difficult to define a 'pure theory': 'All theorists are influenced by what has gone before. Freudian ideas can be seen as representing a creative integration of concepts from philosophy, medicine, biology and literature.'

Many counsellors who initially trained in one approach extend their therapeutic repertoire by incorporating ideas and skills from other approaches. Let me clarify this with an illustration from my own work.

My own initial training (a certificated one-year foundational course) followed the psychodynamic model of working with unconscious processes: resistance, denial and with the transference. The 'blank screen' approach was encouraged, whereby we allowed the client to project their fantasies, projections and anxieties, also allowing an 'optimal frustration' (see Chapter 9) – all to help the client recall, re-experience and finally expunge disturbance through (cathartic) emotional release. This was all very well in theory, but it led to a constant source of discussion between counsellors, allowing the airing of opposing opinions.

I was amongst the counsellors who felt that since the client group we were working with was 14–25-year-olds and many of them had experienced problems with institutionalized systems (e.g. education, the law, abusive relationships with adults), to present counsellors as detached and clinical people was counterproductive in many cases. For example, one of the bones of contention was how to greet the client. The 'blank screen', abstinent approach dictates that the counsellor waits for the client to proceed with what is uppermost in their mind – that they are released from having to begin with distracting social niceties or following the counsellor's agenda. It was very apparent at times that the lack of warm welcome was experienced by the young client as coldness, 'expert' aloofness or even hostility, reinforcing the client's negative view of themselves in relation to others. The general consensus was that while an abstinent approach can be useful for the client, this is unlikely to be so at the onset of therapy when the client is unsure of the surroundings, is embarking on a new psychological relationship with the counsellor, and is troubled and feeling vulnerable.

In the early stages it is important to establish a working alliance, with counsellor–client rapport, and if a counsellor is able to convey empathic understanding, warmth and acceptance then the client is more likely to relax and place trust in both the counsellor and the counselling process.

Person-centred core values are integrated into many approaches as a way of addressing these initial difficulties and establishing trust. Many counsellors working primarily with other approaches concentrate on these at certain times in the therapy; for example, at the beginning and ending. While systematic training in integrative therapy has been established and is commonly adopted in both academic settings and training institutes, some practitioners oppose the appropriation of parts of approaches, which eclecticism is, regarding it as a chaotic hotchpotch of ideas and theories with no clear, consistent rationale. Practitioners who use an eclectic approach sometimes say that they use their intuition to inform them about what would benefit the client at any given time; for example, suggesting visualization at one time and goals as strategies at another. The ability to be flexible, and to use elements of different approaches spontaneously and effectively depends on a counsellor's broad-based knowledge of a range of theories and skills and the ability to use these with competence. Arguably it is an almost impossible standard to achieve.

Eclecticism is also problematic in relation to supervision and training since the individual's methods of working can be highly idiosyncratic and impossible to match. The process of training or supervising another's work depends on a mutuality of terminology, meaning and understanding. A counsellor working in the psychodynamic approach is therefore best understood by a psychoanalytic or psychodynamic supervisor or therapist. The risk a counsellor takes in following an eclectic pattern of relating to a client's needs is that they become a 'Jack of all trades and a master/mistress of none'. Many therapists argue in favour of 'theoretical purity', believing that working in depth with one approach is the most effective method. In contrast, therapists like Michael Khan (in *Between Therapists and Client: The New Relationship*) have shown how two fundamentally different approaches such as humanistic psychology and contemporary psychoanalysis can be synthesized to enhance the client–therapist relationship.

Modalities of relationship

Another method of integrating different ideas, techniques and theories is working with an understanding of relationship modalities, as proposed by the psychotherapist and writer Petruska Clarkson. In *The Therapeutic Relationship* she identifies five relationship modalities which may be useful in the psychotherapeutic client–therapist relationship. These are: The Working Alliance; The Transferential / Counter Transferential Relationship; The Reparative / Developmentally Needed Relationship; the I–You Relationship; and The Transpersonal Relationship. Clarkson believes that these relationship modalities, as a way of relating across the different approaches, are always potentially present in the exchange.

Professional considerations

Towards the end of your course, as you focus on the professional work you might undertake, your attention may be once more drawn to ethical issues and practice. National professional organizations publish copies of their code of ethics and practice for counsellors, which provide a guideline for professional use. A **code of ethics** is likely to encompass values, responsibility, anti-discriminatory practice, confidentiality, contracts, boundaries and competence. Members of professional associations are required to abide by existing codes, which provide a common frame of reference within which to manage their responsibilities to clients, colleagues and the community at large. A code of ethics is translated into a code of practice which applies principles to the counselling situation. The **code of practice** is likely to be concerned with issues which will include client safety, counsellor responsibility and accountability, clear contracting and counsellor competence. Professional indemnity insurance, recommended by professional associations, is another safeguard to be considered. It is worth noting that while counselling for an agency the counsellor is offered protection under the agency's insurance cover. Working to ethical standards, acquiring insurance and having adequate supervision become fully the responsibility of the counsellor when they practise privately. Another consideration at the conclusion of a course is further follow-up training; for example, in a specialist area such as family therapy, or in supervision and training, or in attaining a higher level of qualification, an MA or PhD.

8 THE THREE MAJOR APPROACHES

The psychoanalytic, humanistic and behavioural models of therapy form the foundations from which many other orientations have developed. In counselling the psychoanalytical approach is represented by the psychodynamic models. Humanistic approaches include person-centred therapy, gestalt therapy and transactional analysis. The behavioural approaches include cognitive–behavioural therapy and rational emotive therapy (RET). Although the core approaches are fundamentally different – the psychodynamic places emphasis on the unconscious process and the transference, the humanistic on the congruent relationship between client and counsellor and the concept of self-actualization and the behavioural focuses on monitoring and controlling the individual's thoughts and behaviour – they have proved that they can be complementary to each other. Many counselling training courses integrate elements of all three.

The aim of this chapter is to give you a sense of rather than an in-depth exploration of the three main approaches by outlining the theories, ideas, concepts and techniques particular to each.

SECTION 1:
The Psychodynamic Approach

The psychodynamic approach has direct links with Freudian psychoanalysis. Freud's theories have been developed, modified and adapted by different strands of psychodynamic theorists. Many of Freud's original concepts remain central to this approach: for example, his theories of the unconscious, transference and countertransference; and the importance of formative childhood experiences, relationships and the use of dreams and metaphor as means of understanding the human psyche. These are among the tools used in the work of the psychodynamic counsellor. We can understand the term 'psychodynamic' by dividing it into its two parts. The first part derives from the Greek root word *psyche* which, related to therapy, refers to the tripart combination of the mind, emotions and spirit or soul. The word 'dynamic' refers to the constant interaction and movement between these three forces both internally (within ourselves) and externally in relation to other people and our environment.

The unconscious

Freud was fascinated by material which he believed lay hidden in the human psyche. He identified three categories of mental process:

1 The conscious – material (facts, feelings and thoughts) which the patient is aware of in the present.
2 The preconscious – material (ideas and memories) which are not conscious but are easily accessed.
3 The unconscious – material (desires or impulses) which lie hidden, buried from the conscious mind.

Freud later identified three driving forces of the mind.

The Id (it)

The Id is the part of the unconscious mind that contains the instinctual drives and impulses which motivate our behaviour. The primitive impulses driven by our instinctual needs are at odds with the Ego and the Superego. Both of these parts of the unconscious temper the basic drives of the Id. We may, for example, take a strong dislike towards someone; the Id would tell us to harm them or get rid of them in some way while the other parts of our unconscious mind would apply reasoning to the situation. The Id can be thought of as the child part of the unconscious. Since it forms the underlying motivations and drives of our actions it is our spontaneous 'dangerous' side that wishes to follow the 'pleasure principle'. The Id might say: 'This is what I want, what I really really want.'

The Id has two main driving forces:

- *Eros* – the life-affirming drive of love and sexuality.
- *Thanatos* – the drive towards death and destruction.

The Ego (I)

The Ego is the rational, partly conscious part of the mind which makes decisions and copes with the external world. The Ego says: 'I am, I can and I will.' The Ego can be related to the more grown-up side of our mind; it takes care of us, telling us we are doing OK. The Ego is the means by which we mediate with others and adapt to our environment.

The Superego (higher I)

The Superego is the 'conscientious' side of our mind which contains internalized societal and parental rules and taboos. As we take these into our unconscious mind the taboos are translated into 'I should', 'I ought' and 'I must'. The Superego is the source of guilt and ideals. Both the Superego and the Id are largely unconscious.

The role of the analyst was seen to be to assist the patient (as they were then termed) in translating unconscious material into conscious understanding. Using hypnosis in treatment, Freud's attention was drawn to the workings of the unconscious mind. An aim was to give the patient insight into areas of their psyche where they had 'stored' an experience which had been too painful or threatening for them to acknowledge fully at the time. These remained in the unconscious mind as repressed memories, causing disturbance in the patient's vital functioning. When these occurrences came to light the patient could have more control over their mental processes.

Freud considered that the source of neuroses could always be traced back to early childhood, although the symptoms of the neurotic conflict could manifest at a later stage. 'Neurosis' (or disturbance), lying dormant in the unconscious mind, may cause strong irrational reactions which are inappropriate to what is being experienced in the present. An example of this is demonstrated in our anxious reactions towards other people. Let's look at an example by briefly sketching a case history.

Case study 3

A young man, in his late twenties, has come to counselling because he is feeling depressed and unable to cope with work. It began when a woman joined his team at work as his superior. He took an instant dislike to her. She continued to trigger very strong feelings in him and he is at a loss to understand why. He is aware that his reactions to the woman are ruining his work life and the strong discontent that he is experiencing is permeating other areas of his life. Eventually, through therapy, he can locate the source of his prejudice towards his female boss. He has been talking about his hostile feelings towards his colleague over a number of sessions and some of the themes the counsellor has put together relate the different expressions of fear – for example, loss of control, sudden anger and feeling threatened by an unspecified source. He has also mentioned that he finds it difficult to form words coherently in her presence. The counsellor notes the 'infantizing' effect this woman appears to have on him and asks him if his colleague reminds him of anyone. He smiles and says that she physically resembles a woman who looked after him when he was a child, when his mother went out to work. When he spent time with her in her home, he experienced the woman as mainly indifferent but sometimes hostile towards him. She forced him to eat foods he disliked to the point of vomiting and made him sleep during the day, which his mother seldom did. He felt frightened and humiliated by her. He also reveals that he associated the woman with separation from his mother and feeling helpless and abandoned. This insight proves to be useful to the client, enabling him to see his colleague separately from the 'bad woman' image he had been unconsciously holding.

Freud noted that people repeatedly replay difficult or troubling relationships and situations which were originally experienced in the early years of life. The individual will have the 'compulsion to repeat' the unresolved material, until the unconscious element is brought into consciousness.

Developmental psychology

Psychodynamic theories regard the child's early environment as important and for this reason a psychodynamic training involves the study of developmental psychology. Psychoanalysts, beginning with Freud himself, have formed theories of human developmental stages.

The developmental stages delineated by Sigmund Freud

The early writings of Freud divide the human developmental stages into three: oral, anal and sexual.

1 *Oral, 0–2 years*: At this stage the infant experiences pleasure through the mouth, mainly through gratification from sucking, so toys and other objects are put into the mouth, 'felt' by the mouth.

2 *Anal, 2–4 years*: At this stage of development the child takes a sensual interest in their own faeces, experiencing a gratification in a substance that they produce. This can result in the child experimenting with smearing or eating faeces or withholding as a means of control.

3 *Phallic, 4–7 years*: The Superego develops within this age range as the focus of interest moves from the anus to the genitals as a focus of gratification. The parents become models for role identification. The Oedipus complex occurs during the phallic stage.

The Oedipus complex

The term **Oedipus complex** derives its name from the mythical (Greek) figure of Oedipus, who unwittingly killed his father and married his mother. The Oedipus complex is a collection of unconscious desires to 'possess' the parent of the opposite sex and 'eliminate' the parent of the same sex. The Oedipal stage occurs between the ages of 3 and 6 and, according to traditional Freudian views, is a universal component of development.

Freud said, 'A child's first choice of an object is an incestuous one', and 'Incestuous wishes are a primordial human heritage. The

Oedipal complex (phallic stage) is the central phenomenon of the sexual period of early childhood.' With its dissolution, it submits to repression and is followed by what Freud called 'The latency period'. Disintegration occurs for a number of reasons, due to disappointments growing out of the hopeless longing for the parent who is fixated upon, or to a castration anxiety. Castration enters the boy child's imagination when he first views the genital region of the female child, noting the absence of a penis. The boy then believes that all women, including his mother, have been castrated.

The child's Ego turns from the Oedipus complex, replacing object cathexes (i.e. the investing of his libidinal sexual energy in the parent) with other identifications. The father's authority is at this time introjected into the Ego and forms the centre of the Superego. The position appropriates the prohibition against incest and rescues the Ego from the libidinal object cathexes. The Oedipus complex is thereby 'desexualised and sublimated', and the latency period begins.

The Electra complex

The girl child too develops an Oedipus complex, which Freud initially termed the Electra complex. The girl's clitoris acts as a penis until she becomes aware that she has no penis and considers herself inferior, which results in penis envy. At first she understands the lack is temporary, consoling herself with the belief that as she grows older she will acquire a penis; she does not equate her lack of penis with sexual completion and presumes castration has occurred. Freud wrote, 'The essential difference thus comes about that the girl accepts castration as an accomplished fact whereas the boy fears the possibility of its occurrence.'

The girl's Oedipus complex is a modified version of that of the boy, basically consisting of the girl's wish to take her mother's position in her father's affection and adopt a feminine attitude towards him. She attempts to compensate for the loss of a penis by desiring 'the gift' of bearing her father's child. The resolution of the Oedipus complex occurs because the wish remains unfulfilled. However, according to Freud, the two desires – to have a penis and a child – remain in the unconscious, preparing the female for her later sexual role.

Latency stage

The latency stage is from 6 to puberty. The process which has led to the dissolution of the Oedipus complex has saved the penis, but because its function has been compromised the latency period begins interrupting the child's sexual development. Freud believed that if the Ego has repressed the complex then the latter will persist in the unconscious stage within the Id and is likely at some time to result in 'pathogenic effect' (disturbance or disease). The genital stage, from puberty to adulthood, follows the latency stage.

Erik Erikson's eight ages of man – stages of psychosocial development

Erik Erikson's personality theory places emphasis on the workings of the Ego, rather than concentrating on the unconscious drives of the Id as Freud had. Erikson was a Freudian psychoanalyst whose work extended Freud's stages of development, placing psychological development in the social context within a historical reality in which the child grows up. He suggested that, while the foundations of the individual's personality take form in the first two years of life, the personality is constantly developing, characterized by different stages. Successful development from one stage to the next depends on the resolution of the central task or conflict particular to the stage. These tasks are culturally determined and therefore universal. In *Childhood and Society*, Erikson wrote: 'Each successful stage and crisis has a special relation to one of the basic elements of society, and this for the simple reason that the human life-cycle and man's institutions have evolved together.'

The healthy personality combines individual happiness with social responsibility. For Erikson the quality of interpersonal relationships was all important, beginning with the infant–maternal relationship. He delineates eight stages of psychosocial continual development in his 'whole life' personality theory. (These are well worth reading in their full form and are offered here in a much abbreviated outline.)

Approximate Age	Stage	Conflict	Potential virtue gained	Societal manifestation
0–1	Infancy	Basic trust v. basic mistrust	Hope	Religion
2–3	Early childhood	Autonomy v. shame and doubt	Will	Law and order
4–5	Play age	Initiative v. guilt	Purpose	Economics
6–11	School age	Industry v. inferiority	Competence	Technology
12–18	Adolescence	Identity v. role confusion	Fidelity	Ideology
20–35	Young adulthood	Intimacy v. isolation	Love	Ethics
35–50	Middle adulthood	Generativity v. stagnation	Care	Education, art and science
50+	Maturity to old age	Ego integrity v. despair and disgust	Wisdom	All major cultural institutions

Erik Erikson's eight stages of psychosocial development

Stage 1 – basic trust v. basic mistrust

This early infantile stage of 0–1 years of age is when the patterns for the solution of the conflict of basic trust versus basic mistrust are established, determined by the maternal relationship. The first social achievement is when the infant is able to let the mother go out of sight without experiencing undue anxiety and rage. Bowel movements and teething are part of the infant's internal (bodily) experiencing and a dynamic is set into action between internal and external frames of reference, involving discomfort and loss. Basic trust wins over basic mistrust when the infant experiences the mother's consistency of provision. Erikson's sensory stage corresponds with Freud's oral stage. Religion is the social construct representing the infantile stage of basic trust. Absence of basic trust results in a continued stage of 'infantile schizophrenia' – a schizoid-depressive position. The basic requirement for therapy is working towards a re-establishment of a stage of trust.

Stage 2 – autonomy v. shame and doubt

According to Erikson, at this stage (approximately 2–3 years old) muscular maturation allows an experimentation with 'holding on' and 'letting go'. This muscular maturation stage corresponds to Freud's anal stage. A gradual learning is taking place; the young child has a growing sense of autonomy, experimenting with controlling and directing their behaviour. Alongside this is the potential to self-doubt since the child is aware of their own limitations. The child needs protecting with firm reassurance from the 'potential anarchy of his as yet untrained sense of discrimination' or the outcome is experiences of shame and doubt. This stage corresponds to the social constraints of law and order which, Erikson says, reflect 'The lasting need of the individual to have his will re-affirmed and delineated within an adult order of things.' Within these restrictions the child develops their sense of autonomy.

Stage 3 – initiative v. guilt

The child (4–6 years of age) is developing new locomotor and mental powers and the growing ability to both initiate and carry out actions can give rise to guilty feelings. This stage of increased locomotor power corresponds with Freud's genital stage, which contains the phallic and Oedipal conflicts. It is the 'play age'. Erikson trained in the Montessori method and he focused on child's play as a means of understanding child development. Increasingly the child, who is developing socially as well as physically, is faced with more responsibilities which brings the opportunity to develop a sense of initiative through decision making and action. The increasing responsibilities incurred by the new-found sense of purpose may bring about, Erikson suggests, 'a sense of guilt over the goals contemplated and the acts initiated in one's exuberant enjoyment of new locomotor and mental power'. The social expression of this is economics.

Stage 4 – industry v. inferiority

The child is of school age (5–11 years old) when the task becomes one of industrious focusing and the trying out of new skills. The possibility of failure to do so may result in a sense of inferiority in relation to the achievements of others. It is a time when the early stage of play becomes more technically focused, therefore the corresponding element is technology. The child is industrious, enjoying the tasks of learning when challenges can be met but failure to carry them out or avoidance of challenges can lead to a sense of inferiority, leading to further avoidances. Competence is the potential new virtue gained.

Stage 5 – identity v. role confusion

Integration of a self-identity, that is the Ego identity, is the task of the young adolescent (12–18 years old). The developing youth's prime concern is how they appear to others in relation to their own self-concept. It is a time of emotional flux; there is a great physiological revolution taking place within and a new sexual identity is also developing. Adolescence produces many challenges, including asserting oneself within peer groups, making the transition from childhood to adulthood and making the transition from school to university or the workplace. It is also a time of idealism and the corresponding manifestation represented in society is ideology. The adolescent experiments in different ways in the quest of self-understanding. Although treated like adults, they are not as yet considered to be full members of society. Role confusion is the underside of successful development of identity. Questions such as 'Who am I?', 'What have I to offer?' reflect existential angst. The alienation confusion about who they are causes depression. A sense of identity or a consistent self-concept needs to be established.

Stage 6 – intimacy v. isolation

The young adult (20–35 years of age) is ready to fuse their identity with others. They are ready to meet the challenges of commitment to partnerships and 'concrete affiliations' by the development of an ethical strength. They are willing to make significant sacrifices and compromises in the quest for intimacy with others. The successful progression to achieving intimacy with others necessitates the fulfilling of the previous task of establishing self-identity or Ego strength. If the tasks of this stage remain unfulfilled and the conflicts unresolved, the result is a continuing sense of isolation and alienation from others. The societal manifestation of the conflicts presented in the intimacy versus isolation stage of development is the construction of ethics.

Stage 7 – generativity v. stagnation

Having built a strong sense of identity and an ability to form intimate relationships with others, the challenge of this stage involves engagement with productive activities – putting accumulated knowledge and life experiences to good use. This could take the form of encouraging the young in their endeavours, or the enjoyment of the fruition of the individual's occupation and achievements. The conflicting danger is that the person becomes stuck in their ways and stagnates. The societal manifestation is education, art and science.

Stage 8 – Ego integrity v. despair and disgust

The final stage is maturity to old age (50+). The older person has wisdom to offer from a lifetime's experience. The early phase of this stage is preparation for old age, a gradual summing up of life's achievements and meaning gradually take place. Declining health and vitality makes old age a reality. Retirement from work may bring on a sense of uselessness, despair and self-disgust, fear they no longer have anything to offer society or personal relationships. Approaching death, the individual can either feel at peace with their life experiences, appreciating the contributions they have made – that is, knowing that they have done what they could (Ego integrity) – or view their lives as having been futile. The corresponding representation in society is major cultural institutions as a part of historical heritage. (Chapter 7. pp. 222–42)

Others who have contributed to developmental psychology and personality theories are Gordon Lowe, who also constructed a 'whole life' theory in *The Growth of Personality – from Infancy to Old Age*; Jean Piaget, whose concern was a child's cognitive development; and the psychologist John Bowlby, who wrote studies of 'attachment behaviour' in relation to human psychological development.

Jean Piaget's cognitive developmental stages

The Swiss developmental psychologist Jean Piaget was one of the first to study cognitive development in children, focusing on the importance of sensorimotor (sensory and motor mechanisms) and ideomotor (putting ideas into action) learning – that is, the young child's developing ability to translate their perceptions into actions, organizing their thoughts into a series of actions. Within the sensorimotor (0–2 years) stage the infant develops an ability to interact with their environment through the senses. In Piagetian theory the preoperatory stage of cognitive development (2–7 years) follows the sensory-motor stage. The preoperatory stage is offset by the child's 'object concept' of 'object permanence'; that is, the child becomes aware that physical objects are permanent and exist as a separate entity without his involvement in interaction. It is also the time when the child learns the use of a 'system of symbols' – words and language to relate to the world around – but at this stage the child's thought is intuitive rather than logical. The concrete operatory stage or level (7–12 years) represents a leap in cognitive abilities involving the use of logic to solve problems. By now the child can differentiate between ways of communicating and can cope with concrete situations.

Abstract reasoning comes into play in the formal operator level of cognition development (12 years to adulthood). Piaget called it 'the metaphysical age *par excellence*'. In the preadolescent to adolescent stage of development the young person gradually exercises their 'autonomous reasoning' to test the rules of society with a view to finding personal meaning. Piaget identified a first morality as 'heteronomous' to describe rules which are sacred, external and unchangeable. A second 'autonomous' reality which develops at preadolescent stage wrestles with the heteronomous morality before replacing it.

John Bowlby's attachment theory

The psychoanalyst John Bowlby, whose work has its roots in Melanie Klein's child development theory, wrote extensively on the theme of attachment with regard to loss, sadness and depression. Bowlby wrote *Attachment and Loss*, a three-volume exploration of attachment behaviour from an object relations perspective, identifying the early human need to maintain close contact with parent or mother. A healthy 'secure attachment' develops when the individual as an infant and young child has consistency of care and feels confident and secure in parental availability (mainly that of the mother), having experienced her for the main part to be responsive, loving and safe. An 'anxious attachment' forms through the child's experiencing of inconsistent 'mothering' or the loss of maternal or parental figures. Bowlby wrote that one of the typical patterns of pathogenic parenting was 'discontinuities of parenting'. The early prototypal attachment relationship affects the ability to form healthy attachments to others in later life. In *The Making and Breaking of Affectional Bonds* Bowlby wrote, 'There is a strong causal relationship between an individual's experiences with his parents and his later capacity to make affectional bonds.' He noted that insecure experiencing resulting from inconsistent or poor parenting, involving abandonment or loss, can lead a child or an adolescent to live in a constant state of anxiety, in the fear that they might lose their attachment figure. The anxious attachment expresses itself in diverse ways including anger, sadness and depression and in difficulties in manifesting attachment behaviour.

Object relations

The object relations theorists – D.W. Winnicott, W.R.D. Fairburn, Melanie Klein and others – also saw great significance in the child's first impression of the world. The object relations school moved away from the classical Freudian libidinal theories of instinctual pleasure-seeking drives, placing emphasis on human contact and relationships. The term 'object relations' refers to the central theme of the theory, which is that the baby's emotional well-being and development depends on certain relational needs being met. Melanie Klein, who is sometimes described as having bridged the gap between the object relations school and classic Freudian analysis, retained the idea of infantile instincts and drives as basic to the psyche, while introducing the concept of the infant as 'object seeking' as opposed to 'satisfaction seeking'. The infant's instinctive drive is both to survive and to satisfy their needs in relation to a loving, nurturing 'object' or person, usually the mother or a central figure.

The object relation theorists suggested that the mother's breast is an object of satisfaction and comfort that is not always available, therefore a 'transitional object' like a dummy or a teddy bear is used as a temporary replacement. The 'good breast' and the 'bad breast' are terms used to describe the infant's impression of the breast as 'part object' – as a potentially endless source of nourishment and pleasure it is a 'good object', and the frustrating breast that is taken away is a 'bad object'. Winnicott suggested that the child needs 'good enough mothering'; that is, a facilitating environment to assist emotional and psychological development.

Klein, who regarded herself as a Freudian, believed that the first few weeks of a baby's life were significant. As a child analyst she used 'play analysis', using drawing and simple play materials and toys to help her understand the psychological world of the child. Winnicott also recommended that the counsellor let the client 'play' as a means of unravelling their story or rediscovering parts of themselves. Problems arise for the baby when the relating to the 'object' as mother or significant carer becomes fraught. This could be through environmental factors, or because of incapabilities of the mother or any other circumstance that upsets the symbiotic relationship. When the relating is incomplete, elements will arise within therapy through the transference relationship between therapist and client where issues can be explored in a new and 'holding' environment.

Transference and countertransference

Transference was a term coined by Freud to describe a phenomenon he observed occurring between Breuer and his patient Anna O., who became increasingly dependent on Breuer and fantasized that she was pregnant with his child. Freud was of the opinion that Anna (her real name was Bertha Pappenheim) had fallen in love with or become infatuated by her doctor, but that the manifest feelings really belonged to a relationship from her past and a resolution of the original disturbance would effect a 'cure'. In a paper entitled 'General Theory of the Neuroses' (1916–17) Freud wrote of transference as 'a newly created and transformed neurosis' which within treatment came to replace the original disturbance. He believed that the 'mastering' of the 'artificial neurosis', the transferred emotions, led to the elimination of the illness. However, Freud noticed that his colleague had also become rather involved with his patient, which led him to ponder whether Breuer's overt concern for Anna represented an unresolved conflict of his own. The reaction to client material by the therapist is the **countertransference**, and transference is appreciated as a complex interactional dynamic between the therapist and client that is an invaluable therapeutic tool. Working with the transference encourages that which is in the unconscious to be brought into consciousness in the presence of the therapist. This becomes a possibility when the therapist becomes (represents) a significant other from the client's past, particularly a parental figure. Freud worked with his patient's recall of the primary repressed material.

Transference happens to an extent in all relationships. All of us transfer unresolved 'stuck' ways of relating which have their roots in our childhood experiences onto others around us, especially those we are in close relationships with. If, for example, a person had a domineering, critical father, then as an adult they may view people in authority as having these characteristics and they may regress to a way of relating to them that echoes the childhood relationship with their father, which might include anxiety, resentment or deference. Yet the other person in reality may be nothing like the father in personality or attitudes. Transference can manifest inappropriate ineffectual reaction behaviour that interferes with healthy relating. In the therapeutic setting it can bring old conflicts alive and these can be worked out with the assistance of the counsellor, breaking the old patterns of relating. The 're-experiencing therapist' Merton Gill challenged Freud's belief that therapeutic change came about when the person remembered the conflict. Gill said that remembering alone was not enough and that the client also needed to re-experience conflicts, emotional trauma and impulses in the presence of the therapist. Since the difficulties are acquired experientially, attitudes and meanings can be changed experientially. With the therapist the old conflicts can be emotionally relived under new conditions. When the client experiences and expresses the impulses and anxieties in the presence of the therapist to whom they are now directed in the transference, the therapist must be willing to discuss them with interest, and non-defensively. Finally the therapist helps the client to learn the source of the re-experienced conflicts. The transference offers the client a unique opportunity, in the therapeutic setting, to experience a different response to the original cause of conflict. Whereas in the original encounter the client experienced pain, humiliation or rejection, the therapist's response is one of acceptance.

The **countertransference** is the feelings and attitudes that the counsellor has in relation to the client. Although, like transference, they are initially unconscious the counsellor gradually notices shifts in their inner responses with regard to the client. For example, the person mentioned before who had a domineering and critical father may, in the transference, feel dominated or in awe of a male counsellor. The countertransferential response would arise if the counsellor began to feel omnipotent or critical towards the client or, conversely, the countertransference reaction could be that the counsellor feels that they should have these qualities (that is, they are expected to have them) and are incapacitated by the transference. Although originally countertransference was thought to be a hindrance to effective therapy it is now regarded as very useful. Because countertransference is noted rather than acted upon (the counsellor is always vigilant regarding their own feelings and reactions) it provides the counsellor with insight into the problems of the client that perhaps would otherwise go unrecognized. The counsellor may think 'Why do I feel disapproving' and make the link with what has been said about the client's father, which gives the opportunity to explore these feelings further. Countertransference feelings are often brought to life in supervision and are frequently a source of discussion with regard to the counsellor's own unresolved emotional difficulties.

Malan's triangle of conflict model

The triangle of conflict model helps the counsellor look at the anxieties behind the client's defensive behaviour and thereby understand the underlying hidden feeling or impulse that causes

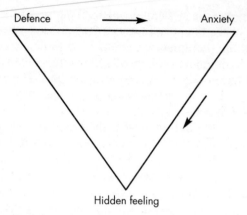

Triangle of conflict

Source: D.H. Malan, *Individual Psychotherapy and the Science of Psychodynamics,* Chapter 10.

disturbance. Expressing painful or conflicting feelings directly can be frightening – the fear might be that others will find the strong feelings unacceptable, hateful, ridiculous, shameful and so on, or that the person themselves becomes overpowered by them. The fear of the consequences of expressing such emotions causes anxiety, which in turn causes the person to defend themselves against both the unwanted feelings and the resulting anxiety by repressing them. The three parts of the process are symbolically represented by the apices of the triangle. The attempt to defend oneself against powerful feelings creates psychological distress, yet the person may not be consciously aware of the feelings at all. Malan's model proposes that psychological distress is brought on by a 'triggering experience' that is congruent with the original damaging experience. The person then attempts to defend themselves against the (repressed) hidden feeling or impulse and the distress it creates. Within therapy it is the defence that the counsellor first picks up. Malan describes the defence and the anxiety as symptoms that indicate both 'expression' and 'denial'. The goal of the therapy is to explore with the client the defence and the anxiety that lies behind the defence, and to help the client confront and contain the hidden feeling. When the hidden material is held in the preconsciousness – that is, the person is (in part) aware of the feelings but is unwilling to acknowledge them – then the exploration of the defence and anxiety can be uncomplicated and the confronting of the hidden problem much simpler. Unconscious defence mechanisms, constructed to avoid mental pain or to control unacceptable impulses, can take a long time to unravel. It is important that the counsellor is tentative in the interventions and interpretations offered, asking questions (inwardly) such as: What are the hidden feelings? Are these feelings accessible? How painful or anxiety ridden are the feelings of past experiences? Can the client express these with me at this time? Psychodynamic therapy is geared towards putting the client in touch with their feelings and the success of this depends on the building of trust and therapeutic rapport. Changes and shifts in perception are monitored by sensitive attention to client responses.

The triangle of insight model

The triangle of insight was first introduced by Karl Menninger in his book *The Theory of Psychoanalytic Technique* (1958). While the triangle of conflict forms a model for reaching and understanding the hidden feelings that are a source of conflict and unhappiness in a person's life, the triangle of insight represents a relational model of the source and effect of the destructive feelings. It is a useful tool in understanding the workings of transference. Often the client alludes to what is going on in the therapy by talking about situations 'outside' in their daily lives – so the client who feels that the counsellor doesn't understand them says that their husband or wife doesn't understand them, the client who feels criticized by the counsellor says that their boss is always criticizing their work. The client may also allude to the therapeutic situation by talking about the distant past; for example, when a break in therapy is pending and the client fears that they won't be able to manage alone, they talk about how their parents sent them to boarding school when they were very young and how lost and frightened they felt. The psychodynamic counsellor tentatively decodes these messages, making the connection for the client: 'I understand that you felt lost and frightened when you were sent off to boarding school at such a young age. I am aware that we are about to have a break in the therapy and I wonder if another meaning of what you say is that you are frightened that you won't be able to cope when I go?' Here the counsellor makes a reference to themselves as the transferential parent figure (potentially abandoning) because the client is already unconsciously making this connection.

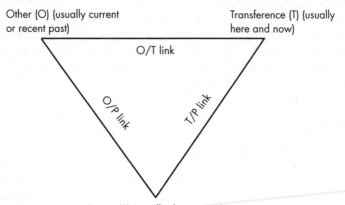

Triangle of insight
Source: D.H. Malan, *Individual Psychotherapy and the Science of Psychodynamics*, Chapter 10.

The triangle of insight model represents three categories of persons and sources of relationship experience from the client's life situations:

- Others (O) – are people recently or currently in their everyday life 'out there' and are connected with the problems they bring to counselling; the person could be a husband or wife, boyfriend or girlfriend, colleague at work or some other person who is strongly impacting on their life at the time.
- Transference (T) – relates to the counsellor in the 'here and now', when the counsellor represents either an 'out there' other person, or a parental figure from the past.

■ Parent (P) – this apex represents primary, formative experiences relating to parents or parental figures from the past.

The model illustrates that all are interlinked; for example, as we have already explored, in the transference the client will at some point in therapy experience the counsellor as a parent and 'transfer' feelings which belong to the past into the here and now and onto the therapist. In a similar manner the client will at some stage in other close relationships experience problems relating to the past unresolved original experiences with the parent. Current or recent experiences with others 'out there', in everyday life, may also be transferred onto the counsellor to be worked out in the session.

Resistances and defences

A major part of the psychodynamic technique is analysing the resistances which put up a smoke screen to protect the defences. Clients demonstrate resistance in various ways; for example, by being late for sessions, by wanting to finish the therapy in a 'flight to health' (in a claim that all their problems are miraculously solved), by missing sessions, and by denial when a counsellor makes accurate observations or interpretations. The resistance betrays a reluctance to discover more, to let down a barrier or open up a protected part of themselves. There are ambivalent feelings; the person wants on the conscious level to have insight into the problems that brought them into counselling in the first place and to deal with life in a more productive self-fulfilling way, but on an unconscious or preconscious level they value and automatically want to hold onto their defences. Defences are a mental armouring that protect the individual from threatening or punitive feelings and were appropriate at the time they were acquired. The client needs reasons to let their defences down, they need to feel safe, accepted and understood and to be able to trust the counsellor to explore painful issues with them. Confronting a defence head on is more likely than not to re-enforce it. A skilled, sensitive counsellor respects a client's defence mechanisms and tries to understand the underlying reasons, interpreting them tentatively and gently exploring possibilities in step with the client, who gains self-insight by making subtle shifts in perception.

The analytic tool of **free association** was introduced by Freud as a means of accessing the unconscious and interpreting defences and resistances. Freud encouraged his patients to talk freely about every thought, feeling, image, memory and association that came into their head, however irrelevant, trivial or disagreeable it seemed. In doing so the patient was likely to let out slips of the tongue (hence the term 'Freudian slip'), making associations that could then be interpreted to bring repressed material into consciousness.

Dreams

The interpretation of **dreams** is another technique employed in bringing unconscious material into consciousness. Freud saw dreams as 'wish fulfilment'; but in dreams too there is a certain amount of repression which forms the latent dream content. The latent dream thoughts are transformed into the manifest dream content by self-censoring functions of the individual's mental activity. The psychodynamic counsellor also uses dreams to, as Freud put it, 'unravel what the dream-work has woven'.

In psychotherapy the psychodynamic approach is differentiated into specific classifications of Freudian, Kleinian, and Jungian, but in psychodynamic counselling the psychodynamic model is likely to be taught, learned, and practised as an assimilation of aspects of all three with a stronger emphasis on Freudian theory as a background. For example, elements of object relations will be included as well as Kleinian theories and concepts regarding 'unconscious phantasies', 'splitting' and 'projective identification'; aspects of Jungian psychology would include his views on the relationship between unconscious and conscious processes and of human growth and creativity.

Michael Jacob in *Psychodynamic Counselling in Action* draws attention to the point that 'Much of the literature upon which psychodynamic counselling draws is written for psychoanalysts or psychotherapists. This does not, however, make it irrelevant for the counsellor, especially where there are case histories to illustrate both technique and the way in which theories of personality development are used in practice.'

Aim of therapy

The psychodynamic counsellor's view of the 'disturbed' person is someone whose everyday functioning is governed by inner conflicts. The psychoanalytic viewpoint understands everyone to have inner conflicts – the point being that normally they are satisfactorily suppressed and therefore manageable. The person experiencing unmanageable difficulties in their life knows something is wrong but not what is wrong, whereas the person who functions in a psychologically satisfied way is untroubled by inner conflict in as much as it is manageable and does not dominate the person's existence. A central aim is to help the client to become more self-aware and to bring that which is unconscious into consciousness. The counsellor's role is in helping the client to gain insight and understanding into aspects of the self which were previously unknown. This is achieved by working with unconscious processes, transference, defences, resistances and dreams, to bring conflicts, impulses and feelings to the surface. Emphasis is placed on self-knowledge and insight rather than on attempting to eliminate problems. Jacob also wrote in *Psychodynamic Counselling in Action*: 'The psychodynamic approach, which the counsellor also shows in action in her or his work with the client, is also often adopted by the client in self analysis.'

Role of the counsellor: the therapeutic relationship

The psychodynamic counsellor adopts a neutral stance based on the 'blank screen' of traditional Freudian psychoanalysis, adopting what is referred to as 'the rule of neutrality', involving a respect for the client's autonomy and an attitude of caring commitment on the part of the counsellor. The 'rule of abstinence' employed by the counsellor is sometimes misunderstood by clients as an attempt by the counsellor to maintain a superior professional distance. The psychodynamic counsellor does not self-disclose, viewing this kind of interaction as a detraction from the client. The more a client gets to know the therapist, in the usual sense, the less likely they are to be able to project and transfer feelings from the past onto them.

It is a kind of withholding, but not one without reason and therapeutic value; the counsellor holds back rather than engaging in conversation, allowing the client to go on talking and revealing their thoughts and accompanying feelings. The counsellor may not answer a question directly; for example, they may address instead the meaning the question has for the client – what is behind the question. The relational frustrations that the client experiences (sometimes referred to as optimal frustration) are regarded as useful to the confronting of conflicts and hidden impulses. The neutral or abstinent role of the counsellor is also helpful to the containing and holding of client material. As the counsellor's own personality takes a back seat, the client is able to feel therapeutically held by them.

Maintaining boundaries is an important aspect of this approach, involving clear contracting as to the frequency and length of sessions and duration of therapy, and creating a confidential and private environment. Assessments and history taking form a baseline of information about the client's early family relationships and experiences. The ending of therapy also has a special significance in this approach – it is likely to stir up past feelings of abandonment and loss which may reassert themselves in last-minute transference feelings. As we have already seen, a central focus of the work is the interpretation of defences and resistances which are brought to the client's attention and confronted with the counsellor. Links are made between past and present and special attention is paid to the client's perceptual world, not only to real experiences but also to how the reality is perceived. Increasingly, the psychodynamic counsellor has adopted person-centred values of warmth, acceptance and empathic responding and an interest in presenting themselves as a 'whole' person. The counsellor's own self-development and understanding is a crucial component of the approach. As personal therapy is encouraged, the psychodynamic counsellor will have experience of being on the receiving end of the therapy as a client, working in the transference, exploring childhood material and confronting defences.

C.G. Jung

The work of the analytical psychologist Carl Gustav Jung needs to be mentioned since his contribution to the analytic, psychodynamic and transpersonal approaches has been immense. Like Freud, Jung was a medical doctor (specializing in psychiatry) who became a pioneering figure in psychoanalysis. Freud, who was Jung's senior by twenty years, was impressed by Jung's pioneering work on schizophrenia. He saw the younger man as a protégé and for a period of six years or so they worked in close association, but in time Jung came to regard Freud's theories on the human sexual drive as limited and restrictive to his own work and they parted ways. Jung's work reflected his diverse interests; from a young age he read extensively, gaining knowledge of philosophy, alchemy, astrology, theology and ancient religions. His main interest was the study of psychotic tendencies in individuals who otherwise functioned normally and he sought answers in the primitive elements of the psyche. The inspiration that he found in the ancient religions influenced his work – for example, his theories of the individual and collective unconscious which manifest in archetypes in dreams and visions.

He admired Hinduism for the way it integrated concepts of good and evil in the attributes of gods such as Shiva – the creator and the destroyer – because he believed that it is important for our mental health that we acknowledge the negative, largely unexpressed side of the human condition, which he terms 'the shadow'. For Jung mental stability was a matter of balance, balance between the conscious and unconscious aspects of the personality, including feminine and masculine aspects and intellect and emotion.

Dreams

Jung considered dreams to be a manifestation of the unconscious mind – a bridge between the conscious and the unconscious elements of the human psyche. He regarded dreams as imbued with meaningful information that guided the individual towards that which could fulfil and nourish them. For example, dreams served as a compensatory or self-regulating form of communication from the unconscious mind which gave expression to neglected or unrealized areas of the individual's true self, or gave warnings when an individual strayed from their 'proper path'. The study of alchemy led Jung to consider dreams as a medium for transforming and purifying psychic energy, which resulted in growth and development for individuals as well as at a collective level when information relevant and significant to the whole of humankind was imparted.

Psychological types

Jung began his work on psychological types through observing the personality traits and temperamental differences between Alfred Adler and Freud and the differences between himself and the other two. His first classifications of the extrovert and the introvert types can be best understood as a frame of reference from which the individual adopts attitudes towards life which affect individual experience. The extrovert character inclines towards the external world of other people and environment, while the introverted character is orientated to the inner world. In his later work Jung added four functions which operated the psyche: thinking, feeling, sensation and intuition. Just as extrovert and introvert are opposites, thinking is opposite to feeling, and sensation is opposite to intuition. (Jung thought that the intellect was too highly valued in the Western world, at cost to the emotional world of humankind.) In the same way as a person was inclined towards either an extroverted or an introverted expression of personality, the individual tends towards being a predominantly thinking rather than a feeling person or is orientated towards sensation rather than to intuition. In drawing a distinction between sensation and intuition as tools of perception, Jung used the term 'sensation' to mean information that is received through the sense organs (i.e. sight, hearing and taste and touch) and 'intuition' to mean information from the unconscious which was independent of sensation.

Individuation

What Jung called 'the process of individuation' is essentially an inner journey embarked on in the second part of life. The first part of life is concerned with being under, then freeing oneself from, parental influence and then establishing oneself as an adult in various roles including useful work, partnering and parenting. Having fulfilled this potential (ostensibly by functioning in the external world), the second part of life was when an individual could achieve a synthesis between their conscious and unconscious self by looking inward. Jung believed the self to be the God within – a 'hypothetical point between conscious and unconscious'. Jung regarded individuation to be a natural psychological process. He wrote: 'The natural process of individuation brings a consciousness of human community precisely because it makes us aware of the unconscious, which unites and is common to all mankind' (from *The Collected Works of C.G. Jung*).

The shadow

To facilitate the recognition and acceptance of the more unacceptable parts of the client to themselves we need to accept what Jung called our 'shadow side'. The shadow is to be found in the unconscious part of ourselves. It is often hidden from us. Our shadow represents all the things that we do not or cannot allow ourselves to do or think. It has been likened to the Mr Hyde part of Dr Jekyll, so it can be the murderous feelings we have towards someone which we would rather not face. Jung saw the shadow as the primitive, uncontrolled part of ourselves. It has been called the inferior side of ourselves, but perhaps this encourages us to deny it. It is part of us but it is a side which is regarded as uncivilized and antisocial. Jung also used the term to describe parts of ourselves which we may have originally expressed as children but then learned were unacceptable to our parents or society. A little girl who shows great ability at something which is seen to be within traditionally male territory, like building or engineering, may revert to a more widely stereotypically acceptable female domain, like playing with dolls and nursing. However, the dormant 'antisocial' part of her lies within her psyche as a source of ill content as her unfulfilled shadow side.

Archetypes

Jung looked at history and the mythology of ancient civilizations for clues to unravelling the human psyche. While working with patients with schizophrenia he noted that the visions that they had were strikingly similar to those in mythology, the details of which were known to only a few scholars. There was no explanation as to how the imagery matched so accurately. Jung was to write that archetypes were: 'Motifs analogous to or identical with those of mythology', and that they were 'found everywhere and at all times in Greek, Egyptian and ancient Mexican myths and in dreams of modern individuals ignorant of such traditions'. This he believed to be more than coincidental. The concept of **synchronicity** recognizes that there are acausal connections between people, places and occurrences in the world.

The collective unconscious

Jung coined the term 'The Collective Unconscious' to describe what he considered to be the true basis of the human psyche. He said that the collective unconscious was 'not individual but common to all humans as the ancestral heritage of possibilities of representation'. Archetypes, he noted, manifest in dreams and visions to help us with human dilemmas. The collective unconscious is like a pool of human situations and experiences which the human psyche can draw on.

Anima and animus

Jung used the word 'anima', the Latin for 'soul', to mean the feminine aspect of the male unconscious; likewise the word 'animus', mind or spirit, is the masculine aspect of the female unconscious. Jung introduced the idea of the sexes having qualities of each other – a man having feminine qualities and vice versa. In order to be whole a person needs to accept and integrate both aspects. He came to these conclusions from studying mythology, fairytales and dreams in which men experienced their souls as feminine and women experienced their souls as masculine. Interestingly, Jung noted that the anima and animus figures tended to come into play in the unconscious when the shadow elements have become accepted and integrated into the opposite sex and further issues come to the fore. In dreams and as outer world projections, figures of the opposite sex represent a collective archetype of relationship which exists between and beyond individual constraints. Jung viewed the anima/animus as functional to our relationship with the collective unconscious.

SECTION 2
The Humanistic/Person-Centred Approach

Abraham Maslow is usually accredited with the title of 'father of humanistic psychology', which reached prominence in America in the 1950s and 1960s. Maslow is perhaps best known for his 'hierarchy of needs' model, which identifies five basic human needs, here listed in the order of importance:

Maslow's Hierarchy of needs model

1 The physiological needs – these are the basic needs for continuing life; for example, water, oxygen, foodstuffs, a need for activity, sleep, bodily elimination, avoidance of pain, sexual expression.

2 Safety and security – these are secondary to the absolute necessities; when the physiological needs are met, then a second layer of needs becomes prominent (e.g. safety, stability, structure, boundaries).

3 Love and belonging – the third layer in Maslow's hierarchy concerns close relationships with others (e.g. bonding, having a place in community). A negative response is a movement towards social anxieties and alienation/loneliness.

4 Self-esteem – Maslow identified two 'esteem needs'. Lower esteem refers to a need for respect from others, for status, attention, appreciation and at times dominance. Higher esteem needs are self-generated (e.g. self-respect, sense of achievement, self-sufficiency, independence).

5 To self-actualize – Maslow equates self-actualization with 'growth motivation' – a continuing desire to 'be all that you can be', which involves a need to fulfil personal potential. However, self-actualization is unlikely to be possible until the lower needs have been met. The self-actualized person is someone who is 'reality centred' – able to differentiate between that which is real or genuine and that which is 'phoney' or dishonest; 'problem-centred' – essentially problem solving and solution orientated; and resistant to 'enculturation' – unyielding to social pressure. Other qualities that distinguish the self-actualized person are spontaneity, creativity and an acceptance of self and others. Living with a 'freshness of appreciation', they have 'peak experiences' more frequently than others. Maslow used the term 'peak experience' to describe mystical experiences; a feeling of awe, exhilaration and appreciation, of being at one with nature or God – similar to what Rudolf Otto called the 'numinous'. Motivating factors of self-actualizers include a drive towards truth, aliveness, playfulness, meaningfulness, unity and self-sufficiency.

The humanistic approach to therapy was named the 'third force'. Maslow is also credited with introducing the 'fourth force', transpersonal psychology. Maslow regarded psychology, in the form of psychoanalysis, to be overly concerned with the neurotic and disturbed, and preferred to work with healthy, creative individuals. He also considered the reductionist, mechanistic theory of behaviouralism to be limited in its view of human functioning. What interested him was 'higher human motivation'. Maslow, along with other humanistic psychologists such as Fritz Perls and Eric Berne, the founder of transactional analysis, was heavily influenced by the philosophy of European existentialists and phenomenologists such as Sartre, Kierkegaard, Husserl and Binswanger. Existentialism rejects the idea of a person as a product of heredity or environment, believing instead that each individual is responsible for their own destiny.

The person-centred approach

The person-centred approach is the main representation of the humanistic approach presented here because its core conditions model and many of its ideas have been widely integrated into other approaches. The views of Carl Rogers and his contemporaries have highly influenced people's attitudes towards therapy. Unlike the cognitive-behavioural approaches, the person-centred model is non-directive and focuses on the quality of therapy, especially the therapist's attitude towards the client. Rogers and his associates shifted clinical models in psychology away from the medically orientated model. He developed 'client-centred therapy' in the USA in the 1940s and 1950s, working in educational and pastoral settings, but it was in the liberal 'flower power' climate of the 1960s that it really came to the fore. Experimental encounter groups became popular at this time and well into the 1970s as a method of working in the 'here and now'. He carried out extensive research in counselling methods and used interviews recorded in the early 1940s on phonograph records as a means of studying and improving psychotherapeutic techniques and supervision. Video recordings are available of Rogers at work both in one-to-one counselling and as a facilitator of large group work (see Resources).

The Rogerian core conditions model

In a paper entitled 'The Necessary and Sufficient Conditions of Therapeutic Personality Change', Rogers set out a set of six conditions that he regarded as necessary and sufficient to initiate 'constructive personality change':

1 Two persons are in psychological contact.
2 The first, whom we shall term the client, is in a state of incongruence, being vulnerable or anxious.
3 The second person, whom we shall term the therapist, is congruent or integrated in the relationship.
4 The therapist experiences unconditional positive regard for the client.
5 The therapist experiences an empathic understanding of the client's internal frame of reference and endeavours to communicate this experience to the client.
6 The communication to the client of the therapist's empathic understanding and unconditional positive regard is to a minimal degree achieved.

(*Source*: *The Carl Rogers Reader*, edited by H. Kirschenbaum and V. Land Henderson, 16, pp. 219–35)

Rogers goes on to conclude: 'No other conditions are necessary. If these six conditions exist, and continue over a period of time, this is sufficient. The process of constructive personality change will follow.' Rogers acknowledged that his six conditions theory was based on the hypothesis that positive personality change occurs in a relationship (condition 1); the other conditions define the necessary characteristics of the persons in the relationship.

In Rogerian theory, and to person-centred therapists commonly, the relationship between the counsellor and client in the 'here and now' is all important. With this in mind, let's look briefly at how Rogers himself defined what has been narrowed down to the three core values or conditions from his original model; that is, congruence, unconditional positive regard and empathy.

Congruence

Rogers equated congruence with genuineness – the therapist's ability to be genuine with the client in the relationship. He wrote that the therapist should be 'a congruent, genuine, integrated person'. By 'integrated' he meant 'whole'; that the counsellor or therapist had self-awareness and was comfortable with their own experiencing, both positive and negative. The therapist didn't hide behind a professional façade but was 'freely and deeply himself'. To put it in another way, using another Rogerian term, the counsellor is in touch with and able to be their 'authentic self'. This entails the therapist being open about their feelings with regard to the client and the relationship. As a guideline on the subject, he wrote: 'Certainly the aim is not for the therapist to express or talk out his own feelings, but primarily that he should not be deceiving the client as to himself.'

The counsellor is not required to relate all their thoughts and feelings back to the client – this would be confusing and unhelpful – but rather the counsellor relates back thoughts or feelings when it becomes apparent that they are in some way either interfering with the therapeutic process or can play a positive role. At other times, Rogers concluded, it may be more appropriate for the counsellor to take the thoughts and feelings that they are experiencing with the client to a colleague or supervisor.

Unconditional positive regard

This term was used by Rogers to describe a thorough, caring acceptance for the client. He wrote: 'To the extent that the therapist finds himself experiencing a warm acceptance of each aspect of the client's experience as being a part of that client, he is experiencing unconditional positive regard.' In agreement with John Dewey, Rogers spoke of 'prizing' the person and of accepting the client as a worthwhile human being. To have unconditional positive regard towards another person means there are no conditions of acceptance, which calls for a non-judgemental attitude rather than a selective, evaluating attitude of accepting some aspects of the client while rejecting others. This stance requires the counsellor to be as accepting of the client's negative expression of 'bad' feelings (e.g. fearfulness, hurt, defensiveness, anger) as of 'good' feelings (e.g. competency, confidence, positive social feelings) and to accept inconsistency of behaviour.

Rogers also defined unconditional positive regard as a non-possessive, non-conditional 'caring', separate from the therapist's own needs, and in terms of valuing the client as a separate person whose feelings and experiencing are facilitated and validated by the therapist. By accepting the client as they are in the present, and extending positive regard without conditions, the person-centred counsellor encourages optimum self-expression in the client.

Empathy

'To sense the client's private world as if it were your own, but without ever losing the "as if" quality' is how Rogers described empathic understanding. He went on to say that empathy involved 'sensing' the client's subjective, perceptual world – fears, anger, confusion – as if they were the counsellor's own, but without 'getting bound up in it'. He wrote of the empathic therapist being able to move around freely in the client's world, helping the client to clarify thoughts, feelings and meanings; and also voicing 'meanings in the client's experience of which the client is scarcely aware'. He concluded that the important elements of empathy were:

- That the therapist understands the client's feelings.
- That the therapist understands the client's meanings.
- That the therapist's comments 'fit in' or reflect the client's mood and the content of what has been said.
- That the therapist's tone of voice conveys the ability to share the client's feelings.

The person-centred view of the person

Rogers had an optimistic view of humankind; he believed natural human characteristics to be positive, forward moving, constructive, realistic and trustworthy, and that every organism instinctively moves towards the fulfilment of its inherent potential. Unlike the psychoanalysts who considered the individual to be a mass of antisocial aggressive impulses which needed to be repressed, Rogers regarded the human as having a deep need for 'affiliation and communication with others'; to become fully socialized, he postulated that a person first needs to be fully themselves. Each person is, as an individual, considered to be unique. Person-centred practitioners regard the human personality to be complex and diverse, resisting diagnostic labelling or prescriptive interpretation.

Self-concept

So, you may ask, what goes wrong? Although the person-centred approach does not focus specifically on childhood experiences as a source of unearthing repressed material, as in the psychodynamic approach, it does acknowledge that many aspects of a false self are formed by the individual's need to fit into family and society. Through the process of socialization and what Rogers termed 'conditions of worth' (the self-concept of the child formed by parental and societal values), the potential to grow to be a 'fully functioning' unique person is quashed. In an attempt to satisfy the need for positive regard, the child learns to please others, understanding primarily what aspects of character and self-expression are acceptable to the parents. Alterations are made and those 'sides' of the self that are unapproved or rejected outright are gradually replaced by behaviour, as expressions of personality, that elicits approval.

Incongruence

Problems arise when the self which has found acceptance, and a sense of being valued by significant others – first parents, then other social groups, friends, a partner – is incongruent with the 'authentic self'. A state of incongruence has established itself within the individual's self-concept when feelings of inner experiencing are at odds with the self which is presented to the external world. A common example of this is the sensitive boy child who, from a very early age, internalizes parental disapproval of any display of emotion. He experiences parental disapproval and rejection when he cries or shows affection or dependency, and yet he senses that he is met with enthusiastic approval when he is 'being brave', keeping emotions in, being independent and self-contained. Such a person can crave a closeness with others all his life but dare not show emotion or dependence on another. At the primary stage of his functioning, when he required unconditional love from his parents, he was given acceptance and love if he met with their requirements of him.

Locus of evaluation

The self-concept is how we learn to define ourselves to meet the criteria required for us to be loved and valued. A 'fully functioning' person would demonstrate congruence between their inner world of feelings and sensations and outer expression, evident in words and behaviour. The congruent person has a strong self-concept, is able to be open, honest with themselves and others, and to live spontaneously. Rogers identified two ways in which we make judgements or evaluations: from our inner 'locus of evaluation' – the 'centre of responsibility' which lies within us – and through external evaluations, the attitudes or belief systems of others (parents, society, etc.). When a person acts on their own internal evaluations, which come from feelings and intuition (gut feelings), they are in touch with the 'organismic valuing process' which comes from the real self, not a second-hand rendition of other people's or institutionalized values. The individual who loses touch with their internal locus of evaluation lives their life by people-pleasing, continually focusing on externally defined beliefs and attitudes. A central aim of the person-centred therapist is to help the client reconnect with their inner valuing processes, to understand what they really feel, what changes they would like to make. The person is ideally then freed from introjected values and self-concepts, and becomes appreciative of their individuality.

Becoming a person

The fully functioning or 'actualized' person is in this way in touch with their inner world, the personal self-concept is extended not only to 'this is what I am' but also to 'this is what I can become'. Rogers talked of the individual becoming everything they 'can be', meaning having fulfilment, integration and acceptance of all the parts of their character, being able to find expression in love and work – to reach their full potential. It can be seen as impossible to reach this Utopian state of personhood, but it is a striving, an ideal and a continuum. Rogers called it 'the good life' – the world of the fully functioning person whose capacity for interpersonal communication is enhanced through positive self-concept and creative interaction with others. The main aim of 'becoming a person', in the Rogerian understanding of it, is the state of fully experiencing; that is, being congruent, able to act on our own feelings, guided by our own organismic valuing processes, and living in the 'here and now'. The concept of person in process is central to the approach.

The therapeutic relationship

While the psychoanalyst endeavours to be a 'blank screen' on to which the patient's transferential material can be projected, humanists regard the willingness of the therapist to engage warmly with the client to be a necessity for therapeutic change. The quality of the interpersonal relationship – supportive, warm, empathic, accepting – provides a safe, validating environment for the client to explore, examine and accept the whole of their being. In order that the client feels safe enough to express themselves freely within the therapy, they need to feel equal to and valued by the therapist. Rogers argued that the neutral stance of the psychoanalyst could be interpreted by the client as hostility or rejection, confirming the client's negative self-concept, particularly with regard to their relationships with others.

In 1958 Rogers wrote *The Characteristics of a Helping Relationship*, in which he presented questions which came from his own studies and clinical experiences; the first (numbered) part, presented here, forms the question and the second contains summaries of his observations and concerns.

1 Can I be in some way which will be perceived by the other person as trustworthy, dependable or consistent in some deep sense?

He recognizes this as a fundamental point. Originally he felt that if he fulfilled 'outer conditions of trustworthiness' such as keeping appointments, confidentiality and acting consistently then this was enough. He realized, however, through his experiences, that to act outwardly as if consistently acceptant while feeling otherwise (e.g. annoyed or sceptical) would mean he was perceived to be inconsistent or untrustworthy. Rogers came to recognize that to be experienced by the client as trustworthy, he needed to be 'dependably real'; that is, congruent.

2 A very closely related question is: Can I be expressive enough as a person so that what I am will be communicated unambiguously?

In connection with this, he states: 'It is safe to be transparently real ... If I can be sensitively aware of and acceptant toward my own feelings – then the likelihood is great that I can form a helping relationship towards another.' He acknowledges that he can never fully achieve the relating of his self-acceptance to the other person; however, striving to be himself fully and convey this to the other person enables him to maintain constructive interpersonal relationships. He concludes, 'If I am to facilitate the personal growth of others in relation to me, then I must grow and while this is often painful it is also enriching.'

3 A third question is: Can I let myself experience positive attitudes towards this other person – attitudes of warmth, caring, liking, interest, respect?

In answer to this question Rogers draws attention to the fear of intimacy with others and 'the professionalization of every field' as a way of staying aloof in an impersonal relationship. He views diagnostic formulations and 'all kinds of evaluative procedures' as means of objectifying others. Again he asserts, 'It is safe to care.'

4 Another question, the importance of which I have learned in my own experience, is: Can I be strong enough as a person to be separate from the other?

Rogers continues with a conglomeration of questions relating to this one, concerned with boundaries; for example, separating out his own feelings, reactions to client material and being affected by the client's moods and dependency, and fears of losing himself in client material.

5 The next question is closely related: Am I secure within myself to permit him his separateness?

He follows this with the concern that as a therapist he may want the client to follow his advice or become dependent, rather than let the client be 'what he is'. In contrast to the less competent counsellor who wants his client to conform to his norms and model themselves after him, Rogers suggests that the more competent counsellor 'can interact with a client through many interviews without interfering with the freedom of the client to develop a personality quite separate from that of his therapist'.

6 Another question I ask myself is: Can I let myself enter fully into the world of his feelings and personal meanings and see these as he does?

Rogers goes on to relate his hopes of losing the desire to judge or evaluate the client's private world; of being sensitive enough to move freely within the client's private world of meaning, helping the client to articulate thoughts and feelings and gain insight by sensing implicit meanings which the client 'sees only dimly or as confusion'.

7 Still another issue is whether I can be acceptant of each facet of this other person which he presents to me? Can I receive him as he is?

By posing this question Rogers addresses the issue of conditional acceptance of another, pointing out that a client can't change or grow unless they are 'fully received' by the counsellor in all aspects of self. In order that the therapist can fully receive the client they also must grow and accept all aspects of themselves, including reactions to client material.

8 A very practical issue is raised by the question: Can I act with sufficient sensitivity in the relationship that my behavior will not be perceived as a threat?

'Sensitivity' is a key word with regard to the person-centred approach. Rogers acknowledges that the client is vulnerable and in a state of 'incongruence' when first entering therapy. He wants to make therapy unthreatening, realizing it (and we as counsellors) can be experienced as another 'external threat'. If the client is sensitively responded to, Rogers concludes, 'he can begin to experience and to deal with the internal feelings and conflicts which he finds threatening within himself'.

9 A specific aspect of the preceding question but an important one is: Can I free him from the threat of external evaluation?

On this subject Rogers notes that institutions and organizations make external judgements and evaluations of individuals throughout their lives and, although these may serve some social purpose, they 'do not make for personal growth' and have no part to play in a helping relationship. He makes the point that a positive evaluation is as threatening as a negative one, 'Since to inform someone that he is good implies that you have the right to tell him he is bad.' When the relationship is free of evaluations and judgement then the client can recognize that the locus of evaluation, the centre of responsibility, lies within themselves.

10 One last question: Can I meet this other individual as a person who is in a process of becoming, or will I be bound by his past and by my past?

Rogers attempts to answer this question by examining the concepts (coloured by his past and upbringing) of others as 'immature child', 'ignorant student', 'a neurotic personality', 'psychopath' – concepts which he regards as obstacles to what the other person can be in the counsellor–client relationship. He says: 'If I accept the other person as something fixed, already diagnosed and classified, already shaped by his past, then I am doing my part to confirm this limited hypothesis.' Rogers considered the therapist's role to be that of a liberator of the client's 'real potentialities' – by accepting and reinforcing 'all that he is'. He concluded by saying: 'I cannot give a positive answer to most of these questions, I can only work in the direction of the positive answers.' For Rogers the counsellor too is in a perpetual state of becoming.

(*Source*: C.R. Rogers, *On Becoming a Person*, pp. 50–6)

Qualities of the counsellor

The chief requirements of a person-centred counsellor are reflected in the questions Rogers posed for himself. The person-centred view is that unless a client perceives the therapist as trustworthy and dependable the therapeutic engagement will not take place. To be able to convey a trustworthiness the therapist must trust in themselves, in their own ability to experience fully in the 'here and now'; full acceptance of the other person requires the counsellor's acceptance of themselves and that they are in tune with their own internal evaluations and authentic experiencing. Unlike other approaches, the person-centred perspective does not rely on complex theories of human personality, nor does the therapist hide behind the professional mask of 'expert'. They engage wholeheartedly in an egalitarian relationship with the client.

The therapist is sensitive and accepts the client as they are in the present, not what they might become. This doesn't mean that the therapist necessarily shares similar values, but means they respect where the person is in their lives. Rogers understood that a person's defences had at least at one time played a useful part in the person's life and need to be respected.

If the counsellor has deep self-awareness, then they are less likely to be overwhelmed by or get lost in client material and therefore are likely to be able to maintain boundaries, while also warmly engaging with the client, encouraging them to experience freely in the 'here and now'. The humanistic therapist has a sense of continuing development as a person in the quest of 'self-actualization', and sees this as an integral part of person-centred work. Being themselves i.e. congruent is at odds with an over-reliance on skills which can lead to formulaic 'professional' behaviour; the skills are the adherence to the core conditions and the employment of a reflective, facilitative attitude.

Lastly, the person-centred counsellor is spontaneous and lets the client guide. Rogers believed in the client's innate intelligence and wrote in *On Becoming a Person*: 'It is the client who knows what hurts, what direction to go, what problems are crucial, what experiences have been deeply buried.'

Aims of therapy

Problems, conflicts, confusions and other presenting matters brought to therapy are seen as a manifestation of incongruence in the client's behaviour and experiencing. The authentic self lies buried beneath introjected (parental, other significant figures and institutionalized) 'conditions of worth'. The 'real' or 'authentic' self has kowtowed to outside 'loci of evaluation' to the extent it is lost, and the unhappiness and frustrations experienced in living under this mantle are a sign of a striving to regain the loss. A central aim is to help the client make contact with the organismic centre of their being, to help them re-experience a sense of self-worth and make movement towards changes in their lives. Signs of movement are:

- The client begins to be less concerned with other people's attitudes and judgements and begins to trust in and value their own.
- They increasingly enjoy living in the present and appreciate the process of personal growth and expression rather than being governed by impersonal objectives.
- They demonstrate greater respect for others and self, showing a deep understanding of others and self.
- A valuing of intimacy and close relationships with others.
- A valuing of honesty and 'realness' in self and others.
- Accepting responsibility for their own life.
- A capacity to make considered choices with regard to the direction taken, and to live with a new spontaneity and enjoyment of life, 'towards a valuing of all forms of experience and a willingness to risk being open to all inner and outer experiences however uncongenial or unexpected' (W.G. Frick, *Humanistic Psychology; Interviews with Maslow, Murphy and Rogers*).

Process of change

Change takes place in the psychological environment of the therapy. Negative self-concepts can, person-centred therapists believe, be changed by the valuing and respect given by the counsellor and experienced by the client. Through the non-possessive warmth and acceptance demonstrated by the counsellor the client experiences their own 'essential worth'. At the onset of therapy the client typically finds expression in self-destructive or self-denying behaviours that reinforce a negative self-concept. The counsellor provides a facilitative, supportive environment that is safe for the client to explore behaviours, attitudes, thoughts and feelings. Movement towards a healthy expression of the 'organismic self' – the true inner core of the person's being – takes place because the counsellor is willing to engage wholeheartedly with the client in their experiencing as it happens in the 'here and now' present of the session. The counsellor too is 'human', willing at times, when appropriate, to self-disclose if it will benefit the client or the client–counsellor relationship.

When the facilitative attitudes (core conditions) are steadily present in the relationship, the client begins to gather that they are worth the attentive care and valuing – a case of 'if someone else is willing to take the time to listen attentively to what is really happening to me in my life, then maybe I will too', 'if someone else is willing to risk an emotional intimacy with me, then perhaps it is safe to reciprocate' and 'if someone else can accept all the disparate sides of me, then perhaps I can too'. Change is made possible by the counsellor's acceptance of the client in their entirety, thereby encouraging the client to explore and accept different aspects of themselves. All aspects, both negative and positive, can then be owned and integrated in a more realistic, healthier self-concept.

Some fundamental differences between person-centred and psychodynamic counselling

Psychodynamic	*Person-centred*
1 Working with unconscious processes – emphasis on dream work, free association and the transference	Working with conscious processes – neither the transference nor dream work is emphasized.
2 Makes connections between client's past and present	Focus moves where client wishes, to past, present or future
3 Focus on content of client–counsellor relationship	Focus on quality of client–counsellor relationship
4 'Rule of neutrality' absistent approach, professional stance of counsellor	Warm engagement, congruence of counsellor
5 The counsellor does not self-disclose	The counsellor is willing to self-disclose
6 Focus on defences as a route to underlying anxieties and (hidden) feelings	Focus on experiencing feelings
7 Assessment orientated	Non-diagnostic, no initial assessment
8 Counsellor's expertise	The client is considered to know best
9 Immense volume of written work	Limited theoretical framework/literature
10 Knowledge of client's history is considered crucial to the work	Allows history to unfold; option that past may be irrelevant
11 The counsellor makes interpretations for the client	Interpretations come from client's changing perceptions
12 People are regarded as being driven by hidden hostile drives/impulses/instincts	People are motivated towards self-actualization and are basically social beings
13 Looks for hidden material	Respectful, acceptant of client as they are presently
14 Promotes personal understanding	Promotes personal growth

SECTION 3:
The Behavioural/
Cognitive-behavioural Model

Origins

Behavioural therapy, in its various forms, originated from the scientific discipline of psychology. At the turn of the century and in the early 1900s psychologists like J.B. Watson and E.L. Thorndike conducted experiments on animals to observe their behaviour. They considered the methods of psychoanalysis and introspection which were prevalent at the time to be unreliable, based as they were on the subjective, inner thought processes of the patient – an area that was neither measurable nor observable and therefore unscientific. Thorndike was influenced by Charles Darwin's theory of evolution and the laws of 'the survival of the fittest' and believed that parallels could be drawn between animal and human behaviour. He went on to systematize a theory of human behaviour, based on the observation of animal behaviour, in laboratory experiments. Watson, accredited with coining the term 'behavioural psychology', also believed that research and a body of empirical evidence would lead to psychology being regarded as a scientific practice.

J.B. Watson, who termed himself a behaviourist in 1919, was the forerunner of B.F. Skinner. The main concern of Watson and his contemporaries was the process of learning; they surmised that the basic principle of learning applied to all organisms, including human beings. Just as behaviour is learned, so too can it be unlearned. The traditional behaviourist understands all human behaviour to be determined by learning through classical and operant conditioning. 'Inappropriate', 'dysfunctional' and 'maladaptive' are all terms used to describe behaviour which can be changed through a process of unlearning.

It wasn't until the end of the Second World War, when psychiatric services were stretched to their limits, that behavioural psychology moved from its scientific research base to practical use as a form of therapy. At this time, B.F. Skinner refined Thorndike's theory of operant conditioning, and it was his version which was widely adopted by behaviourists. Behavioural theory is based on two experimental paradigms: Pavlov's dogs, used to demonstrate classical conditioning; and Skinner's operant conditioning.

Operant and classical conditioning

B.F. Skinner and E.L. Thorndike – operant conditioning

Thorndike used the term 'operant conditioning' to describe behaviour which is largely determined by its consequences. He noted that animals learned responses because they affected their environment. Following a particular behaviour led to a reward of some kind – for example, touching a latch resulted in food becoming available. The learning of a task was strengthened when an action resulted in reward. Thorndike termed this 'law of effect', and understood it in terms of trial and error on the part of animals rather than an innate intelligence, thus linking his observations with Darwin's theory of evolutionary selection; that is, species that adapt to their surroundings adapt their behaviour and therefore stand a greater chance of survival.

Skinner built on the work of Thorndike and it was his method of studying operant conditioning which was eventually widely adopted in behavioural therapy. Skinner's theory was based on the idea of reinforcements playing a motivational role in the learning of new tasks. **Positive reinforcement** describes the strengthening of a response by the incentive of a stimulus as reward. **Negative reinforcement** describes the strengthening of a response by removing an unpleasant stimulus (e.g. by removing a loud noise). Reinforcements can be food, stroking, praise or encouragement; a reinforcement signals to the participant that they have done something that is correct or that is working for them in some way. A gradual dawning takes place – that the behaviour ends with favourable results, which leads to a mastering of the task. In contrast, an operantly conditioned response which is not reinforced will gradually die out – this is referred to as 'extinction' in behavioural terminology.

A Skinnerian experiment

A rat (or pigeon) is placed in what has come to be known as a 'Skinner box', the interior of which is empty apart from a dish and a protruding bar situated above it. There is a light above the bar which can be switched on by the researcher. The rat begins by exploring its new surroundings. Occasionally, as part of its inspection of the box, it touches the protruding bar. The rate at which it is pressing the bar at this stage, is termed 'the baseline level'. The researcher then activates a food dispenser (magazine) outside the box. When the rat now makes contact with the bar, a food pellet is delivered to the dish. The rat eats the pellet, then presses the lever again – the food has reinforced the action of bar pressing and therefore the activity increases accordingly. This is an operantly conditioned response called an 'operant'. If the source of food is disconnected and the action no longer results in food becoming available, then the rate of pressing the bar will also diminish, undergoing extinction. A further dimension of the experiment tests the animal's powers of discrimination.

Food is dispensed only when the light is switched on, thereby conditioning the rat through selective reinforcement. The light is a discriminative stimulus that controls the rat's response. The conclusion reached was that operant conditioning increases the likelihood of a response by following the behaviour with a reinforcer – this can be food, drink and so on. The rate of response is a way of measuring the operant's force. (The operant's effects operate on the environment, and have a consequence – reward or punishment.)

Classical conditioning – Pavlov's dogs

A definition of classical conditioning is: 'One particular event follows another.'

In the early 1900s a Russian psychologist called Ivan Pavlov held experiments to observe the associative learning of animals. In a typical experiment a capsule is attached to a hungry dog's salivary gland to measure its saliva flow. The dog is placed in a cage in front of a container in which meat powder is dispensed automatically. A light is turned on in a window facing the dog. A few seconds later a portion of meat powder is delivered to the container and then the light is switched off. A copious amount of saliva is registered because the dog is hungry. At this point the amount of salivation is an unconditional response (UCR), because the dog has not as yet learned a new response. The meat powder is an unconditioned stimulus (UCS), a substance which the animal naturally responds to when hunger equates with food. The sequence is repeated many times as before – the light coming on followed a few seconds later by meat powder being dispensed into the container, then although the light is turned on no meat is delivered to the bowl. However, the dog continues to salivate, now associating the light coming on with the distribution of food. This new development is a conditional response (CR), and the light is a conditioned stimulus (CS) which has been formed through association, causing the dog to continue to salivate. The dog has been conditioned to associate the light coming on with food and responds by salivating. Over a period of time a neutral stimulus (e.g. the light or the bell) is associated with a reflexive stimulus (food), resulting in a CR (e.g. salivation) to the neutral stimulus alone.

Characteristics, techniques and applications

Experiments carried out on animals – such as these, which formed the basis of behaviourist theories – may seem to bear little relevance to human behaviour. Behavioural psychology is often criticized as presenting a picture of human beings as malleable and passive victims of external stimuli. Perhaps the greatest contributions behavioural models have made to human psychology are their observations on motivations and learnt behaviour: for example, how young children look to their parents, or other significant figures in their lives, to 'model' behaviour.

Child development

Albert Bandura's **social learning theory** stresses the prominence of vicarious, symbolic and self-regulatory processes in psychological functioning. Social learning theory views human behaviour in terms of a reciprocal interaction between cognitive, behavioural and environmental determinants. The child learns vicariously from their parents, acquiring behaviour modelled by significant others. Bandura doesn't propose that individuals simply react to external influences, but rather they select, organize and transform stimuli around them. From a behavioural point of view a child who has repeated temper tantrums or is aggressive to others has learned that this behaviour elicits attention from their parents and others in contact with them – in other words, it pays off. The attention is the reinforcer which tells the child that their behaviour is having an effect. If steps are taken to demonstrate to the child that their behaviour is not working, they will gradually drop it (extinction). If they found, for example, that when they had a tantrum their behaviour was ignored or that they were required to stay alone in their room for an interval as a consequence of that behaviour, and if this was further reinforced by their receiving attention through other means (e.g. through appropriate, approved-of behaviour), then the original inappropriate behaviour would cease. Reinforcers of the new behaviour could be praise, encouragement, privileges or treats. The behaviour of others in the family may also have to be readjusted. A child may have learned inappropriate behaviour through vicarious factors; for example, from observing antisocial or maladaptive behaviour in their parents.

Through laboratory experiments psychologists found that immediate reinforcement is the most beneficial form. There is a temporal (time-related) relation between a response and its reinforcer. An operant response is weakened when the reinforcer is delayed. It is more effective to praise (reinforce) appropriate social behaviour immediately; for example, when a child shares toys with a friend or attempts a task with care. It follows that it is best to discipline a child for antisocial or inappropriate behaviour when it happens rather than later, when the behaviour and consequences may have less association. (The old tricks reverted to by desperate mothers of fractious children – 'Wait until I get you home' or 'Wait until your father gets home' – prove to be mainly ineffective and are probably bewildering to the child.)

Behavioural therapy follows the basic assumption that some psychological problems are acquired through learning experiences and are subsequently maintained by the pattern of events. Its method of treatment focuses on the challenge and reversal of the negative or ineffective learnt experiences. Behaviourists are not concerned with the abstract (such as feelings) and there is little emphasis on the therapist–client relationship. Unlike psychoanalysts, behaviourists regard the symptom as the problem, not the underlying causes.

Who and what problems behavioural therapy can help

A candidate for behaviour therapy would be someone who is finding it difficult to fit into what is predominantly regarded as normal behaviour within their environment. Their behaviour is considered antisocial and is in some way interfering with the smooth running of their lives. They may be an uncontrollable or hyperactive child, or an adult suffering from panic attacks, or a person suffering from an obsessive–compulsive disorder who continuously washes or checks numerous times that switches are turned off before feeling safe in their environment. Whatever the problem, it is likely that the person is suffering in some way from social reinforcement deprivation as their problem sets them apart from others in particular ways. The young child is regarded as a 'spoilt brat' because of their actions and the parents are ridiculed. The adult who suffers from panic attacks or a phobic disorder is restricted by the problem and may become reclusive or secretive, feeling criticized by others. The well-adjusted person receives positive social reinforcements that those who violate social norms seldom get.

Problems tackled by behavioural therapy

- Antisocial behaviour – social learning – development of new behaviour (social skills deficit – unlearning inappropriate behaviour).
- Anxiety associated behaviour – including obsessional and compulsive behaviour, phobias, sexual dysfunctions.

■ Appetitive behaviour – including anorexia nervosa and sexual deviance.

Widely used in the treatment of anxiety, phobic and obsessive–compulsive disorders and sexual dysfunctions, behavioural therapy also lends itself to social learning programmes in child development and to helping to extend social and communication skills in adults who exhibit inappropriate, dysfunctional behaviour. The criteria for client suitability include:

■ The problem can be defined in terms of observable behaviour.
■ The problem is ongoing and to some extent predictable.
■ The situations or objects triggering the response are identifiable.
■ The client is motivated – willing to co-operate with the therapist – and wants to change their behaviour and to take an active role in the process.

Treatment plan

Behavioural treatment incorporates a variety of techniques which aim to solve problems by bringing measurable and observable change to the client's behaviour, altering behaviour patterns in specific areas which are currently dysfunctional. The treatment is modified to suit each individual's needs. In the case of panic attacks or phobias, the exposure principle is followed wherein the client is gradually exposed to the disturbing object or situation (gradual emersion) in a process called **systematic desensitization**. This technique is widely used to treat phobic and obsessional–compulsive disorders. There are two types of exposure:

1 Vivo exposure – when the actual feared object or situation is confronted.
2 Imaginal or fantasy exposure – this entails imaging the act of dealing with the problem while in a state of relaxation. The technique of pairing relaxation with the troubling conditioned stimuli was pioneered by J. Wolpe.

The client is given 'homework' in the form of tasks between sessions. Goals are discussed and negotiated.

The client is often asked to keep a diary to note progress and setbacks.

Stimulus and responses

The stimulus is the object or situation which stimulates and elicits the negative behavioural responses. The responses are the inappropriate, dysfunctional or maladaptive behaviour manifested in response or reaction to the stimulus. The object of the therapy is to neutralize the power of the stimulus to create the destructive negative response.

Avoidance and passivity and exposure

A person who suffers from panic attacks has become a passive slave to the fear the stimulus evokes and its incapacitating effects. The reaction to the fear is avoidance of the feared object or situation (stimuli); the agoraphobic stays within the safety of home and the person who is terrified of crossing bridges, at great inconvenience, takes a much longer route home. Part of the treatment plan of action is what is termed **exposure**; that is, the client is usually gradually introduced to the feared stimulus. The length and amount of exposure to the object or situation would be suggested by the therapist at an appropriate learning stage, agreed to by the client. For example, a first stage for someone who is terrified of birds might be to look at photographs of birds then visit a menagerie to view caged birds at a distance, either with a friend or with the therapist (therapist aid). At a later session, when both the client and therapist consider the client to be ready, a bird may be let free to fly around the room or be held by the client.

Coping strategies

These are basically elements that help alleviate anxiety and stress and help keep stress levels down to a manageable level. Strategies are planned with targets and goals. Tasks are given between sessions, often to reinforce work achieved in the session or in therapist-aided outings. The ultimate goal is to give the client not only an understanding of the maladaptive behaviour, but also ways first of coping with it, then modifying and overcoming it so that passivity is replaced with assertiveness.

The therapist

The therapist is highly active in the treatment. They are directive, taking on the role of coach, motivator and supporter – offering encouragement and praise, modelling behaviour, offering therapist aid which may involve accompanying clients on excursions and continually assessing the client's needs and monitoring progress.

<u>Before</u>

Picture yourself coping

Stay relaxed

Breathe slowly and calmly

<u>During low anxiety</u>

Stay as relaxed as possible

Stay in the situation

Breathe slowly and calmly

Don't add secondary fear (this situation need not lead to a worse situation)

Use distraction

<u>During high anxiety</u>

Breathe slowly and calmly

Accept your feelings

Notice your NATs – negative automatic thoughts

Replace them with rational, coping thoughts

Stay in the situation if possible – if not, return as soon as you are calmer

Wait for the uncomfortable feelings to pass

<u>Afterwards</u>

Note the positive ways you coped

Continue with what you were doing

<u>The golden rules</u>

Accept your feelings

Try not to avoid situations

Strategies for coping with anxiety

Sometimes a member of the family acts as a co-therapist whose role it is to support and encourage. The co-therapist will be guided by the therapist and informed as to progress and difficulties. The therapist will advise the helper not to comfort or collude in ways which might encourage avoidance of difficult tasks.

Behavioural therapy is primarily concerned with analysing and assessing problematic behaviour and helping the client to understand and conquer it. The lines of enquiry that the therapist is likely to pursue include the following:

- Circumstances – what triggers (brings on) an attack or particular behaviour? Where? When? How?
- Levels of anxiety – what happens to the body in physical manifestation, e.g. sweating, shaking, numbness?
- Thoughts and feelings that accompany the behaviour while it is taking hold.
- Anticipatory factors – what the thoughts and feelings were directly before the onset of the episode (panic attack, tantrum, etc.), e.g. anticipating catastrophe, dreading confrontation.
- What is experienced after an attack? Is there relief or does the unease continue for a period of time?
- What the consequences of the behaviour are; e.g. antisocial; effects on work, play, relationships; self-defeating, restricting aspects.
- Variables – are anxiety levels or behaviour worse at particular times or do particular situations cause exacerbation? Is the situation fluctuating or constant? What factors contribute to improvement or deterioration?

Systematic desensitization

This method is based on the learning laws of operant and classical conditioning.

The behaviourist Joseph Wolpe wrote a paper called 'The Systematic Desensitisation Treatment of Neuroses' (1961), describing techniques to decrease, in an organized manner, levels of anxiety over the causal factors. The term 'neurosis', which was used to refer to a collection of psychological problems – the central characteristic of which was acute anxiety – has now come to be included collectively under the heading of 'anxiety disorders'.

Systematic desensitization, which Wolpe is accredited with perfecting, is used in the treatment of phobias, obsessive–compulsive disorders and panic disorders.

Since phobias and other forms of anxiety disorder are accompanied by physiological ('fight or flight') responses like sweating, heart palpitations and dizziness, Wolpe suggested the use of relaxation in the form of progressive muscle relaxation (see Chapter 6) to help the client gain control over the anxiety-producing condition. First the client would be trained during therapy sessions, by the therapist, in the relaxation techniques; then when these became familiar to the client, they could be self-applied in stressful anxiety-producing situations. Wolpe recommended deep relaxation as an anxiety-inhibiting response because he believed that we cannot experience deep relaxation and fear concurrently. The same practices are used in adapted forms today by behaviourists.

The anxiety hierarchy

Following a relaxation programme, an anxiety hierarchy is constructed by the therapist. The client makes a list of anxiety-producing situations or scenarios (in the case of phobias and panic attacks), listing them in order of manageability (e.g. those which cause mild discomfort, proceeding to increasingly frightening and therefore challenging situations, culminating in situations which would produce the most anxiety). The contents of the list constitutes the number of steps in the client's hierarchy of 'tasks', which vary from individual to individual.

Description and imagination technique

Wolpe recommended the use of description and imagination in the treatment of certain anxiety disorders. The idea was to 'unlearn' the phobia which was learned through the process of association. Adopting this technique, the therapist begins by describing a first-step scene from the anxiety hierarchy list. The client imagines the scene while maintaining a state of relaxation. For someone suffering from acrophobia this may be sitting by a window in a room on the first floor of a building.

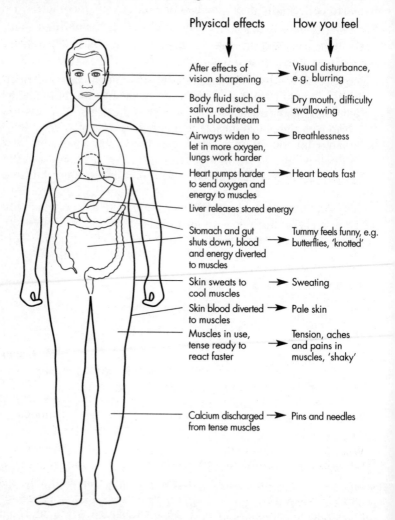

Physical effects | How you feel

After effects of vision sharpening → Visual disturbance, e.g. blurring

Body fluid such as saliva redirected into bloodstream → Dry mouth, difficulty swallowing

Airways widen to let in more oxygen, lungs work harder → Breathlessness

Heart pumps harder to send oxygen and energy to muscles → Heart beats fast

Liver releases stored energy

Stomach and gut shuts down, blood and energy diverted to muscles → Tummy feels funny, e.g. butterflies, 'knotted'

Skin sweats to cool muscles → Sweating

Skin blood diverted to muscles → Pale skin

Muscles in use, tense ready to react faster → Tension, aches and pains in muscles, 'shaky'

Calcium discharged from tense muscles → Pins and needles

Physiological manifestations of anxiety panic attack

The description and imaging process proceeds through the steps of the anxiety hierarchy until eventually the client is able to hear the most difficult step described in detail and to imagine being in the scene while maintaining a state of relaxation; in the case of the acrophobic this might be standing at the edge of a clifftop.

To understand Wolpe's theoretical propositions, read Roger Hock's excellent book *Forty Studies that Changed Psychology* (see **Suggested further reading** at the end of the book). Wolpe's theories were based on the work of Pavlov, Watson and others on classical conditioning. He believed that phobias are learned behaviour, that at some point the object or situation became associated in the sufferer's brain with extreme fear.

The therapeutic relationship

A criticism of behaviourism has been that in an approach built on empirical investigation (knowledge based on experimental research) the therapist has taken a clinically detached and highly directive role. The client could easily be made to feel powerless or worthless. Although traditionally the client–therapist relationship has not been considered central to the therapy, more recently it has come to be recognized that the relationship is important, for the following reasons: The co-operation of the client is necessary since the approach is task and target orientated requiring negotiation.

In a supporting role, the therapist demonstrates that they are trustworthy, warm and accepting, and also directive as the client's motivation may depend on encouragement and praise. Therapist-aided tasks, when the therapist accompanies the client on anxiety-inducing tasks, necessitate sensitive modes of communication. Client and therapist work closely together.

When a client comes to therapy they may have had their problematic behaviour for some time. It is often a huge step to enter into therapy and the client is likely to feel frightened, embarrassed or angry. As they feel vulnerable, the first impressions of the therapy offered and the attitude demonstrated by the therapist may influence the client's decision to continue or not.

If a therapist demonstrates sustained empathic understanding throughout treatment, that will encourage a client through times of difficulty. Setbacks and lapses are less likely to be experienced as overwhelming.

Cognitive-behavioural approaches

Cognitive-behavioural approaches include cognitive therapy, stress inoculation therapy and rational emotive behaviour therapy. Since the 1970s cognitive science has emerged, partly in response to behaviourism's deterministic view of human behaviour, which has been accused by some (e.g. Thomas, *Dialectics of Schizophrenia*) of reducing the human being and human consciousness to the level of the machine. The central focus of cognitive approaches is the individual's thought patterns and beliefs and how these link with self-defeating behaviour. Clients are helped to alter the way they think; irrational, self-destructive thoughts are, through therapy, replaced by more realistic rational thoughts.

Aaron Beck

Aaron Beck, the founder of cognitive therapy, began his professional life as a psychoanalytic psychotherapist. In his work he came to the conclusion that an individual's cognitions (i.e. mental messages) affect both feeling and behaviour. He noted the irrationality behind self-critical cognitions, which he terms 'automatic thoughts'. These are also sometimes termed negative automatic thoughts (NATs).

The psychoanalytic understanding of emotional disturbance, or behavioural dysfunctioning, is that it is rooted in unresolved trauma from childhood. In contrast, the cognitive approach considers such problems to arise not directly from the events themselves but from how the individual interprets and creates meaning for them. Another difference between the two approaches is that while psychoanalysis considers thought to be dictated by emotional needs, cognitive behaviourists are of the opinion that cognitive processes govern the emotions. Cognitive behavioural counsellors use a model of cognitive processing called the

cognitive distortion model devised by Beck. In this model Beck proposed that when a person perceives a situation to be threatening it results in a reduction in the reasoning of functioning of normal cognitive processes.

Cognitive distortions include:

1 Over-generalization – the tendency towards sweeping conclusions made from limited evidence.
2 Personalization – the tendency of distorted thinking which involves the individual imagining that events are the result of their (faulty) actions.
3 Dichotomous thinking – the tendency to take a polarized view of situations, e.g. regarding people as either all good or all bad (similar to the theory of 'splitting' from psychoanalysis).

Memory

Memory is another area associated with cognitive distortion. Research has shown that people suffering anxiety or traumatic times lose the ability to recall details of painful events accurately. The sufferer generalizes and the power of recall is diminished. This is thought to be because of a connection between the events and recalled negative emotions (as repressed material). In cognitive-behavioural counselling this causes a problem because of the need for client contribution in the construction of micro-analysis of events used as part of therapy.

Metacognition

Metacognition refers to the ability of individuals to deconstruct and understand their own cognitive processes; this involves reflection and awareness of the various steps in thinking or problem solving, as in the use of strategies – for example, strategies such as simplifying tasks to make them manageable by selection; planning action and systems, creating order and so on. Parents pass on metacognitive strategies to children when they 'model' the use of sets of strategies.

Examples include the following:

- ■ Play:
  - games played with rules and turn taking,
  - assembling complex jigsaw puzzles,
  - putting up a tent (careful unpacking, placing the tent pegs together, lining up and grouping different sizes of poles, constructing the tent systematically);
- ■ Work:
  - building some form of structure (selecting and buying materials and tools, ordering the tasks);
- ■ In a social context:
  - cooking for and entertaining others,
  - relating to other people in different social contexts and situations.

Albert Ellis

Albert Ellis, the founder of rational emotive behaviour therapy (REBT), also originally trained as a psychoanalyst. REBT (also referred to as RET) adopts a robust directive therapeutic style which challenges and confronts the 'irrational beliefs' of clients. 'Crooked thinking' governed by 'shoulds' and 'musts' was, in the opinion of Ellis, the cause of emotional problems and maladaptive behaviour. Internalized irrational beliefs lead to 'catastrophizing', anxiety and depression; 'catastrophizing' means to view things in an absolutistic, exaggerated or overstated manner – an 'it's the end of the world' scenario. Irrational beliefs are replaced by rational belief statements which allow clients to deal with problems constructively.

Ellis's ABC theory of personality functioning

A – represents the **activating** event – a person's action or attitude or an actual physical event.

B – represents the **belief** the person has about the event.

C – represents the **consequence** of the event, in terms of the individual's emotions and behaviour in relation to their experiencing of the event.

The rational emotive therapy counsellor teaches the client, through the ABC formula, how to engage in metacognitive processing of their thoughts with regard to events. Cognitive reactions to events can be monitored, reflected on and understood, giving the client more choice of perspective.

A, the activating events in Ellis's theory, do not cause C, the consequence, but rather it is B, the client's beliefs, that colour the relationship between the event and the consequence (i.e. the resultant feelings and conduct). For example, one person may believe that a missed opportunity means that all opportunities are now closed to them and, feeling depressed, give up trying to achieve their goal; while another person believes the missed opportunity is one of many that will come their way and feels OK about the situation, continuing to work towards their goal.

Cognitive theories were added to the behavioural approach to therapy in the 1970s, because therapists realized that cognitions (e.g. thoughts, beliefs, perceptions) played a major part in individual experiencing. Behavioural and cognitive practices have merged as the two are acknowledged to complement each other. The combined theories have produced a therapeutic approach for the treatment, in particular, of depressive and anxiety states. As a 'scientific' therapeutic approach that relies on observation and monitoring (of behaviour and cognitions), the model has been widely endorsed and adopted by the medical professions. A central aim of cognitive-behavioural therapy is to replace irrational beliefs or negative automatic thoughts with realistic self-accepting beliefs that are constructively self-affirming. With the counsellor's help, the client learns to monitor and gain control of how they think and behave.

Cognitive contents are the components of our thinking that motivate us. D. Meichenbaum, writing in 1986 (see **Suggested further reading**) drew attention to the effects of 'self-talk' and internal dialogue. A.T. Beck wrote about automatic thoughts as dysfunctional, and Ellis lists in *Reason and Emotion in Psychotherapy* 'irrational beliefs' as the main contributing factors of self-depreciating and defeating behaviour. The following are examples of irrational beliefs linked to situations or events:

1 I made a mistake – I am so stupid, I do everything wrong/I can't do anything right (arbitrary inference).

2 The end of a relationship – He doesn't love me. I am totally unloveable/unattractive to everyone (over-generalization).

3 I will never meet anyone else who will love me. My life is over (catastrophizing).

4 I was placed third in an activity that I always win – I am a complete failure (dichotomous thinking).

The cognitive-behavioural counsellor picks up on these types of distorted belief statements and with the client questions the underlying assumptions that form them; for example, the counsellor may say: 'You are used to being the best at your subject; now you've come third, which is a very high placing, yet you think you are a total failure?'

Anxiety-inducing and reinforcing self-statements

The cognitive-behaviourist Meichenbaum draws attention to the statements which accompany behaviour as internal dialogue. Internal dialogue involves talking to ourselves while we go through situations or events. In exams or interviews we may be telling ourselves during the proceedings that we are failing or messing things up if any slight difficulty or hitch in the proceedings arises. The (negative) self-statements can sabotage hopes of success by 'feeding' feelings of anxiety; also, the inner dialogue distracts attention from external details, which may cause further incapacitation of 'performance' behaviour.

The cognitive-behavioural counsellor uses various techniques to assess cognitions, including asking the client to apply methods of monitoring self-statements by:

- thinking out loud while doing a task;
- working with a tape recorder to record spontaneous talk;
- completing worksheets on which they are asked to record details of the activating events, belief and behavioural consequences/outcome.

Once the client is in touch with their beliefs or automatic thoughts they can begin, with the guidance and encouragement of the counsellor, to experiment with alternative (realistic) beliefs or self-statements in relation to particular events.

The focus of work is to bring to the client's awareness cognitions which can be either: appropriate or inappropriate, functional or dysfunctional, constructive or destructive, rational or irrational, adaptive or maladaptive. In simple terminology, cognitions can either work for us or against us, and the cognitive-behaviourist helps the client to decipher what changes can be made to lessen, if not totally eradicate, negative self-messages and the corresponding behaviour.

Intervention techniques or methods

These are techniques or methods used to accomplish behavioural objectives after the initial stages of contracting, explaining the rationale for treatment, problem assessment and setting of goals or targets has been established. In *Introduction to Counselling* (pp. 77–8), John McLeod has identified intervention techniques as including:

1 Challenging irrational beliefs.
2 Reframing the issues; for example, perceiving internal emotional states as excitement rather than fear.
3 Rehearsing the use of different self-statements in role plays with the counsellor.
4 Experimenting with the use of different self-statements in real situations.
5 Scaling feelings; for example, placing present feelings of anxiety or panic on a scale of 0–100.
6 Thought stopping; rather than allowing anxious or obsessional thoughts to 'take-over', the client learns to do something to interrupt them, such as snapping a rubber band on his or her wrist.
7 Systematic desensitization. The replacement of anxiety or fear responses by a learned relaxation response, the counselling takes the client through a graded hierarchy of fear-eliciting situations.

8 Assertiveness or social skills training.

9 Homework assignments. Practising new behaviours and cognitive strategies between therapy sessions.

10 In Vivo exposure. Being accompanied by the counsellor into highly fearful situations, for example, visiting shops with an agoraphobic client. The role of the counsellor is to encourage the client to use cognitive-behavioural techniques to cope with the situation.

Relapse prevention

Cognitive-behavioural approaches address the problem of relapse with clients who have addiction problems, such as alcohol or drug abuse, by providing strategies and skills for dealing with periods of relapse. These are based around identifying typical situations such as times of emotional crisis, or a social situation which triggers a response back to pretherapy behaviour. This might be an alcoholic drink at a family get-together, encouraged by others (social situation) or a person with a drug problem (re)turning to drugs because of a painful or stressful situation arising which they feel unable to cope with (emotional crisis). Other techniques used include: reframing or redefining distortive self-statements to acknowledge that although the client has lapsed this time, it does not imply total relapse; and the counsellor and client working out a plan of action for particular situations, given to the client as written instructions to use as a coping strategy if a temptation to lapse occurs. Social skills are also learned as a method of helping the client; for example, in declining invitations to join in (alcoholic) drinking sessions or handling a conflict situation.

Affect and non-conscious processes

As we have seen, there was first a development from an exclusively behavioural perspective to the recognition of the role of cognitions – it was realized that human behaviour is more than learning through experience, it also involved associated thought processes. More recently there has been a recognition of 'affect' or feeling. It appears the various different schools of therapy are moving closer together. Wessler and Hanklin-Wessler (1986) developed a psychotherapy approach utilizing 'the concept of nonconscious algorithms for processing social information and the motivational principle of re-experiencing certain emotional states' (R.L. Wessler, *Affect and Nonconscious Processes in Cognitive Psychotherapy*).

Non-conscious states are similar to Freud's preconscious state where material is accessible, not buried in the unconscious, but is not fully conscious. Individuals adopt 'defence manoeuvres' whereby affective (mood, feeling, emotion) states are avoided. 'Security manoeuvres' produce desired affective states. These are similar to Freudian defence mechanisms and the 'armouring' of resistance. The learned affective state (LAS) refers to the vicarious, learnt imitating of parental emoting; in the same way as the child imitates the parental model of thinking and behaving, the child learns to express emotions. The environment becomes the controlling factor of the emotional process. As a means to understanding the origins of the individual's emotion reactions cognitive-behavioural therapies have acknowledged the need to explore the client's early developmental years of past experience. The individual's view of their life, with emphasis on the early years, is termed the phenomenological developmental history (PDH).

Advantages of the cognitive-behavioural approach

Highly structured approach which suits some people
Gives client a sense of 'doing'
Active and directive
Can be combined with other approaches
Gives practical coping strategies and skills
Encourages self-responsibility
Encourages self-awareness – links between thoughts, moods and actions

Disadvantages of the cognitive-behavioural approach

Lack of emphasis on feelings
Little emphasis on client–counsellor relationship
Ignores reality of misery

The socializing and normalizing elements make a person
behave in a more socially acceptable way but can be seen as
a form of restriction and control

In a situation where you have events that are very emotionally
charged – for example, sexual abuse – the use of the cognitive-
behavioural approach will not be very helpful because of the need
to deal with the associated powerful feeling. Cognitive-behavioural
methods are most effective when carried out with an awareness of
their limitations.

9 | DEMYSTIFYING
THE JARGON

Many of the terms used in the psychodynamic approach derive from psychoanalysis. Psychology dictionary definitions give clinical meanings, the understanding of which sometimes depends on foreknowledge of other 'technical' terms. While some therapists regard specific terms as necessary – useful for dialogue between therapists as a type of shortened language – others (like the ex-psychoanalyst Jeffrey Masson, who warns against diagnostic labelling) consider the jargon to have meaning for the particular exclusive world of therapists only, and that the use of categories to describe clients' mental processes is dehumanizing.

Freud identified various categories of 'defences' which have become widely accepted in psychology, psychiatry, counselling and psychotherapy alike. Even therapists who do not consider themselves to refer overtly to psychoanalytic theories are usually familiar with the psychoanalytic theoretical meaning of defences such as denial, repression, regression and so forth. In fact, terms like these are also used in everyday life as a form of psychological language for the lay person.

The traditional Freudian view is that a defence mechanism is a weapon employed by the Ego (the reality principle) to protect from anxiety, conflict, shame and other types of painful experiencing. The source of the potential anxiety is the Id (the pleasure principle), which motivates the person to satisfy its basic biological urges (including sexual impulses) in any way possible. The Id calls for immediate gratification, irrespective of logic or moral reasoning. The Ego and Superego develop ways of containing the deviant expressions of the Id. The function of the Ego, as the (predominantly) conscious part of the psyche, which is aware of social restraints and consequences of behaviour, is to satisfy the demands of the Id by reasoned and socially acceptable means. As 'piggy in the middle' the Ego, in turn, is influenced and restrained by the Superego. The Superego (the conscience) demands that the Ego utilizes internalized moral and ethical views (rules and taboos) to regulate the rampant Id.

The psychodynamic counsellor treats defences with respect, acknowledging that most were formed many years before, possibly in early childhood. Although the defence was appropriate to the client's survival at the time (to withstand anxiety, trauma, shame, etc), it may now be limiting or incapacitating – for example, interfering with self-development or the development of close relationships with others. The person-centred approach believes that by offering unconditional positive regard to the client their defences will gradually diminish as they recognize that the whole of their being is acceptable to the counsellor.

In a series of books on 'attachment behaviour', John Bowlby explored attachment and loss. He noted how a person who has experienced abandonment as a child attempts throughout life to protect themselves from further anxiety by distancing themselves from others. This results in an 'attachment anxiety' – further abandonment and the pain of separation and loss. It is at a later stage as a spouse, partner or parent – when the person finds it difficult to show affection or commitment to a relationship – that the defence mechanisms prove to be most destructive.

The defences

Denial

We hear people use the term 'in denial' quite commonly these days, meaning that a person (usually not the speaker) is refusing to face up to something about either themselves or what is happening in their lives. This type of denial, by implication, is conscious; the speaker is suggesting that the person has made the choice to deny or refuse an unpleasant reality. In contrast, the psychoanalytical meaning of 'denial' is that it is an unconscious mechanism which refuses to acknowledge thoughts, emotions, needs or wishes that can cause anxiety. As an unconscious process its function is to deny difficulties which cannot be dealt with consciously. In the therapeutic setting, something a therapist suggests to a client (an observation made or an interpretation offered) is rejected; denial is indicated when this is done with some speed, 'automatically' – without any consideration or reflection.

Displacement

Displacement is another defence which involves the redirecting of feelings and impulses (see below for an outline of the meaning of 'impulse') from the original source to another object, person or situation. An example is when a person feels angry with their boss but is unable to express it; on arriving home their anger is displaced onto their spouse. Displacement is evident in the transferential relationship between the counsellor and client when impulses or desires arising from the original sources (usually relating to the client's parents) are replayed.

In a behavioural context, displacement refers to the substitution of one response for another, particularly if the original response is thwarted or blocked in some manner.

Fixation

Like regression (see below), fixation is a defence which relates to earlier developmental stages. The term is used to explain when an individual gets stuck at a certain stage or fixed in their outlook, demonstrating failure to progress from one stage of development to the next – hence the term 'a mother/father fixation', used to describe a situation when an adult is highly reliant on nurturing, approval or guidance from the parental figure (e.g. tied to their mother's apron strings).

Erik Erikson's 'whole life' scheme of psychosocial development makes the point that movement to the next level of development (e.g. adolescence to young adulthood) requires the fulfilment of tasks in the resolution of the problems particular to that stage. In stage 5, that of the adolescent, the issues and tasks that the young person has to grapple with are concerned with the establishing of an individual identity or development of a consistent self-concept. Incompletion of the task causes 'role confusion'. An individual who has failed to resolve certain issues and deal with the many challenges of the adolescent stage of development, for example, may in later life find the ageing process particularly difficult to deal with. Inevitably there is always unfinished business regarding stages of development; it is extremes of these which are relevant to the fixation theory.

Idealization

Idealization is a form of denial in which an object of attention (parent, partner, sibling) is presented as 'all good' to the therapist, masking ambivalent feelings towards the other. So instead of declaring feelings of jealousy and hatred towards the sister who excels at everything she does, the client says how clever and marvellous she is and how well the two have always got on; rather than stating that their father was a cruel, bullying megalomaniac, the dutiful daughter says that he was a kind, considerate father whom she adored. When the client talks about the person in exaggeratedly glowing terms, this may be a signal that opposite emotions lurk beneath the acceptable ones. The 'all bad' representation of illicit emotions of hatred and fear (products of the Id) towards the other person is too dangerous to acknowledge and has therefore been repressed, replaced – via the Ego as a mediator or by the moral internalized views of the Superego – by an idealized view of the person. Idealization as a defence applies to groups of people, nationalities or locations when the object of idealization is revered, idolized or elevated to extremes.

Projection

This is the defence of attributing to others feelings or aspects of self which cannot be directly owned. Projection takes the onus of responsibility from the one who projects by placing (often negative) attention on the other person where unconscious urges can be safely identified. An example of projection is when one person accuses another of being angry, unhappy or bad tempered, when it is the speaker who is secretly feeling the emotion. The anxiety-provoking feelings are externalized by disassociation from the self and by reallocation to another person.

In *Still Small Voice*, Michael Jacobs gives an example of a client-to-counsellor projection, common to the early stages of counselling. When the client says, 'I think I may be wasting your time', Jacob comments: 'Although this may indicate a difficulty in allowing themselves to claim attention, it can also disguise the client's feeling that counselling is a waste of time, because it has apparently got nowhere in the initial meeting.'

Projective identification

This term, used by Melanie Klein to describe a type of object relationship, means the placing of part of oneself into another person, then identifying with them. It has close associations with other defence mechanisms: denial, idealization and splitting (see below). Projective identification is the paranoid-schizoid position, when the baby and later the child disowns their own destructiveness by placing it in someone else (i.e. mother; as **part object** – the breast). (See page 200.)

Projective identification is a psychological interpersonal process in which the recipient begins to think, feel and behave congruently with the projections – the recipient gets pulled into the manipulations of the projector, identifying with the attributed material.

Another aspect of projective identification is that the projector reinternalizes the modified material when it has been 'psychologically processed' by the recipient.

Rationalization

In psychoanalytic theory, as a defence mechanism rationalization conceals the real motivations for the individual's thoughts, feelings or actions. Irrational, obscure and confusing material is 'rationalized', made sense of, by the client, as a defence against the therapist's probing, disapproval or interpretation. Rationalization can take the form of 'philosophizing', explaining away anxiety-producing material, 'staying in the head' (i.e. the realm of rational thought) rather than getting in touch with feelings. It is a process of making that which is experienced as confusing, non-rational and hidden into that which is clear, rational and ordered and therefore manageable.

Intellectualization is similar. The more highly educated client retreats 'into the head' to avoid deep feelings. The client may philosophize or expound 'life theories' or attempt to foil the counsellor with their analytical knowledge.

Reaction formation

Reaction formation is a term used for a process through which unacceptable thoughts, feelings or impulses are controlled by creating opposing attitudes or behaviours to mask the feared ones. Anxiety is averted by outwardly engaging in behaviour urges of the Id. It may be helpful to think of reaction formation as a red herring detracting from qualities or attitudes of the self that seek expression, when a person has strong 'anti' opinions and feelings which indicate a 'fixed' position in reaction to the submerged urges. Reaction formations are so convincing a part of a person's personality that they become a permanent feature.

The psychoanalytic belief is that the original thoughts, feelings and impulses are repressed. Since they are stored in the unconscious mind, they emerge from time to time in free association and in the content and relating of dreams where the 'Id will out'. For example, a person who is fanatical about her appearance, who follows a strict diet regime, may dream about herself as plump and happy indulging in an orgy of food.

Regression

Regression is another defence activated by the Ego. At a simple level it refers to a person resorting to actions that have provided security in the past. In psychoanalytic theories the implication is that anxiety or stress causes the individual to retreat from reality into an infantile state or pattern of behaviour. (Remember the young man in Chapter 8 who regressed to an infantile use of language.)

An individual may begin to display infantile behaviour when they have not actually engaged in this particular activity in the (primitive) infantile stage of development; for example, an 11-year-old begins to suck their thumb, behaviour which they did not display as an infant. Regression occurs at times of adaptation when an unconscious aspect is brought to the fore. Jung said, 'By activating an unconscious factor regression confronts consciousness with the problem of the psyche as opposed to the problem of outward adaptation' (*The Collected Works*). In this light, regression can be seen as a type of distracting device or a refusal to go forward at that point in time until unresolved material held within the psyche is satisfactorily addressed.

In the cognitive-behavioural model of working and in cognitive-developmental theories regression refers to when a client goes back to a previous mode of behaviour before learning how to cope with more complex material. An example of this is when a person who has been terrified of flying has reached the point that she has taken a short journey in an aeroplane, but when the time nears for her to embark on a longer flight for a family holiday, the old anxiety and panic return and she reports to her therapist that she can't go anywhere near an aeroplane. This 'going back before going forward' is regarded as a temporary resting phase on an otherwise progressive pattern of cognitive processing.

Repression

Repression, as a means of blocking an unpleasant experience from memory, is at the root of many other defences. The psychodynamic understanding of the term is when anxiety-laden thoughts, feelings and experiences have been totally forgotten, hidden away in the deep recesses of the unconscious mind. These may have been disturbing impulses which were experienced as dangerously threatening and were not allowed into consciousness or painful memories which have been 'stored' in order that the person can go forward with their lives as best they can. In the understanding of the working of defences, it helps to remind ourselves that they are always designed to protect, although in the long run they can work against the emotional development of the individual.

It is a psychoanalytic view that repressed material is stored in the body, causing psychosomatic symptoms. The psychoanalyst Wilhelm Reich, a contemporary and close associate of Freud, also believed that repression was a defence against unacceptable sexual desires. He designed a therapeutic system of 'bodywork' to release repressed (usually libidinal) pent-up thoughts, feelings and memories stored in the body as armouring, which manifested in psychosomatic symptoms. Reich identified a source of life energy which he called the 'orgone force'. His pioneering work included the patient exercising deep breathing and receiving massage from the therapist to encourage the release of blocked emotions and buried traumas. The breaking down of these tensions in the body was accompanied by a cathartic response from the patient of crying, spasms, laughter or screaming. Reich's work was developed by practitioners like Alexander Lowen, the founder of a therapeutic technique called bio-energetics.

Resistance

Resistance is a term which encapsulates the use of the various forms of defence (e.g. denial, projection, 'flight into health'). See Chapter 8 for an exploration.

Splitting

This is a term used by Melanie Klein, who placed emphasis on the first few months of life and referred to the mother's breast as 'part object' to the infant, who experienced it as either 'wholly good' (e.g. an available source of comfort, sustenance and pleasure) or 'wholly bad' (when not available for gratification). The good/bad splitting occurs because the young infant has no appreciation of good and bad co-existing in the mother (the object in relationship to the infant). The resultant rage that the infant experiences when the breast is absent leads to anxiety, guilt and fear of loss.

Sublimation

Freud regarded this defence as normal and necessary as it serves a compromising, mediating function. It is usually defined as a redirecting expression of feelings and desires or impulses in a 'grown-up' manner. The individual who has reached a mature level of personal development is capable of expressing feelings openly, while at the same time appreciating what constitutes appropriate behaviour in relation to others (in the larger social context). Excesses of feeling find expression in other socially and culturally acceptable constructs. Freud believed that the growth of civilization necessitated the sublimation of the primary expression of the Id, but that the Id asserts itself in science, technology, literature and art. The idea of the Id finding expression in art is evident in aspects of the work of surrealist artists like Salvador Dali and Paul Delvaux who, inspired by psychoanalytic ideas, promoted dreams and the unconscious in their work. The surrealists experimented with 'automatic' drawing in an attempt to capture forms of art from the unconscious, inner world. Picasso's tortured *Guernica* is another example of the Id's *thanatos* (death drive) as are the more recent death portraits of animals preserved in formaldehyde by Damien Hirst. In technology, the urge to create without addressing long-term consequences manifests in its side-effects of pollution and ozone destruction. Currently in science we have the workings of the Id exemplified by the wish of some scientists to clone humans and genetically alter crop sources (sometimes referred to as 'playing God' – a moral and ethical Superego statement). The Id is most often seen in its potentially destructive context but it is also powerful as a creative motivating force of individual (and Jung would say collective) expression.

Other terms

Acting out

This term is used to describe uncontrollable outbursts of behaviour. A 'problem' child may 'act out' for the rest of the family, in so much as they are the one who expresses or displays (in outbursts because the problems and feelings are unfaced by all of the family) the anxieties, conflicts and aggressions that are held within the family dynamic. Equally, acting out may be evident in the neurotic symptoms of an adult. In psychodynamic theory the term is used when a client is acting out (as in putting into action) some of the issues which are being worked out in therapy, outside of therapy. A young man may talk about being very angry with his father but never be able to confront him; instead he becomes angry with another male authority figure 'out there' in his life.

Borderline personality disorder

The client or patient who is considered to be a 'borderline' case lives in a precarious position between normal adaptive functioning and 'real psychic disability', which makes the forming of relationships with others extremely difficult. The therapeutic relationship is complicated by the client's dependency and reactive expression of anger.

The Kleinian view of 'borderline' personality disorder is that the person's development has been arrested in the early years of the 'paranoid-schizoid' stage of development, when the infant experiences in terms of 'wholly good' or 'wholly bad' (splitting), and the persecutory anxieties of this stage persist.

Catharsis

From psychoanalytic theory, the term 'catharsis' refers to the release of tensions and anxiety experienced when repressed feelings from the past – memories, wishes and urges – are brought into consciousness through therapy. Catharsis often involves 'emotional discharge' – weeping or laughter. In 1893 Freud and his colleague Josef Breuer called their methods of psychoanalytic investigation 'catharsis'. Freud believed that psychoneuroses were based on sexual, instinctual forces that maintained pathological manifestation. Symptoms could be turned back into 'emotionally cathected ideas' brought into consciousness, thereby giving insight into the nature and origins of formerly unreachable unconscious processes.

Complex

A complex is an idea filled with emotionally charged content which interrupts our attention and redirects our thinking and behaviour; also a cluster of feelings around an association with a person (like the mother) or an event. The terms 'inferior complex' and 'superior complex' are familiar to us all.

Depression

A mood state characterized by a lack of self-esteem, and by despondency, lack of motivation and decrease in activity with accompanying sadness and defeatism. Bouts of depression are considered normal when they are of relatively short duration. Depression is classified as a disorder in various ways in psychiatry, depending on the extremes and intensities of the moods and their effects. The two most useful classifications for counsellors are: neurotic depression – severe depression (in terms of depths and duration) which does not involve the sufferer's loss of contact with reality; psychotic depression – the sufferer demonstrates a variety of impairments of normal functioning. The term 'clinical depression' is used to denote that the sufferer would benefit from medical or therapeutic attention.

Free association

Freud used the technique of free association to investigate the unconscious mind as an alternative to hypnosis, which was a method used at the time. In free association unconstrained associations between words, thoughts and ideas are encouraged as a method of accessing unconscious material. This technique is still used by psychodynamic counsellors, who let the client talk and express what is uppermost in their minds.

Impulse

The term, used in Freudian theory, means an instinctual act, an unconscious force arising from the Id. The cognitive-behavioural use of the term refers to an event or an act that is 'triggered' by a stimulus (something that rouses into activity) over which the individual has insufficient or no conscious control. Impulses interest those of behavioural and psychodynamic orientation alike in the analysis of certain behaviour; for example, what makes a person who has never displayed antisocial behaviour experience a sudden incitement to act uncharacteristically, with violence towards others? Both would acknowledge the activation of unconscious forces. A characteristic of an impulsive act is the speed at which it occurs.

Introjection

Introjection refers to the internalization of parental and societal views, rules and taboos. Introjection has positive and negative aspects – positive qualities and attributes can be instilled through vicarious means. They may be modelled by the parents; the young child introjects a picture of themselves through parental views and opinions which can be both positive or negative. A child may experience heavy criticism from a parent throughout childhood and internalize this as a self-view. Consequently, as an adult, they continue the internal criticism, considering themselves to be worthless, with resulting low self-esteem.

The **paranoid-schizoid position** refers to the earliest phase of development when the infant responds to the breast as 'part object', experiencing the breast as both 'good' and 'bad'. The 'splitting' in both the object and the Ego (internalized) is an expression of paranoid anxiety.

Part object refers to objects which are introjected into the Ego from earliest infancy, beginning with the introjection of the part ideal (feeding) and part persecutory (withdrawn) breast. Part objects are the result of conflicts within early experiencing and are characteristics of what Melanie Klein termed the paranoid-schizoid position (as above). A glossary of terms, which includes those introduced by Melanie Klein, may be found in Hanna Segal's *Introduction to the Work of Melanie Klein*.

Phantasies/Fantasies

Early childhood experiences mould our perceptions of our world. These perceptions, particular to each individual, affect how we process our thoughts and feelings in our internal world.

Freud termed these 'fantasies' because of their idiosyncratic nature. The term 'fantasy' does not mean that the perception is untrue, but rather that understanding/experiencing of the world in infanthood and as a young child can be distorted as fantasy. Fantasy is best regarded as an idiosyncratic distortion. Fantasies are real to the individual, buried in the unconscious mind in association with other people, experiences, surroundings and so on. Fantasies relate to how we perceive ourselves, our inner world, and how we interact with the external world, others and our environment.

The counsellor who uses the psychodynamic approach may intervene with: 'What is your fantasy about …?' to help the client elucidate personal meanings.

The spelling 'phantasy' is used to distinguish the Freudian meaning from the 'fantasy' characteristics of daydreaming and wishful thinking. The *ph* spelling indicates the nature of the fantasy as an unconscious process.

Narcissistic personality disorder

The original psychoanalytic term was Narcissistic neurosis. Freud introduced the concept of narcissism, taken from the Greek myth of Narcissus, who fell in love with the image of himself reflected in a pool of water. The diagnostic description of the term is that the Narcissistic personality is totally self-absorbed, having an exaggerated sense of self-importance and displaying an exhibitionistic need for attention. There is a propensity to fantasize about success, power, riches and so on, and a general grandiose self-glorifying attitude towards self. Freud wrote that the characteristic feature of Narcissism was 'loving oneself'.

Psychoanalytic theory defines narcissism as 'primary' or 'secondary'.

Narcissism (primary)

Primary narcissism refers to the young child's libidinal drives being focused on the self, the Ego (in auto-erotic satisfaction). This is a normal stage of development; only when this stage continues into adulthood does it become a neurosis.

Narcissism (secondary)

This refers to the love of self that precludes love of others – emotional investment in oneself.

Narcissistic neurosis

A neurosis characterized by extreme self-love that excludes normal feelings of love for others, preventing the individual from forming a transference in therapy.

Neuroses

The dominant meaning of the term originates from Freud's use to describe a personality or mental disturbance due to a conflict involving the blocking of instinctual urges. Neuroses was once thought to be a neurological or organic dysfunction, originally viewed as a disease of the nerves.

Optimal frustration

Optimal frustration is a term used to describe feelings that the client has in response to the blank screen or abstinent approach of psychoanalysis and the psychodynamic approaches. It refers to the frustration that the client experiences when the counsellor 'holds back' from comforting or reassuring, or from directly answering questions posed by the client. Instead the counsellor offers interpretation, addressing the underlying or unconscious meaning of a question. For example, the client may ask, 'Have you got someone coming here after me?' If the counsellor answers 'yes' or 'no', this does not allow exploration of what lies behind the question.

The counsellor's response might be, 'Do I have a client coming here after you ... I wonder if what concerns you is that you may be one of many clients that I see and that you are not important to me?' The client's first reaction may be to deny that this is their concern and they may feel a frustration that the question has not been directly answered, but the frustration that the client experiences acts as a stimulant which causes inner conflicts to emerge and be discussed.

Psychosomatic disorder

Psyche originally meant 'soul' and the psychological meaning is 'the mind'. *Soma* pertains to the body or general physical components. 'Psychosomatic' refers to the interaction between the two.

10 DEALING WITH ANGER

This chapter is concerned with anger and how to deal with it in an adaptive and constructive manner. It is easy to project outwardly on this topic as a problem of others, and for this reason the trainee counsellor is advised to get to know their own anger. As I have pointed out elsewhere in this book, both stress management and assertiveness techniques help us understand and cope with our anger and the symptoms and underlying reasons, such as tensions and unrealistic self-goals and expectations of others. Anger can usually be managed and can even be used productively.

Anger and the trainee counsellor

Anger in itself is not 'bad' – it is a human expression; part of the age-old 'fight or flight' stress response. A certain amount of stress and angry impulse gives us the will 'to do', but inappropriately high levels of anger can be harmful to self and others and violence is always unacceptable. Before being presented with the anger of clients it's advisable to explore our own experience with dealing with anger, our own and others'.

- What makes you angry – presses your triggers? Prejudice? Being ignored? Criticism? Insensitivity? Rudeness? Feeling vulnerable? Feeling humiliated? Incompetence?
- Whom do you most commonly get angry with? Your partner, spouse? Friends? Your immediate family? People in authority?
- How do you express angry feelings? Do you tolerate so much, then 'blow up'? Accuse, blame, criticize?

■ Do you take time out to assess the situation and approach the problem assertively?

■ Do you ignore your angry feelings?

■ Whom do you feel safe enough with to express angry feelings? With a close friend? With your partner or spouse? With a parent? Do you feel it is something you have to deal with alone?

We are more likely to feel afraid of other people's anger if we are afraid of our own. If we feel we have no right to be angry ourselves then our attitude to other people's expressions of anger is also going to be dismissed. As counsellors we need to self-challenge and accept our imperfections in the interests of being genuine with clients.

Accepting responsibility for our anger

Expressions like 'You made me angry' and referring to ourselves in the abstracted second-person form (e.g. 'When that happens you feel so angry') allow us to relinquish responsibility; we don't have to own our anger as we do when we state, 'I am angry.' No other person makes us angry as such; others behave in a certain way by doing or saying something, and if we have an opposing agenda, problem or issue, we respond with anger. Our 'trigger' or 'button' is pressed – we react in a negative way. I say 'negative', but we need to be careful here because anger expressed appropriately, as means of reasonable self-assertion, is both valid and necessary (and at times we need to acknowledge that a client has a right to be angry in relation to their experiences). This kind of anger is not aimed at hurting people or gaining revenge or winning an argument; it is more to do with expressing your right as an individual and it never threatens with physical violence. Before we meet the anger of our client, we need to recognize and understand the manifestations of our own.

Associations

As a way of getting in touch with your anger, take time to think of what associations you have. Complete these lists:

■ Other people – parent, siblings, childhood friends, bullies etc.

- Metaphors and imagery – 'pressure cooker', 'bottled up', 'roaring like a lion', 'shouting like a fishwife', 'eaten up with anger', 'a whiplash tongue' etc.
- Symbols and archetypes – fire, war, animals (wolf, tiger, lion), bared teeth, demon eyes, warrior, devil, witch, destroyer etc.

Exercises

When you have added your own contributions, ask yourself which have most meaning to you. Are you able to put them into any specific context? For example: 'demon eyes' – as a child when certain 'grown-ups' were very angry with me their eyes appeared to me to bulge out of their heads.

Where do you hold anger in your body? What does it feel like?

Try to image your anger in a drawing or painting. What thoughts accompany your anger?

Avoidance

Unless as counsellors we become familiar with and work at understanding and accepting our own anger, we may devise ways of avoiding facing the anger of our clients, as it presents itself, by deflection or collusion, or by other methods of keeping discomfort at bay. We may fail to pick up on angry statements, on body and facial expression and important associated feelings, or collude in the client's avoidance and efforts to keep angry material hidden; or perhaps we may encourage the client, through the use of reflecting skills and open questions, to explore their anger, only to find that our skills are insufficient to support the client through the expressed anger. The therapist's work includes dealing with hostile feelings in the 'here and now', making sure they are not avoided or acted out.

Safety procedures

Before we move on to helping techniques, remember the importance of safety procedures. When considering working with clients who have demonstrated a propensity towards violent action the following needs to be established:

1 Your suitability to work with the client – i.e. have you sufficient training and experience?

2 The client's suitability for counselling – i.e. do they require a more experienced counsellor than yourself? Would psychotherapy (of a longer duration than you can offer) or other medical help be a better option for them? Extreme aggression can be physically or organically based.

3 Is the client currently taking any medication?

4 Do you have sufficient support from a supervisor who can advise you on the above?

5 An awareness of safety procedures and facilities in the building. If you work for an organization they will have specific safety policies; for example, an alarm system in each room and an understanding that at no time should a counsellor be working with a client alone in the building. There should always be at least one other counsellor as a back-up or witness if anything goes wrong. Safety is equally important for those working in a private setting, although those available in organizations may not be possible. This raises questions that you may like to consider regarding personal safeguarding.

When working with clients who are experiencing difficulties with either expressing or controlling anger, reflecting feelings is unlikely to be enough. The counsellor needs to encourage the client to talk about and express their anger in the 'here and now'; for example, saying, 'Tell me how you are feeling now as you talk about these past events.' This helps the client to bring past and present feelings together and to deal with them in an adaptive and constructive manner. The client can also be helped to 'own' their feelings by being encouraged by the counsellor to say angry statements out loud, such as 'I feel angry when …' and 'I feel angry now because …' Expressive methods of therapy, such as those used in psychodrama – techniques like imagining and role play – are useful because they help the client address their anger towards the actual person(s) or situation that they feel angered with, rather than holding it inside or off-loading it onto the counsellor.

A gestalt method

This is a variation of the 'empty chair' method (see also Chapters 6 and 11). An empty chair is placed to face the client, at a distance of four to five feet.

Begin by asking the client to identify the source of their angry feelings and then direct the client to imagine that the person (if it is a few people, they can be addressed one by one) is sitting in the chair. Let the client know what you are feeling; for example, 'I sense that you are very angry; I don't care to be the target of your anger, so rather than telling me how angry you are feeling, I would like you to express your angry feelings towards the imaginary person in the chair.'

You can then be alongside the client facing the empty chair. They may choose to sit or stand – standing when the imagined person sits gives the client an advantaged position, which they may prefer. In your role as supporter and coach you are no longer likely to be the recipient of the client's anger. They may at first find it difficult or embarrassing to talk directly to the imagined person and may turn to you, beginning: 'Well, I am really angry with my father: he is always criticizing me and interfering with my life.' As counsellor you can help the client by 'modelling' direct communication with the imagined person to help them get started; for example, 'I am angry with you, Father. I don't like how you criticize me and I feel that you interfere with my life.'

Another method of addressing the anger is to coach the client to be aware of physiological signals activated by anger (see the chart). Individuals react differently, but often reactions include a pounding heart, headache, tension in the shoulders, sweating and clenching of fists. It is also useful to adopt methods used in cognitive-behavioural therapy, asking the client to keep a journal and note what happened before an angry outburst, how they felt during it, what the consequences were and what they felt when the anger had subsided (e.g. relief or shame). The before, during and after assessment helps the client to make connections between cognitions, emotions and associated behaviour, heightening self-awareness.

	Physiological signals	
	e.g increased heart rate, rapid shallow breathing or sharp intake of breath, muscle tension	
	Acknowledge anger	
Express anger		Take time out

Assertively	**Aggressively** **Possible consequences**	**Mentally step back**	
Clear, direct communication with others	Damage e.g. to relationships with others/self-esteem	Count to 10	
	Danger	Take deep breaths	
Escalation	Inappropriate, out-of-control anger Threatening to others	Relax tension in body	
	Habitual	Take time out, remove self from situation	
	Becomes a 'stuck' way of relating without addressing the actual sources of anger or facing problems	Relax Lie down Meditate or practise simple relaxation technique	Redirect attention on task

Aggression to punching cushion, bag etc. |
| | Escalating levels of non-communication with others | | |

Anger chart – based on assertiveness training and stress management techniques and guidelines

Appropriate and inappropriate expression of anger

We express anger in many ways, ranging from raising our voices to threatening violence verbally or physically, or even carrying out violence. Feeling angry is normal. The suppression of anger is unhealthy, as we are likely to store anxiety in our bodies and develop aches and pains or more serious illness. We can learn to express anger in appropriate ways as opposed to giving vent to inappropriate high levels of anger.

Appropriate expression of anger includes:

Dealing with angry feelings assertively, being firm, raising our voice level, stating clearly what we feel, think and mean; taking action which does not involve physically hurting other people; being specific and concrete regarding our needs and wishes.

Inappropriate expression of anger includes:

Physical threats or actual harm to other people, destruction of other people's property, verbal bullying or harassment, making unrealistic demands of others.

Make a fuller list to help you explore what you consider to be appropriate and inappropriate expressions of anger.

Alternatives to 'blowing a fuse'

Look at the chart. Note body cues, what your body tells you. To use a behaviourist term, we can 'unlearn' destructive behaviour. We can learn to pause and think, and to redirect our energies by learning to stop when we recognize the physiological body changes – by reducing heat from the situation we can choose to step back mentally, following learned procedures to calm the mind and body. Count to 10, take deep and slow breaths and relax, 'self-talk' the body – tell yourself you can be calm, relax, lessen the tension in the body by shrugging your shoulders up to the count of 3 and then let them drop, circle your shoulders. Most importantly at this point, take 'time out' from the situation and try to get away from the anger-reinforcing environment. Give yourself a break – time to 'mull over' and assess the situation. This can be achieved by:

1   Taking time to meditate or practise a simple relaxation technique.

2   Redirecting energy by engaging in physical exercise or energetic activity, such as scrubbing the floor, hammering nails in wood etc.

3   Redirecting attention or aggression by focusing on a task. Redirect aggression by employing a Gestalt technique of hitting a pillow or cushion, or similar, with fists or an implement such as a tennis racket while verbalizing the grievance. This method of expressing anger is safe for non-violent persons only (a violent person's anger may be further activated by an exercise like this, when it unleashes pent-up anger). The angry person is more likely to be in a position to assess what appropriate steps need to be taken when the heat is taken out of the situation. Everyone is different and needs to find something that works for them. Helpful tactics to let off steam include taking a vigorous walk, listening to music, screaming and shouting with the windows closed, singing at the top of the voice or writing a vitriolic letter – it doesn't have to be sent. None of these things hurts other people.

How best to deal with the problem

The client is then in a position to be more objective about the situation and can decide what (if any) further action needs to be taken. Anger often escalates as personal relationships become more strained. The individual can feel increasingly misunderstood and unloved. Irrational thoughts and beliefs increase proportionally.

Examples of irrational belief

Irrational (negative) thoughts

1   I've got too much to do, I'll never get everything done and they'll think I'm a failure.

2   I have been humiliated and I'm going to get revenge.

3   I'm trapped and I'm powerless to change my circumstances – it's up to my husband or wife to make decisions.

---

4 I've got to win this argument; if I don't then people will think I'm a fool.

5 He is ruining my life. He always lets me down and criticizes me.

6 It's just not fair; she got promotion when I am better qualified for the job – it's the story of my life.

7 Other people don't show me any respect, they use me and then when I need them they let me down.

Corresponding alternative (positive) thoughts

1 I will do what I realistically can. What other people think doesn't matter. I know I am doing the best I can.

2 People are not always pleasant and I can learn from this experience and survive it. Thoughts of revenge are a waste of my energy and stop me enjoying myself.

3 I can decide what I want to change in my life. Not all the changes I would like to make may be possible right now. I can negotiate with my husband or wife as a first step.

4 I don't always have to be right. I can respect my own point of view and respect other people's right to have different views.

5 My happiness comes from within me and is not dependent on other people's behaviour towards me or their opinion of me.

6 Life is not fair and it is unrealistic to expect it to be. I will have other opportunities, as I have in the past. This person's promotion doesn't diminish my abilities.

7 I am a worthwhile person. If people don't treat me with respect then that is their problem. I can't control the way others behave towards me. If I help another person in any way it is my choice and it does not mean that they have to reciprocate.

Let's compare the self-statements from both columns.

Column 1

The negative, irrational thoughts are self-defeating, defensive and self-denying, demonstrated by words and phrases like *failure, humiliated, trapped, powerless, I'll never get, I've got to win, ruining my life.*

Feelings from Column 1

Overwhelmed – with responsibilities, powerlessness, entrapment, humiliation, hurt, abandonment, loss, let down, reflection, dependency on others for happiness, approval, expectations, life's unfair, shoulds and oughts of self and others. Irrational beliefs which accompany angry feelings reveal our high expectation of both ourselves and others.

Column 2

The positive, rational thoughts are self-affirming and responsible, demonstrated by words and phrases like *realistic, worthwhile, I can negotiate, I am doing the best that I can, I can learn and survive* (from the experience), *I don't always have to be right.*

Consider the statement, 'I don't always have to be right'. My own reaction is to give an inner 'Phew – what a relief!' I wonder what your reaction is?

Feelings from Column 2

Relief – which comes from a dropping away of shoulds and oughts – targeted towards both self and others; humility, I am human, it's OK to make mistakes, be wrong; tolerance – other people have their own opinions – it's OK if they don't agree with mine; self-respect – I am capable of making decisions, I do the best I can, I can survive, inner strength, I am a worthwhile person; hope – in affirmation of self and capabilities.

Working with a video

If working with a video is available to you, the client can role play situations which they recognize as producing angry responses, practising appropriate adaptive and more constructive ways of dealing with other people and potentially problematic situations. This could be a past unresolved experience or a conflict that is currently taking place. You, as counsellor, can practise with your client, 'modelling' adaptive behaviour and demonstrating methods used until the client is familiar with working with this medium. It will not suit everyone and, of course, the client must always be presented with a choice as to whether they would like to try this kind of work or not. People who have been physically, mentally or sexually abused may abhor the idea of working with a camera because of its intrusive probing nature. They may, for example, feel humiliated by seeing themselves 'performing' in an inappropriate way. The client needs enough Ego strength to appreciate that their angry behaviour only constitutes a part of them. They also need to believe that their behaviour can change. The client with very low self-esteem may need to build up to working with a video recorder; consider it as an option when they can see that some progress has been made.

Suitable candidates for video work usually enjoy the exploratory nature of it. Viewing the playback and trying out different responses and reflections can be a valuable learning process. By role playing a recent real situation which made the client angry, the client will see their behaviour more objectively and see themselves as others perceive them – as, for example, out of control, frightening, ridiculous or vulnerable. The client gains insight into the effects of their behaviour on others if they role play both themselves and the person they are in conflict with by alternating roles. Again, the counsellor first models this technique. By reviewing the video recording the client witnesses the dynamics of the relationship; they gain a sense of being angry and what it feels like to be on the receiving end of that anger. They can also examine the responses they anticipate. When challenging situations are looming that are known to the client to bring on anxiety, and are therefore likely to produce anger, they can rehearse more appropriate responses in preparation. The counsellor and client can discuss the recording together, replaying and homing in on particular parts. The counsellor can ask the client what they were feeling or thinking as both themselves and the other person in the role play. The video frame can be frozen while asking such questions as: 'You look very sad here – what is going through your mind?' 'Your mood seemed to change at this point – what are you feeling?' The observation of body language is also useful.

The methods used in this chapter have been mainly of the directive cognitive-behavioural approach; that is, looking at behaviour and thoughts and beliefs (cognitions) and coaching in and modelling certain corrective thoughts and behaviours. The cognitive-behavioural method teaches or 'coaches' the client to 'self-talk', replacing irrational incapacitating thoughts with rational ones. The psychodynamic approach addresses causal factors and underlying (repressed) material. The counsellor will also be attentive to dreams and psychosomatic symptoms.

The psychodynamic perspective

The psychodynamic counsellor would approach the client's problems by considering anger in terms of the transference, introjections, defences – such as denial, repression and displacements – and working with the sensitive confronting of resistance. Childhood-related material such as feelings associated with abandonment or loss are likely to be re-experienced through the transference, especially when the end of therapy is approaching. The object relations concept of 'good enough mothering' and holding and containing the client's anger will come into play. The good enough mother can contain her infant's destructive rage while remaining loving and nurturing; she doesn't retaliate or take revenge on her child. The client who holds deeply rooted anger may have not had 'good enough mothering' (or adequate valuing from a significant other). The 'not good enough mother' may have been emotionally wounded and therefore stunted in her ability to demonstrate love, afraid of her own anger and possibly unable to control it, resulting in anger turned towards the self. This could manifest in various ways; she may desperately attempt to satisfy the infant's every demand promptly, behave inconsistently, be cold, punitive or rejecting or place a rigid regime on the infant or child. The child of dysfunctional parenting has introjected many negative views of themselves and self in relationship to others; for example, I am stupid, I am not worth loving, I am responsible for my mother's inability to cope. Families who avoid unpleasant topics or express anger by physical violence or abuse fail to 'model' appropriate methods of expressing and dealing with anger. The anger gets 'split off' as something to be feared because of its destructiveness and denigrating potential. As psychologists and sociologists alike attest, unresolved problems with anger in the parents can result in repercussions down the generations.

As we have seen, destructive anger is often displaced anger, directed towards someone other than the person or situation that provoked it. The angry client may demonstrate destructive idealization of the therapist, a form of splitting and an acting out of destructive anger. The client feels an emotional ambivalence towards the therapist, being unable to tolerate the therapist as having 'good' and 'bad' potential, and may attempt to make the counsellor manageable by assuming an idealized view of them. Feelings of strong need and helplessness can result in rage, which hides an impulse towards relational closeness. Extreme anger is often a defence against painful feelings of sadness, vulnerability or helplessness, linked to loss, abandonment and fear of separation, which will most probably be recalled in therapy and re-experienced in the negative transference as an echo of the client's past.

The main focus of the psychodynamic counsellor is to help the client get in touch with vulnerable feelings, bringing denied anger out into the open, which in itself can be a great relief to the client. The dangers are that the client hides behind defences and verbal and non-verbal manifestations of defensive reactions, by being vague, becoming silent, changing the subject, offering rationalization or fending off feelings with continual chatter; that the anger felt towards the therapist is reallocated to other people outside the therapy (acted out); defences are acted out through resistance to therapy (not turning up for the session, being late) and that hidden destructive anger will be detrimental to the therapeutic process. The 'angry client' who initially finds it difficult to communicate thoughts and feelings most probably lacked parental 'mirroring' and the counsellor's support and willingness to face the source of the destructive impulses is reparative.

The need to be mirrored, brought to our attention by Heinz Kohut in his developmental theory of self-psychology, is a grandiose-exhibitionistic need of the child. Kohut was of the opinion that to develop a healthy self-concept the child needs to be shown that at least one of the parents derives great pleasure in having them around. The parent demonstrates love and regard for the child from the subtle cues of gesture, expression and tone of voice. The child looks into the mirror of the parent's face and, seeing love, approval and pleasure, forms a picture of themselves. The self-concept then is positive – I am a lovable, worthwhile person. However, the parent cannot always be the mirror that reflects a positive self-image. Kohut said that when the parent fails to 'mirror' it presents an opportunity to draw on the memory of the positive experiences, when the child can be their own mirror. Kohut called this process **transmuting internalizations**. Over time the transmuting internalization contributes to part of a 'strong and cohesive self'. By conveying a genuine interest, acceptance and empathic responding, the counsellor 'mirrors' self-worth to the client, accepting the mothering role in the transference. While appreciating the effects and importance of past relationships and experiences, the counsellor keeps the client's attention in the emotional experiencing of this minute, in the here and now in relationship to the counsellor, encouraging them to be both more responsive to their own feelings and emotions and attentive to their emotional interaction with another.

The reparative relationship

People who have been well mirrored as children appreciate themselves to be acceptable, lovable and attractive and are not solely reliant on others for their self-esteem. The child of dysfunctional parenting, with parents who exhibited low self-esteem and a disposition towards angry outbursts, has rarely received enough positive messages. The grandiose-exhibitionistic needs which sought fulfilment at the early developmental stage are frustrated and repressed since there is no opportunity for these wishes to be satisfied. The counsellor's work can be seen to attempt to repair some of the lack experienced. The reparative relationship is a useful reference for working with anger. Therapy can provide nurturing and a form of corrective reparenting, supplying an emotional experience lacking in childhood. It is the re-experiencing of old conflicts and impulses in a non-judgemental, non-threatening supportive, empathic environment that makes reparation possible. The counsellor 'mirrors' a self-worth by valuing the client and extending positive regard. The reparative model encompasses person-centred qualities and values of warmth, acceptance and empathy. The client experiences in the 'here and now' of the therapy that anger can be confronted, can be talked about, explored and understood. Rather than being devastatingly destructive, the outcome is positively constructive.

General checklist for confronting anger

Do

Be caring and empathic
Confront sensitively and tentatively
Confront the defence, not the client
Accept and respect the client's true feelings
Be supportive and strengthen the client's Ego
Be optimistic and realistic
Hold the boundaries
Have adequate supervision

Beware of

Becoming aggressive, punitive or defensive
Colluding with the client's resistance
Losing yourself in the transference/reparative intention

11 | UNDERLYING ISSUES

When people decide to go for counselling, they have decided that they need specialized help, recognizing that they have problems or difficulties that they are presently unable to cope with alone. Having made the decision to do something about the situation, the prospect of talking to a stranger about intimate problems can still be daunting and often it is difficult for a person to 'open up' in the first session – no matter how sensitively the counsellor handles the intake session, the 'presenting problems' (i.e. the problems that the client openly expresses to the counsellor) may be only symptomatic of more deeply rooted troubles. The client may present problems as generalizations – they are depressed, or not getting on well with others in a close relationship, or dissatisfied with life. These feelings are very real – sometimes the clients themselves are not fully aware that 'bigger' issues lie below the surface manifestations. But the client who initially says they are depressed may, a few sessions into the therapy, intimate or tell the counsellor directly that they have been considering suicide; or the person who at the onset of therapy cited their main problem to be trouble in close relationships may eventually reveal that they are suffering from a form of unresolved grief. With this in mind, the focus of this chapter is the client who suffers from unresolved grief, the client who has been abused, the suicidal client and the self-harming client – all real-life situations that people go through and present with in therapy. On occasions these surprise and sometimes incapacitate the inexperienced counsellor or willing helper.

Grief

Grief is always associated with some form of loss which involves change. The person who grieves is attempting to acclimatize or reorientate themselves to the new circumstances that they find themselves in. This is not always straightforward, for a variety of reasons. When we think of someone as grief stricken we usually associate the condition with the death of a loved one (bereavement), yet there are other sources of grief to consider which require deeply challenging readjustment, including:

- Change of circumstances – e.g. loss of job, on-going financial problems that are status/security related.
- Change in relationships – e.g. death of a loved one, a child growing up or moving away, divorce or separation.
- Change in body – e.g. loss of limb, internal organ, persistent illness.
- Change in physiological functioning – e.g. due to ageing, fitness deterioration, loss of mental faculties, deafness, eyesight deterioration.

People grieve for many reasons and in differing ways. Grief is a normal process through which we work out and eventually resolve our deeply felt loss and the accompanying pain and anxieties. Grief therapists like J.W. Worden and E. Kubler-Ross have, through their writings, greatly enhanced understanding of grieving processes. One of the main reasons a person suffers prolonged grief is that they have been unable to express, in their own time and in their own way, all the complexities and stages of their grief, their thoughts and emotions, and do not feel heard, acknowledged and supported. In bereavement this may include a yearning for the deceased, a need to blame others and to express guilty feelings. When a person is having to cope with a fundamental change (physical, or in life circumstances), feelings of frustration, anger and depression can contribute to a prolonged grief.

An example of unresolved grief

If grief is not fully expressed at the time of the original loss, it can lie submerged as a source of pain and inner conflict. What follows is an account of how a client was helped with problems originating from unresolved grief.

Case study 4

Susan was a woman in her late 20s. Her presenting problems were: she felt generally depressed, she had no interest in sexual relations with her husband, she felt that their relationship was on a downward spiral, she had no energy or enthusiasm for anything, suffered from severe headaches and had heavy, painful menses. During the first few sessions of counselling Susan was composed and appeared somewhat distant both from what she was saying and the counselling experience. Although she talked openly about her deteriorating relationship with her husband and her lack of sexual drive, she spoke without feeling, completing most statements by rubbing her eyes. I sensed an underlying sadness which was incongruent with her matter-of-fact outward manner. When I related this to her, she told me that two years previously her 4-month-old son had died in a 'cot death' (also termed Sudden Infant Death – SID). When I asked her how she had felt at the time of the death she used the word 'numb'. She related that she cried at the time but there had always been an air of unreality about it, especially when her husband and relatives kept telling her to 'try for another baby as soon as possible' as if he were replaceable. She began to cry when I asked her the baby's name, saying that neither her family nor her friends ever referred to him any more. For everyone else's sake she had tried to behave as if she had fully recovered but she never had. Instead, to protect herself, she had cut off from her feelings and this had inadvertently caused close relationships to suffer.

In the sessions that we had together, Susan experienced the grief that she had clearly repressed. She talked about the initial shock, the pain, guilt, sadness, anger and helplessness she had felt and continued to feel. She felt immense guilt – blaming herself for the infant's death. Visits from various sympathetic personnel, including a police interview, only confirmed her fears. She was angry with herself and others 'for letting it happen' and angry towards the child for going, as if he had changed his mind about accepting her as a mother. She recalled that she was producing breast milk after he had died and this, and the way those around her had adopted a 'hush hush' approach to the tragedy, left her feeling rejected and 'lost'; she yearned to hold and touch her baby.

> By acknowledging and re-experiencing the grief she had originally been unable to express fully, she began to understand why she had distanced herself sexually from her husband. She acknowledged that she was terrified of the possibility of having another child; she also felt that she had no right to experience love or pleasure, judging herself to be a bad, neglectful mother who deserved punishment.

In the above example we see many of the known symptoms of grieving: shock, denial, guilt, anger, emotional withdrawal and physical symptoms accompanying the psychological effects. The client had become 'stuck', suffering acutely from the death of the child because she had not been able to go through the grieving process fully and at her own pace. There was what the Gestalt approach terms 'unfinished business'; the infant's death had not been accepted and integrated into her being as part of her life experience, which would allow her to move on and live in the present. Susan commented that what helped her in counselling was being able to 'say anything I felt like saying'. She felt supported because nothing she said or felt was dismissed but was explored with interest. She felt that she had been 'given permission' (when everyone else expected her to be stoic) to talk about feeling angry and how depressed and 'dead' she herself felt; and it helped. She was able to identify fears and misconceptions, recognizing that SID is a *bona fide* medical problem which affects families across the social cultural spectrum, and occurs in the families of doctors and other medically trained individuals.

Normalizing the grief

What is needed to work with someone who is suffering from unresolved grief? It is important to acknowledge what they are going through, to help the client to actualize the loss. Another important factor is the 'normalizing' of their feelings, thoughts and behaviour. The grieving person who has not come to terms with the death of a loved one will inwardly ask themselves what is wrong with them, why they can't get over it. There can be many reasons, including a disbelief that what has happened has actually happened. The reason a person has not actualized the death is more often than not because they have never been allowed to experience it fully in their own way.

The counsellor can help with this, encouraging the client to give full expression to the ways that will help them to come to terms with their loss. The person might like to bring in photographs of the lost loved one to show the counsellor, they most certainly will want to talk about the person and can be encouraged to share their memories with you. Susan brought in some of her baby's clothes and toys to show me; other clients have shown me poems that they have written about the deceased. Because people are very sensitive and vulnerable at such times, there is a tendency for them to think that what they experience is abnormal. For example, some people talk to the deceased person or hear their voice; experience bouts of copious crying or moments of spiritual euphoria; feel unconnected from what's going on around them, becoming increasingly alienated from their own experiencing and from other people. Counsellors may choose to self-disclose to help the client to appreciate that they are not alone in thinking 'different' thoughts or feeling extremes of emotion. The counsellor, if they think it will be useful to the client, might say something like, 'I felt like that too when my mother died' or 'It took me a long time to accept my friend's death' – just enough to share a little of the counsellor's own experience without distracting the focus from the client.

The counsellor can help the client to:

1 Actualize and accept the reality of the loss (whether this is bereavement, broken relationships or physical change).

2 Identify, focus on and experience the pain of grief.

3 Adjust to life as it is now, without the loved one or in the changed circumstances.

4 Get in touch with inner resources, e.g. by reality testing and drawing attention to achievements.

5 Redirect emotional energies from the deceased one or 'life as it was', and reinvest energies in new relationships and life interests.

Stages of grief

Various stages of grief have been identified by grief therapists writing on the subject. There can be considerable movement between the stages – all of which are normal. Variously they have been described as follows.

The initial stage

In the first stages of grief recognized normal reactions include: shock, denial, unreality, emotional outpourings, psychological and physical symptoms (e.g. inability to think straight, feeling panicky, bodily aches and pains, depression).

The middle stage

While the first stage consists of immediate, shocked grief responses, the middle stage relates to expectations and disappointments of ourselves and others; these include:

guilt – e.g. we could have done so much more for the other person;

anger – e.g. at self and deceased for envisaged inadequacies in the relationship;

resentment towards the deceased – e.g. they have left behind the one who is still living;

idealism – the deceased was a 'perfect' person.

The last stage

The final stage represents the resolution of grief – a realistic coming to terms with the life and death of the loved one:

the realistic overview – e.g. 'I did what I could' for the deceased, 'She was a lovely person but could also be difficult at times', appreciating both positive and negative aspects of their lives;

acceptance – e.g. understanding of the person's death, that they are no longer physically present in the person's life, letting go;

readjustment and emotional investment – e.g. moving on;

personal growth – the client's development of a stronger inner self, acknowledging, appreciating and cherishing the contributions the deceased person made in the client's life and an internalization of the person.

Supporting roles

It is the opinion of grief therapists that no specialized skills are needed when working with grief. The process of grieving requires time and the free expression of thoughts and emotions. The main thing is just being there with the client, acknowledging and supporting them through their expressions of grief, listening, using reflecting skills and gently encouraging them to get in touch with and explore their feelings to assist with actualizing the loss. Person-centred skills are particularly important, especially empathic responding. Because people are vulnerable when they hold on to deeply painful emotions, the counsellor's ability to convey acceptance and to hold and contain the client's catharsis of grief is all important. In the Western world we tend to hurry most experiences along, including those in the areas of self-care and reflection. 'Normal' life calls us back to work, to relating to others – even those close to the person who mourns may give a time limit, expecting the person to recover from the loss in as short a time as a few weeks. Individual need and expression is, more often than not, subjugated to conventional ideas of normality and 'getting on with life'.

In *Death – the Final Stage of Growth*, Rabbi Zachary Heller looks at the support systems religious communities offer. For example, he writes about the Jewish way of mourning as a collective experience. Jewish tradition confronts death directly; the loved ones of the terminally ill person 'surround, comfort and encourage the patient'. The deathbed confessional as a rite of passage allows the dying person to express any residual concerns and fears. The ceremonial involvement of family and community is a comfort to those who survive, children included. The Jewish tradition of maintaining a vigil at the bedside of the dying is of immense value, both for the dying person and those about to face bereavement. Judaism shields mourners from being overwhelmed by guilt because the community shares in the care of the dying. The Jewish mourner is not protected from the death of the loved one, being called on to make funeral arrangements at the beginning of the grief process.

Religion may be or not be a comfort to the mourner, but it is important that the counsellor respects the person's religious beliefs. When the client is from a different culture it would be helpful if the counsellor familiarizes themselves with the practices and customs surrounding death. It can be a source of distress to the surviving members of a family if the person has not been treated with respect in accordance with the traditions of their culture, in hospital, on their deathbed or in funeral arrangements. For example, the dying Muslim patient will wish to face Mecca to die, and may wish to have a relative whisper the call to prayer or family members to recite prayers. If none of this is done it can complicate the grief process.

As we have seen, many complex feelings are involved in loss of any kind. These include abandonment – being left behind; anxiety – about coping without the person or with the disability or the impoverished circumstance; sadness – at the loss and the separation, yearning for and missing the person; and fearfulness – of facing life in this new situation. The subject of fear is not widely addressed in association with mourning, yet it is a primary emotion which feeds the other emotions. People may be fearful that they will be alone, will have no one to love them, that they can't look after themselves, can't manage financially; or they may fear their own impending death.

Depression

The depressed person is likely to be fearful about life ahead and may be constantly defeated by irrational thoughts and beliefs such as 'my life is over'. The woman who has recently undergone a hysterectomy may consider herself to be no longer fully a woman. Underneath these thoughts lie fears of leading a lonely, meaningless or impoverished life. The elderly survivor may feel that since their spouse has died they have nothing to look forward to but joining the deceased. When a person's spouse dies, they often have real worries that they might be unable to cope alone with day-to-day practicalities of life, like paying bills, mending appliances and running a home. This is exacerbated by physical symptoms such as listlessness. Feelings of dependency may result in anger: 'How could he leave me with this financial mess?', 'I don't know where anything is; my wife used to do all that.' A child whose parent has died may fear that they have somehow killed the parent. Fear issues need to be addressed before a person can move on; the counsellor can challenge these thoughts by normalizing the person's beliefs as normal and appropriate to hold, but also help the client to 'reality' check. The term 'irrational' is perhaps misleading in this context because feelings of inadequacy and dependency on the lost person (or object) are a normal stage to go through. The counsellor's acceptance of these, conveyed by empathic responding and verbal acknowledgement of fears, frees the client to express associated emotions.

Reality testing

This is a method of challenging the client to look at their 'one-sided' thinking. For example, someone who experiences guilt turns in on themselves and believes that they have been neglectful of the deceased, telling themselves that they should have done more, even to the point of thinking that their neglect had indirectly or directly caused the death. In relation to the example of Susan, who blamed herself for being a bad mother, the 'reality testing' came in the form of asking her what she did with the child and what her relationship with him was like. By re-exploring many details of occurrences in his short life she could appreciate that she had on the whole been a very attentive, loving mother. Sometimes reality testing may involve the counsellor (sensitively) providing specific information which contradicts an irrational belief or challenging the client to check medical facts with a physician. For example, Susan may have thought she was physically unable to have another fully healthy baby (genetic factors), and a woman who has had a hysterectomy may have believed that her sex life was over.

The letter and the empty chair technique

The letter and empty chair are simple techniques which have been used effectively to help the grieving person to resolve 'unfinished business' and say goodbye to the person who has died. As a first step the counsellor can ask the client if they would like to write a letter to the deceased to say all that they want to say, identifying unresolved issues – perhaps what they wished they had been able to say to the person when they were still alive – as a way of saying goodbye. It is important that the counsellor doesn't give too many suggestions about what the letter might contain – it needs to come from them. It is up to the client what they do with the letter. Some people may find the writing down of their thoughts, feelings and wishes enough to bring relief, but bringing the letter to a counselling session is also presented as a possibility.

The technique of the empty chair has been explained in Chapter 10. To recap, the client addresses an empty chair as if the person they are addressing was sitting there. The client is then able to talk to the person. In the letter and empty chair technique the client can read out the letter, addressing the person who is imagined to be in the chair. The client can express strong emotions such as anger, resentment, bitterness, guilt, love and tenderness through these media. This technique is particularly helpful to clients who are finding it difficult to get in touch with their grief and are harbouring complex and debilitating emotions.

An example from my own counselling experiencing was a young woman whose brother had killed himself in particularly tragic circumstances a year before she sought out help. The letter writing, followed up by reading out the letter in therapy using the empty chair method, released an immense amount of guilty feelings (she should have helped him more) and also angry feelings (how could he do that to her and the rest of his family) – which proved to be cathartic for her. Often grief is hard to resolve because of the ambivalent feelings felt towards the dead person; this is especially true when a person has taken their own life.

To sum up, there are many reasons for unresolved or complicated grief. Possible reasons include:

- ■ Cultural issues – not being able to mourn or carry out ceremonies in a way that is appropriate to a religion or culture.
- ■ Shut-down time – not enough time has been allowed (because of self-censuring or the requirements of others) to grieve.

- Lack of support and understanding from others – a lonely experience, accompanied by emotional withdrawal.
- Ambivalent feelings towards the deceased person – resulting in an idealized view of the dead person – or unresolved issues between the two at time of death.
- Complicated guilt feelings – often related to those above; watching the dying person suffer; in cases of suicide, not being able to say goodbye – the person who is left behind wishes they had been able to tell the dying person that they loved them or to say goodbye in a way which would be meaningful to them (e.g. having input in the funeral ceremony).
- Inability to accept the person is gone – related to shock and denial, especially with sudden death through accident or illness.

The suicidal client

In the spirit of a mini-research project over a period of time, I asked a number of people what they thought a counsellor's role was with regard to people who say they are contemplating suicide. All but a few said, in varying ways, that it was the counsellor's job to stop those persons from killing themselves by making them feel better about themselves or their life situation. Some said words to the effect that the suicidal person should be made to understand how devastated the people they leave behind would feel; a few advocated strong intervention strategies. Generally, people have strong reactions to the subject of suicide. The question 'Does a person have the right to choose to end their life?' brings up uncomfortable feelings for most of us. Having someone say to us, 'I really don't want to live any more' is a challenging situation. It would be wise to examine our personal attitudes and beliefs with regard to suicide before we are faced with a client who says just that. Take time to think over the following questions.

■ Do you think it is a person's right to choose?

■ Do you think that intervention – e.g. hospitalization, psychiatric treatment – is justifiable when suicide is inferred?

■ Do you think the person contemplating suicide is incapable of making a considered choice?

■ Do you think suicide is wrong, an act of selfish self-pitying?

Now, replacing the word 'think' with 'feel', work your way through these questions again.

The counsellor's anxiety

It is a normal reaction to feel anxious at the thought of another human being ending their life. Not surprisingly, counsellors may feel swamped by feelings of responsibility for the fate of the client. Anxiety can cause the counsellor to collude with the client by intervening with a change of subject or promoting a positive attitude towards life. Anxiety is often linked to impossible expectations of ourselves as counsellors. Individual counsellors need to assess their experience and training and accept their limitations. We actually do the other person an injustice if we attempt to work at levels beyond our experience and capabilities. It may be appropriate, for new counsellors especially, to refer on. The first time a client reveals that they intend to kill themselves, the new counsellor's functioning is likely to be impeded by 'self-talk' like, 'If they kill themselves, I'll be blamed.' Other irrational self-statements may go something like:

1 I am personally responsible if the client takes their life.

2 If I am a competent counsellor I can persuade them to change their mind.

3 Through the therapeutic relationship I can give them a sense of self-worth and save them.

Are these types of self-statements realistic? Examine any irrational beliefs you might hold on the subject of the counsellor's responsibility towards suicidal clients and replace them with realistic ones, taking into account the client's responsibilities and free choice. All talk containing suicidal intention needs to be taken seriously. People do make repeated attempts at killing themselves and some succeed. They may be cries for help or they may equally be considered decisions that the person has made having weighed up the pros and cons of their life situations.

Some of the reasons and situations of suicidal intention

The suicidal cry for help

This might come from the person who repeatedly thinks of killing themselves but has not attempted to do so to date. Suicidal references are a plea to be heard and responded to in relation to the pain and inner turmoil a person is experiencing and can only express in imagery of self-destruction. The person feels alone and may be holding a great deal of unexpressed anger, resentment and frustration towards themselves and others. The person may feel persecuted or unloved. There can be an underlying wish to control or manipulate the behaviour of those close to them – 'I'll make them see what they've done to me', 'I'll make them sorry.' It would be a mistake to dismiss the person as merely attention seeking. The number of young males committing suicide is disproportionally high in most societies. This may be due to many reasons, but is likely to be related in some way to internalized pressures and expectations of family and society. The pressure to 'succeed' in life can cause tremendous stress and the person who in his own eyes consistently underachieves, failing to live up to his own or others' expectations, can suffer from chronic low self-esteem. The suicidal person usually feels that they, and their lives, have little value or meaning.

The crisis situation

Another reason a person may have suicidal thoughts is a desperate reaction to trauma or a crisis situation. For example, they may arise when a person close to them dies; they feel they 'can't go on' without them. The survivor may be in a state of shock and feel that the only solution to the desperate psychological pain they are experiencing is to end their life. A further instance of this crisis category is the person who loses all material wealth or is shamed or outcast by their community and has no sense of 'place' or worth.

> An example of the latter was a client I saw, an Indian woman who had been ostracized by her community for leaving her husband, taking their two children with her. Her husband had been abusive – physically, sexual and mentally – and her self-worth was very low. Her decision to leave the comfortable middle-class family home meant that she was, along with her two young children, living under great duress, with Social Security funding, in temporary accommodation. In this atmosphere she felt she couldn't go on; she felt diminished in the eyes of her community and of society, and she had no self-respect and no hope of providing adequately for her children. She felt doubly oppressed and discriminated against, as a member of an ethnic minority group by society as a whole, and as a rejected member of her community and culture.

Quality of life

Those who experience poor quality of life and who have no chance of improving their situation – including the heavily disabled person, people who are terminally ill and those who live with continuous terrible pain – may have weighed up their situation and having taken into account all considerations decided that they want to put an end to their lives. What is the position of the counsellor in this case? What may be a temptation is to attempt to buoy the person up or to deflect what they are conveying, to make both of you more comfortable, when what is needed is to stay in the feeling world of the client, to give them a full opportunity to state their desperate state of mind and the pain and hopelessness they are feeling.

It can also be helpful to explore with the person what they do value in life, what it might be hard to leave behind if they did decide to end their lives. Appropriate questions may reveal, for example, that the person feels that they are a terrible burden on a carer and it may be appropriate to 'reality test'. The client may also like to talk about dying and religious beliefs. The topic of dying is still a taboo subject for most people and a person contemplating dying can find much relief in talking to another person who does not shy away from the reality. Details like these may be enough to highlight that there are some ambivalent feelings about living. The people in the above situations are liable to be depressed because of their dire conditions; some types of depression require medical treatment. If depression is linked with indications of mental illness such as hearing voices that instruct the person to end their lives, then the client needs to see a doctor immediately. The counsellor needs to be aware of the medical history and any medication the client is currently taking. Mostly people who talk about suicide have a considerable ambivalence about wanting to die – some may see it as the only solution at the moment, others who have considerable physical difficulty and live daily with heavy pain have made a considered and conscious decision.

Possible reasons for the client to relate suicidal intentions:

1 They feel overwhelmed by their problems and are unable to see any other solution.

2 They feel alone and unloved.

3 They see no value in themselves or their life.

4 A 'cry for help' – they are emotionally disturbed, fearful that they may kill themselves and want to be stopped.

5 A way of saying goodbye, a preparation for death.

6 An imploding expression of anger: revenge on others.

7 The person is suffering from mental illness and needs medical help – e.g. referral to a psychiatrist; they may hear a voice telling them to kill themselves, suggesting schizophrenia.

8 To manipulate the actions or attitudes of others.

9 Because they have decided to end their life, having considered it carefully. They are sure they want to do it and would like others to understand, respect and accept the reasons for the decision.

10 To have supportive contact with another person before dying.

11 To 'admit' to suicidal thoughts/considerations – bringing them out in the open (there may be ambivalence about dying).

12 To seek help and affirmation or confirmation of self-worth.

13 A reaction to crisis.

How can a counsellor help?

Firstly, the counsellor needs to keep in focus how vulnerable the client is and strike a balance between sensitivity and mild challenging. The counsellor can help the client to clarify and make thoughts concrete, in particular by being aware of 'clues' – what is being implicitly said and asking the client about feelings, especially angry ones. The counsellor can be direct and say, 'Are you saying that you are having thoughts of killing yourself?' Without trying to change the person's mind about whether their life is worth living or not, the counsellor can help them to explore relationships or the problems they are experiencing. Because there are many taboos generally around the subject of suicide it is helpful to encourage the client to talk about their self-destructive thoughts, bringing them out into the open. Empathic, attentive responding will give the client a sense that what they are revealing is acceptable in that you are able to hear it and contain it, being neither shocked nor overwhelmed by it. As a counsellor, be aware of both your own body language and that of the client, looking for signs of stress, awkwardness or withholding of feelings. It may be appropriate to self-disclose; for example, if you become aware that the client has become very anxious, you might say, 'I'm aware it is very difficult for you to talk about your feelings and I am aware of my anxiety too.' The person who feels suicidal usually feels very isolated and genuineness and warmth from the counsellor may be the only nurturing they are receiving. Your conveyed concern will give them a sense of being valued, which is likely to be something they are presently lacking.

Self-harm

Self-harming comes in many guises, but always involves some form of sustained injury such as cutting, bruising or burning. It is not an easy means of self-expression for others (non-harmers) to understand. What makes a person cut their own arms or burn holes in parts of their bodies, or bang their head repeatedly against a wall?

A very high percentage of young people who have been abused go on to self-harm. It has been described as an attempt to express the unspeakable, a way of 'letting bad out', of telling the world what has happened to the victim. Although the injuries are usually hidden under clothing, the abuse experienced is re-enacted in a different form and 'written on the body'. For example, some women will cut or burn themselves on parts of their bodies where the initial abuse and injury was carried out.

Issues of control

Some people who self-harm have spoken of letting something out from their inner world. Others see self-harming as a way of taking control; their body or mind was hurt by other people in the past and by doing something to themselves they then appropriate the ability to injure by owning the act. Instead of 'our secret' of sexual abuse, the injury becomes 'my secret'. It is also a way of feeling 'alive'. A young client told me that after she cut herself (usually on her lower arms), 'I know that I exist – I see the blood coming out and I feel better.' The person often experiences signs of acute disassociation with their feeling world of emotions, and from other people who know nothing of their experiences. Self-harming is, for some, a way of registering and controlling boundaries between the internal and external world. The 'marking' or scarring that ensues after injury is also regarded as a form of branding, saying 'This happened – I am affected for life.'

Shame

Often people feel great shame and hide their injuries. Although great relief often follows the act, the effects of the act perpetuate self-disgust.

To the outside observer self-harm or injury may seem punitive and self-destructive, but we must remember that it is a mode of survival. Sometimes when an individual is rushed to hospital with a severe cut or burn, doctors and nurses mistake the act as a suicide failure or dismiss it as a manipulative attention-seeking behaviour.

Anger and depression

Counsellors and other therapists working with clients who self-harm say that self-hate and self-disgust are always contributing factors. The client experiences numbing depression and loss of a sense of self. They may be stuck on self-thoughts of 'Who am I?' or 'I am worthless.' The initial harm done to them has been taken into their bodies (internalized) and there they hold the anger until they 'let it out'. The survivor of sexual, physical or emotional abuse may be angry at themselves for 'allowing' the injustices to happen to them, as well as angry at the perpetrator. Instead of 'acting out' the anger on the person or persons involved, they express it towards their own bodies. Because children are often the targets of abuse of various kinds, being defenceless and malleable, they have no resources to deal with either the perpetrator of the act or the act itself. Subsequently feelings of powerlessness extend into adulthood and the revenge is enacted on the victim's own body, reflecting the accumulation of self-hatred. As a child they had no one to talk to, or any other way to relieve their distress and confusion.

Frequency

Self-harm takes on many forms, involving cutting, burning, scratching or injuring the body in any way. One of my clients banged her head against a wall or punched herself when she was distressed. Injuries are usually carried out on parts of the body that can be hidden – for example, the inside of arms or legs – and for this reason it can be shrouded by secrecy. A person may self-injure several times in the same day or once a month – frequency is variable, depending on situations, triggering events and emotional reaction.

The cycle of self-harm and self-care

For some people the post-care of their injury offers solace – a nurturing they lack in their lives. Just as the body has become a focus of punishment, it then becomes a focus of caring in changing bandages, cleaning the wounds, applying ointments. Although this may initially be done by another person, perhaps a nurse or helper, some people take comfort in nursing their wounds. A 'split off' part of themselves – a part that loves and respects themselves – comes into play to care for the abused, hurt part of the self.

Who self-harms?

At one time medical health professionals thought that it was predominantly young females of between the ages of 15 and 25 who self-harmed, and variance from this pattern seemed rare. Psychiatrists, clinical psychologists and others working in the mental health field regarded self-harm to be linked to the young women's maladaptive approach to sexuality. Yet a considerable number of men self-harm too; it affects both sexes across the age groups.

A counsellor who worked in a telephone crisis centre told me that she had experience of women in their 70s calling when they had self-harmed. Diane Harrison, author of *Vicious Circles*, works as a counsellor with those who self-harm and is herself a survivor of many years of self-injury. She has told me that carers of the elderly note how some older people who have become highly dependent on others begin to self-harm, possibly as an expression of frustration, in the form of scratching themselves or knocking and bruising their hand or legs against bed frames or pulling their catheters out. Lack of self-worth, loss of autonomy or having little regard or respect from others are possibly contributing factors.

In an article in *Openmind* (1994), the mental health magazine, Diane Harrison expresses some of the complex feelings associated with self-harm:

> Self harm is about getting through each moment. It is a symbolic language from the unconscious where you are trying to tell yourself what is going on inside even though you can't make the conscious links. It can be a way of trying to rid yourself of dirty feelings inside that seem to take over, like a poison. The pain and rage finds an outlet through self mutilation, even though women are often unaware that they

are angry at all. Men who self injure tend to be more overtly angry and may be more open to talking about it.

Responses to self-injury

Unhelpful responses include:

A shocked reaction
An angry reaction
Criticism – regarding self-harm as attention seeking or manipulative
Any kind of punitive measure
Contracts that insist that the person agrees not to self-harm
Bombarding with questions
Avoidance – minimizing or dismissing self-injuries

Helpful responses include:

Being warm, accepting and supportive of where the client is now
Maintaining clear boundaries – be clear about what you or your agency can offer
Taking the self-harming seriously – facing it with the client
Empathic responding, conveying concern
Thinking of self-harm as a consequence of trauma and an expression of a trauma continuum
Being clear about agency policies and guidelines
Being 'real', honest, congruent with the client (holding on to negative feelings)
Exploring 'buttons' or 'triggers' – patterns of behaviour
Exploring existing coping strategies and establishing new supportive ones
Helping the client bring the 'secret' world of self-harm into the room, in relationship with the counsellor
Developing a trusting environment for client exploration and disclosure

Some of the reasons given for self-harming

Feelings that precipitated the action:

■ Painful emotions – grief, sadness, desperation, helplessness, hopelessness

■ Anger – rage, frustration, powerlessness, injustice
■ Anxiety – fear, panic, stress, tension
■ Self-hatred – shame, 'contaminated', dirty, guilt
■ Unreality – numbness, dead, unconnected, alienated
■ Loneliness – unsupported, lack of contact, unheard, unloved

Effects of the act of self-harm:

■ Outlet for feelings – relief, expression, externalization of pain, soothing, distracting
■ Control – of body or self, owning the anger, repulsing the abuser
■ Self-punishment – cutting out 'bad' or 'dirty' parts, atonement (linked to guilt)
■ Feel alive – reconnecting with feeling world
■ Communication – way of telling others about emotions and problems

What can help the counsellor

To help you manage the feelings that cutting or other forms of self-injury evoke in you:

■ Use supervision and group support to discuss difficulties.
■ Try to respond – not react.
■ Recognize powerful feelings evoked – be prepared to look at them, not deny or push them to the back of your mind.
■ Ask yourself questions about your feelings, questions like:
  – What is it about self-harm that threatens me?
  – What do I bring to this experience from my past?
  – What does being in control of oneself mean to me?

You may hold polarized views about rescuing or rejecting. Part of you may want to rescue the person; another part may want to reject the person. You may feel repulsed or afraid. Try to see the whole person, not just the injury or scars. Appreciate that the self-harm is there for a purpose and has helped the individual survive.

A clinical psychologist would use behavioural techniques such as asking the client to keep a diary as a means of monitoring self-harming episodes, noting thoughts and feelings that precipitate the injuring, what the client is feeling during the actual harming and what feelings follow on, and finding other channels of expression. Some counsellors consider these methods to be superficial, that emphasis on 'cure' and methods of stopping the behaviour ignores underlying associated feelings. Failure to comply with behavioural programmes can, where the symptom is regarded as the problem, lead to the withdrawal of help. If the person continues to self-harm in this climate of expectancy, the feelings of self-disgust and failure become re-enforced.

Above all, make sure you, the counsellor, are working at a level you are comfortable with. You will be working with distressful and powerful feelings. It is important to acknowledge your own limitations and refer on if necessary. It may be appropriate to give the client information about other agencies and about crisis services.

Clients express their emotions in different ways: anger, hostility, emotional pain and sadness can be expressed overtly or as a 'baseline'. The client may seem detached, sullen or depressed. The counsellor can easily be drawn into the client's feelings of hopelessness or feel overawed by the client's problems or inadequate. In the countertransference the counsellor can feel weighed down or that they have to be all powerful for the client or a nurturer. Nurturing can be useful, but a counsellor needs to be realistic about what they (or the agency or organization) can offer; otherwise they will be restricted by an unrealistic wish to fulfil all the client's needs. For example, the counsellor probably cannot be with the distressed or suicidal person for more than an hour a week and therefore a network of support is needed for the client. In this case the counsellor can make sure that they and the client have identified other support systems. This could involve a key social worker, a doctor or a specialist agency. Counsellors can prepare themselves for demanding client work by building an awareness of helping techniques, strategies and interventions to give the client the feeling of being therapeutically 'held'. Counsellors also need to look after themselves when counselling people who have experienced deep trauma and emotionally discharge in sessions. Adequate supervision is necessary for the holding quality it offers the counsellor (see the 'parallel process' in Chapter 7). The supervisor will be aware of the potential impact of working with high levels of client distress. For example, a client's grief may set off feelings of grief in the counsellor in relation to a past loss.

Abuse

The person who thinks about or attempts suicide, the person who self-harms, the person who has problems with their expression of anger and the person who has suffered abuse all usually have low self-esteem and sometimes feel extremes of self-hatred. Past abuse may be at the root of their problems. Prolonged repeated abuse is likely to seriously damage a person's sense of self-worth. In *Counselling Adults who were Abused as Children* Peter Dale draws our attention to the fact that 'there are no commonly accepted definitions of abuse'. The main categories given below can be extended to include mental abuse and others more specific to the individual experience. Dr Alice Miller, who was a practising psychoanalyst for twenty years, holds the conviction that methods of conventional child rearing and education effectively thwart self-expression of the child, and that it is commonplace and in fact an accepted part of Western societal norms that adults bully, criticize and humiliate children.

Those who suffer abuse from others are often children or adults who are physically and mentally less strong than the perpetrator of the abuse. The victims have learned first hand, sometimes at an early age, that adults and other people are untrustworthy, cruel and unpredictable. The most difficult aspect of the abuse is that it usually comes from the people who are expected, by society and by the child, to love, care for and protect the child. The child who sustains physical injury or endures sexual abuse feels 'all mixed up' (as one client put it) in their feelings towards the perpetrator, who may be a parent or some other member of the family. Because of the complexity of feelings the sufferer experiences – which might include love, hate, anger, helplessness, vulnerability and self-disgust – the child or young person keeps the abuse hidden. After all, if they can hardly believe it is happening then how will others believe it?

Definition of abuse

Four main categories of child abuse are commonly cited: neglect, physical injury, sexual abuse and emotional abuse.

1 *Neglect*: The persistent or severe neglect of a child, or the failure to protect a child from exposure to any kind of danger, including cold or starvation, or extreme failure to carry out important aspects of care, resulting in the significant impairment of the child's health or development, including non-organic failure to thrive.

2 *Physical injury*: Actual or likely physical injury to a child, or failure to prevent physical injury (or suffering) to a child, including deliberate poisoning, suffocation and Munchausen's syndrome by proxy.

3 *Sexual abuse*: Actual or likely sexual exploitation of a child or adolescent. The child may be dependent and/or developmentally immature.

4 *Emotional abuse*: Actual or likely severe adverse effect on the emotional and behavioural development of a child caused by persistent or severe emotional ill treatment or rejection. All abuse involves some emotional ill treatment. This category is often used where it is the main or sole form of abuse.

(Supplied by Social Services – Child Protection Unit, 1999.)

Confidentiality and client disclosure

Children under 17 are protected by the law and other social constructs designed to safeguard the child. A counsellor needs to be aware of legal obligations and implications of working with those who have been or are presently being abused in any of the above categories. Remember too that these categories can merge; for example, a person may suffer physical, emotional/mental and sexual abuse.

Counsellors, whether working with young people privately or with an agency within Social Service settings, are required to have the relevant skills and knowledge of appropriate procedures to implement action if abuse is disclosed. It is ethical practice, during an intake session or at the onset of therapy, to give clients information regarding the service offered so that the client understands what to expect, what counselling involves. The counsellor should address the where, when and how concerns. The client's history, family details and other relevant details are also taken. It is at this time that the issue of confidentiality needs to be raised. It should be made clear to the client that, although the service offered is in the main part confidential, there are circumstances under which confidentiality may not apply. It should be explained in advance of any disclosure that if the counsellor thinks that something the client has told them suggests that the client or another young person in the family is in immediate or potential danger then other authorities may have to be involved. The client would be assured that if the counsellor decides that a situation necessitates the passing on of disclosed information to other parties, which may be consulting with a colleague or supervisor as a first step, the client would be told of this move prior to its happening.

Working with young children who have experienced abuse is highly specialized work, requiring specific training in the sensitive responding to the problem. The newly trained counsellor who is setting up in private practice needs to consider carefully the responsibilities that accompany working with children and young people. It is a complex area of counselling and there are many issues to become acquainted with, with regard to how and when information is passed on to child protection agencies within Social Services, which may lead to police involvement and giving evidence in court proceedings.

Survivors of abuse

The remainder of this discussion will focus on the adult client who has experienced abuse either in childhood or as an adult. Some clients decide to have counselling following the advice of a social worker or a doctor, some self-refer. The reasons they give for deciding to have counselling sometimes conceal a history of abuse;

self-harming and suicide attempts or suicidal thoughts can be a consequence of abuse. In the case of sexual abuse, the victim may have never told another person. Multiple physical abuse is hard to conceal; usually others in the family, friends or neighbours are aware of it. A social worker or doctor who is unaware of the abuse history may refer the person to counselling because they demonstrate antisocial behaviour, or are suffering from depression.

Trust

Trust is a central issue with most people who have experienced abuse of any kind, and possibly more so when the abuse experienced was sexual. It is acknowledged that children are unable to fend for themselves or stand up to their abusers. The victims of abuse often have to rely on the people who abuse them to 'care' for them in fundamental ways – to feed, clothe and house them. The result is an uncomfortable dynamic between loving and hating the perpetrator of the abuse. The child's perception of what is appropriate behaviour becomes blurred as boundaries and roles are transgressed. It can be difficult to form a working alliance with the abused child part of the adult client who demonstrates a low tolerance level for intimate personal interaction. It will be difficult to trust a warm, positive regard from the counsellor if the client has been consistently humiliated and criticized or has had their trust betrayed. The consequence is an inability to trust or a tendency to trust indiscriminately. It is necessary to maintain clear boundaries because the client may have little sense of what is appropriate behaviour. They may demonstrate a compliant 'learned helplessness', being unable to assert autonomy and remaining highly dependent on others in meeting the challenges of everyday living or for feelings of self-worth; or reveal the 'caretaking syndrome', compulsively assuming responsibility for the needs of others as a way of attaining self-worth and control. The abused child sometimes displays a pseudo-maturity at a cost to their own developmental needs. Learning assertiveness skills can be useful in identifying and understanding personal needs, boundaries and how to assert the self positively.

Sexual abuse

The experience of sexual abuse in childhood can lead to sexual dysfunctioning later in life, manifesting as promiscuity, oversexualization or the repression of a sexual identity. The stress is on the word 'can', because there is documented evidence that not all individuals who have been abused benefit from therapy in later life. Some people are fortunate enough to establish loving relationships with others, including satisfactory sexual relationships, but many others have difficulties in establishing a sexual identity that they themselves are happy with. As children their experience of sexuality was confusing and frightening, often involving secrecy, threats and hostility. There can be a propensity to self-blame: 'I could have stopped it', or 'I sometimes had an orgasm, so it was my fault too.' They may consider themselves to be 'damaged goods' and associate sex and sexuality with hostility, fear and guilt. As an adult the victim of sexual abuse may find it very difficult to trust both their own expressions of sexuality and those of their partner in a loving context. Parenting can also bring back past complex associated anxieties: for example, a mother who was sexually abused by her father may fear that her husband will do the same to their daughter.

Power issues

The person who has been abused physically, emotionally or sexually is likely to have reservations about trusting those whom they regard as in a role of authority – including a counsellor, who may be experienced in the transference either as a potential abuser or another link in a chain of bureaucracy, part of a system alongside social workers, doctors and other 'official' figures. One of the key rules is that a counsellor should never put words into a person's mouth, even when they think that the client is giving strong hints that there has been abuse in their background. Rather than ask probing intrusive questions, the counsellor needs to let the person unfold what has happened to them in their own way. Since they haven't been able to own what happened to them emotionally, physically or sexually in the past, it is important that they own the experience of disclosing what they choose to. For example, when the client says, 'My father refused to put a lock on the bathroom door and when Mum wasn't around he would come in when I was having a bath', an appropriate response from the counsellor could be: 'He didn't respect your privacy ...' or 'It seems to me completely understandable that at that age you would expect to be able to take a bath in privacy' (the second response 'normalizes' the client's feelings, encouraging her to go on if she chooses to). An inappropriate response would be if the counsellor asked, 'Did he touch you?' or 'Was he sexual with you?'

While a counsellor needs to be aware of the dangers of being intrusive, too direct or voyeuristic, they also need to convey to the client that the material is bearable to hear. The countertransference feelings can be the 'good parent' who will not abuse but who also will not engage enough with the client to encourage them to talk as freely as they wish to. Another possible countertransferential response could be that the counsellor feels abusive or powerful in response to the client's expectations of potential abuse. Abuse experienced in the counselling setting by the client can entail feeling humiliated, criticized, punished or having their feelings dismissed. These issues need discussing and careful monitoring with the supervisor. In *Against Therapy*, Jeffrey Masson, who was a practising psychoanalyst for some years, has chronicled details of how eminent analysts have abused their position with their patients or clients. These include Fritz Perls – who, according to Masson, had sexual relations with many of his female clients. Counselling organizations stipulate the inappropriateness of a counsellor engaging in a sexual relationship with a client and a counsellor member who does invites official disqualification from membership and accreditation. It is recognized that a client is in a disadvantaged position when they put their trust in a counsellor, being in a disempowered and vulnerable state.

An integrative approach

Increasingly it is acknowledged that no one approach to therapy is complete in relation to depressive states. The person who has been the victim of abuse suffers 'real harm' – mental and emotional distress. Since mind, body and spirit are all involved, various approaches contribute to healing. The psychoanalytic/ psychodynamic models, survivor/recovery models (which encourage group support) and eclectic/integrative models are amongst the theoretical approaches described in clinical literature. The psychodynamic model offers an object/relations insight through 'attachment theory', transferential material and the sensitive working with defences; for example, denial – 'It didn't affect me much', repression – 'I don't remember a lot about what happened in my childhood', minimizing – 'It wasn't full sex; other people have to put up with much worse', rationalization – 'I must have encouraged it', disassociation/splitting – 'I used to think about something else when it was happening, I didn't feel anything.'

The person-centred core conditions model provides a safe environment, a warm non-judgemental and accepting relationship in which the client can talk openly, exploring the reality of their experiences and creating new meaning. In contrast with the abstinent stance of the psychodynamic mode of counselling, the person-centred paradigm offers an opportunity for the client to improve on interpersonal and social skills. Adopting the person-centred values, the counsellor reassures and encourages the client to be more self-affirming; for example, 'It wasn't your fault – it was wrong of the person to take advantage of you. You were a child.' An adult, perhaps a woman who is the victim of her husband's violent aggression who rationalizes the situation by saying, 'It's probably my own fault, I make him go mad – I deserve it', may be equally reassured by the counsellor's assurance that she is not responsible for acts of aggression towards her.

The cognitive-behavioural approach addresses the learned and maladaptive responses towards others in relation to the acts of aggression and exploitation experienced and the potential to re-enact dysfunctional modes of relating within the social environment. Cognitive states are challenged by focusing on self-defeating, distorted thinking patterns and replacing these with more realistic perceptions with regard to what happened and to the individual's low self-esteem. Behavioural difficulties, learning difficulties and lack of social skills are all possible effects of abuse.

Themes of therapy include:

■ Physical
  – the individual's ownership of and respect for their own body

- developing a sense of appropriate boundaries and ways of relating to others in interpersonal contact

■ Emotional
- helping the client to express freely and explore their emotional inner world
- helping the client to release and express anger
- helping the client to express and accept ambivalent feelings with regard to the abuser
- conveying to the client that they are valued and accepted as a worthwhile person
- providing a holding and containing safe environment in which fear is reduced
- helping the client make contact with the survivor resourceful side of themselves
- developing a capacity to trust self and others

■ Mental
- changing distorted thinking, perceptions and imaging (e.g. not 'damaged goods' or a 'despicable person') and negative automatic thoughts
- clarifying responsibility issues – who did what to whom?
- developing a survivor consciousness – proud of their achievements in surviving
- increasing self-esteem/self-worth
- increasing contact with adult coping self and inner locus of evaluation
- developing autonomy and personal integrity

■ Social context
- increasing social skills
- use of appropriate boundaries
- appropriate behaviour
- self-mastery
- increasing interpersonal skills
- encouraging assertive behaviour

12 | CULTURAL ISSUES

Background

An awareness of the need to address cultural concerns grew in the counselling and psychotherapy world in the 1960s and 1970s in the climate of equal opportunities, when racial inequalities also became a focus of concern. At this time counsellors attempted to develop and integrate an awareness of cultural considerations in training and practice. It has been acknowledged that in multicultural societies counsellors often work with clients from a variety of cultural backgrounds. Working within counselling with persons from a different culture has been termed 'transcultural', cross-cultural and intercultural counselling. The multicultural approach, so termed by P. Pedersen in 1991 (see **Suggested further reading**), recognizes that membership of a particular culture influences psychological development and personal identity, and acknowledges that emotional or behavioural problems can reflect the cultural milieu of the client. It rejects an ethnocentric approach, whereby cultural differences are perceived as deviations from the 'norm' of a dominant culture.

The concept of culture

The concept of culture is complex and multidimensional. The cultural dimension of human experience affects behaviour and relational patterns, and encompasses the way an individual has constructed 'selfhood' in relation to how they perceive – for example – reality or morality, both of which are likely to be viewed differently by a collectivist or individualistic culture. The complexities of cultural diversity therefore have important implications for counselling. Counselling calls for sensitivity to the possible ways in which different cultures express themselves in their outer and inner worlds. It is unrealistic to expect counsellors to be experts in different cultural orientations. Social anthropologists are of the opinion that unless a person is immersed in a particular culture for a considerable length of time they will be unable to understand fully the social networks, use of language, religious rites and myths particular to it, or to have a sensory perception of that particular milieu. In reality a counsellor will have few or no opportunities to see the client interacting within their own culture. Observation and experience of the client is likely to be restricted to the client–counsellor relationship, the counselling process and what the client chooses to reveal. However, the counsellor can become sensitized to the nuances of language, the structures and traditions through input gained directly from the client (by demonstrating genuine interest), from relevant reading matter, from other members of the culture and through art, dance, religion or other expressions of the culture. It may help the counsellor to 'enter into' the client's world, by attending a ceremony, for example. The possibility of this could first be discussed with the client, demonstrating a genuine interest and a willingness to engage in a dialogue of cultural difference.

What is useful is creating a working framework that encompasses elements of the client's world view, by which counsellors can understand how the client relates to others; that is, social behaviour, their perceptions and assumptions with regard to health, help and cure. Although there is no one 'right' way to understand a culture, working guidelines can help counsellors understand the complexity of cultural identity and the multiplicity of cultural influences. While guidelines cannot offer 'expertise' in any given culture, nor be specific to any school of counselling, they can provide a way of raising awareness about clients' cultural differences and help the counsellor to demonstrate a willingness to engage fully.

Awareness

In order that a counsellor is able to work transculturally, they need to build an awareness of the intricate and complex dynamics of the relationship between personal issues and cultural context. A counsellor working across cultures needs to understand which of the client's cultural experiences will be useful in moving the therapeutic process forward. They will need to be aware of the family and social networks of the client's culture; the religious, spiritual and ethical background of that culture; and its approach to healthcare, education and employment. The counsellor must strive to avoid 'cultural encapsulation', 'crystallization', stereotyping or making assumptions, and be aware that if family ties or religious affiliations are perceived by the client as liberating forces, the counsellor must accept this. They also need to be aware that the different ways of perceiving the world may manifest themselves in non-verbal behaviour, family patterns, gender relationships, expressions of emotion, theories of healing and issues around power.

Non-verbal and verbal behaviour

Non-verbal behaviour

Cultural practices may differ with regard to eye contact, facial expression, touch, proximity, the giving and receiving of information and gestures. For example, while in Western culture direct eye contact is considered a sign of openness, in some cultures it is regarded as an affront to dignity. Also, issues of 'modesty' may restrict both the giving and the receiving of specific information.

Verbal behaviour

Clients conditioned by a culture that cherishes individualism may express themselves in linear or logical accounts, displaying a strong sense of self as an individual with an autonomous identity; for example, I am a lawyer, my hobbies are ...; whereas the collectivist culture's form of self-expression may be more abstract, reflecting family and community orientation and collective responsibilities. Story-telling, dreams, symbols and myths are media used to relate individual experience in relation to community, identity and culture.

Emotions

People from different cultures have different ways of demonstrating emotions. Emotion is a mode of communication, and what is deemed appropriate in one culture may be inappropriate to another. Arab people, for example, can be elaborate and poetic in their interactions. People of non-Western cultures may hold a longer or shorter gaze than is usual in Western-orientated social interaction. Women may wail at a funeral in non-Western cultures in a way that diverges from Western notions of reasonable behaviour. Conversely, Westerners may appear disrespectful and inappropriately forthright to people from a different culture. There are many variants and it is folly to make assumptions about 'knowing'. Instead, take the position of a learner. A healthy curiosity and an appreciation of differences form a foundation to build on. At its best the experience is mutually enriching.

Family, community and gender roles

Community patterns of bonding and living together may vary considerably from culture to culture. These encompass notions of family, extended families, arranged marriages, child-care, inheritance and so on. It is important to take account of the structures within the client's community that serve to strengthen and support them as regards natural support systems crucial to healing or problem solving; for example, in Western societies the strongest bond or source of support is likely to be a spouse but in other cultures the strongest bond may be that of the parent and child. Gender roles differ in various cultural settings. In some traditional Asian communities the woman's role is primarily in the home as a nurturer and she has secondary status to her husband. A middle-aged Indian woman visiting a counsellor for the first time may be intimidated by a younger white 'professional' woman counsellor. Equally, a white male client may be intimidated by an older Asian female counsellor. Age, race, culture, professional standing and social status are all factors that need to be taken into account, as do the restrictive nature of conventional or traditional gender relationships within the home, family and community within the context of the majority culture of society. We must listen to and be respectful of our client's cultural norms, leaving our own values to one side. We can only be of help from the 'frame of reference' that the client normally functions within. A feminist approach to counselling wherein the client may be asked to reject patriarchal constraint could prove totally inappropriate to a female from a culture where masculine supremacy is a norm. Issues of gender inequality may be the last thing on the client's mind and would only be introduced as part of the counsellor's (inappropriate) agenda.

Healing

Each cultural group has its own methods and techniques for dealing with people who suffer emotional or psychological disorders. These attitudes may reflect the rich diversity of sources for healing available and may include traditional healing techniques and spiritual perspectives. Counsellors need to understand different cultural perceptions around the meaning of 'well being', 'illness', 'normality' and 'cure'. Increasingly, counsellors are realizing that Rudyard Kipling's adage 'East is East and West is West and never the twain shall meet' is defunct. Different therapeutic systems are not always 'worlds apart' and there is a growing awareness that an integrative approach (including the application of techniques such as yoga, meditation, body work, dreamwork, dance and sound) can have enormous possibilities and benefits in the therapeutic process. Psychosynthesis and the transpersonal approach to counselling embrace Eastern religion and philosophy and many of the above techniques.

Skills

A counsellor would be required to have reached a level of proficiency in the use and practice of theory and skills before embarking on work with persons of a different culture, for which additional skills will be required. Clearly, working with people of a different race and culture requires a flexibility of approach. The counsellor needs to be prepared to negotiate a mutually acceptable mode of working. Considerations may be how important is it for the client that the counsellor is able to converse in the client's first language or whether an interpreter is required, what would constitute helpful boundaries and the inclusion of family support during sessions. For example, in *Transcultural Counselling in Action*, Patricia d'Ardenne relates how she held an assessment session with a Bangladeshi couple who had sexual problems, in the company of their grandmother, two uncles, an aunt and a small baby. All the adult family members present at the session contributed to the assessment, offering practical help at home regarding baby-sitting and more privacy for the young couple. This is an example of how counselling can be adapted to meet the needs of clients' collective culture.

Language use is important. Abstract 'middle-class' therapeutic discourse, as a product of the dominant majority culture, is likely to be inappropriate when addressing people from ethnic minority groups. Any reference to psychotherapeutic terms such as 'fantasy', 'projection', 'transference' and 'denial' may be experienced (as indeed it may by many Western people) as clinically 'foreign', over-intellectualized, and as a cold, detached, superior stance. Humanistic terminology like 'being real' or 'phoney' is also unlikely to be helpful. The counsellor can try to match the cultural and cognitive manner of the client, initially 'modelling' culturally flexible behaviour and enabling and encouraging different experimental forms of expression.

The therapeutic relationship

The client of a minority group can establish and integrate a positive identity within the therapeutic relationship where the white counsellor acknowledges the difficulties encountered by the client through prejudice and discrimination against themselves and their community. To form a working alliance with the counsellor, the client needs to feel that they can trust the counsellor's integrity by experiencing them as genuine, sincere and open to the client's perceptual world and the complexities of another culture. At the same time, the counsellor, if a white person, is a member of the race/culture that discriminates against that of the client. As a representative of a majority 'host' culture, and as a person who views themselves as a helper, a white counsellor may adopt an attitude which is in denial of oppression. In an attempt to promote a positive white identity the counsellor may cut off from certain aspects of themselves and project other aspects that they hope are more acceptable and productive. The relationship with the client of different racial or cultural origin may be restricted by feelings of guilt, shame and fear of 'difference'. Both the white counsellor and the black client are psychologically impoverished when inequality is upheld rather than addressed. Personal development and consciousness raising are the fundamental tasks of those who accept that as advantaged members of society they bear some responsibility for the oppression of disadvantaged groups.

In an article in *Counselling* called 'Working with Issues of Race in Counselling', Aisha Dupont-Joshua stresses the importance of personal developmental work in transcultural counselling, in understanding the dynamics of the relationship:

> Until white counsellors start owning their whiteness as part of their identity, and working on their racial identity development, they will be ill equipped to work across cultures, because their attitudes, who they are and what they represent to their black clients, are vital ingredients in the counselling relationship ... As counsellors we are mirrors to our clients and to keep our mirrors clear we have continually to work on ourselves and our attitudes. Our attitudes on how we perceive 'the other' are very largely based on how we see ourselves and what we have been taught is socially normal.

Dupont-Joshua points out that the black person's view of what it means to be a 'normal' white person is likely to be that, as part of the majority, they are used to 'being historically dominant, having access to privilege, being considered aesthetically attractive, being in control'. These factors need to be acknowledged in the relationship so that the black client can comfortably air their views in an exploration of self-identity.

The counsellor needs to demonstrate to the client a willingness to engage enthusiastically and fully in the relationship, which involves confronting and working with cultural issues. Differences in belief and value systems – for example, notions of dependency, individuality, emphasis on history taking or the abstinent stance (blank screen) of the counsellor – may be totally puzzling and disorientating to clients who do not originate from the dominant culture. Counsellors need to be aware of what has been termed the 'myth of sameness' whereby they posit caring, respectful 'core conditions' – positive regard, empathy, genuineness and warmth – as the only requisites for working cross-culturally and ignore other methods of engagement. Areas of difference are covered by a benevolent 'we are all the same under the skin', which may mask uncomfortable feelings of awkwardness or hostility. Counsellors need to demonstrate actively to their clients that they take responsibility for their own historically held attitudes by conveying a willingness to examine difficult cultural conflicts and prejudices within themselves.

Patricia d'Ardenne and Aruna Mahtani (*Transcultural Counselling in Action*, p. 37) suggest practical issues for the counsellor to consider:

  how your cultural or racial background affects your attitude to your client;

  whether or not you see the client's culture or race as a cause of the present problem;

  whether or not you see the client's culture as part of the solution to the present problem;

  whether or not you can accept, acknowledge and understand your client's culture;

  whether or not your expectations about the client's culture affect the counselling outcome;

  whether or not your cultural prejudice has a bearing on the counselling relationship;

  whether or not any cultural prejudice or racism experienced by you affects the counselling relationship.

Transference

Transference in the usual sense of the term occurs when the client brings unresolved issues from past experiences with significant others (usually parents) into the relationship with the counsellor. In the counselling relationship the counsellor 'becomes' the parent, giving the client an opportunity to re-experience and work through the original complex emotions. When the client is from a minority culture the usual parent–child transference is likely to occur but another dimension of transference will also occur, that of the counsellor representing the oppressor/dominant or rejecting 'parent'. The parent in this cultural context may also be the 'state', society, colonialism or some other dominant force that has been experienced as racist and rejecting. A white counsellor, for example, may at times be experienced by a black client as a white oppressor who regards themselves as superior. Since the counsellor is experienced as racist at this point in therapy (in fact, the counsellor is likely to be experienced as potentially racist from the onset), the counsellor needs to draw attention to and willingly face these feelings with the client.

What follows is an example from my own experience.

A young male client (20 years of age) of mixed-race origin whom I shall call L came for counselling because of what behaviourists call a compulsive–obsessive disorder. The training I had at this point was an integrated mix of psychodynamic with Rogerian values. I knew very little about cognitive-behavioural theory and technique, so rather than dabble I decided to stay with the approach I was familiar with. He was spending up to four hours a day washing and cleansing himself. He locked himself in the bathroom for sometimes two hours at a time. Without going into too much unnecessary detail, I will outline some of the language and imagery he used in relating to me in the client–counsellor relationship. His self-image was such that he thought that people perceived him as 'thick' – he talked slowly as if deliberating and he understood this mannerism to stem from early school days when he sought to extend his teacher's attention. It became a habit that backfired on him (one wonders if the teacher's attitude was racist). The pupils at the school he had attended were almost exclusively white and he was always the only child of mixed race in his class. His appearance was akin to his mother's African–Caribbean background. People regarded him as black. He was very confused about his identity. He described himself as neither black nor white – and as having 'no chance' with women. He treated his mother with disdain.

My hunch was that we were working with issues (amongst others) relating to race and internalized racism, manifest in his negative self-image. His black origins were a source of self-disgust but the point was that it was 'learned' disgust – a product of (probably covert) racism. Imagery that he used also spoke of despair, loneliness and unexpressed anger. One example was a repeated image of himself spinning for ever in time, all alone, in a 'black void'. He had described the time he took cleansing himself as 'filling in time' because he said each day went on for ever. Since early childhood he had experienced trouble making friends, being convinced nobody would like him. Focusing on the imagery of the friendless, helpless state of being in a black void gave an opportunity for us to explore his experiences of rejection from both black and white groups of people. His mother had exclusively white friends and regarded other black people as 'nosy' and 'gossips' (she may have suffered negative internalizations from both black and white sources because of marrying a white man).

L's view of young black men was that they were 'fast talking' (unlike himself) and 'a lot of trouble'. When I asked him if he saw himself as a lot of trouble, he said, 'No, cos I never do anything – I stay in.' His washing regimes could be not just a way of expressing self-disgust or washing the 'black away', but also a way of keeping himself occupied or out of trouble. My attempts to address his white origins were usually deflected. An opportunity to bring into this the issue of having a white counsellor came when L came to a session following a job interview. He was surprised to find that the interviewer was a black woman, who reminded him of his mother. He talked about his problems in getting a job, which led to discussion of how black people are usually allocated menial work. During this session I asked him what it felt like having a white female counsellor. This was not the first time I had posed the question but it was the first time that he was able to make use of it. He replied that he initially expected me (like others) to dismiss him as a black person. He also had the opinion that a counsellor would be a white middle-class 'do gooder' with no sense of what it was like to be of mixed race.

This was a turning point in the counselling work because I realized that I had been colluding with L's denial of his white identity for two reasons; firstly, because it brought up my own uncomfortable feelings of being part of the majority (dominant) race/culture and, secondly, because he looked black. I saw him as predominantly black. I didn't consider myself racist but clearly there were race issues here.

Similar mistakes can be made when as white counsellors we view other Europeans – or, other white people – as culturally similar. One of my first clients as a new counsellor was a young Eastern European woman. Unaware as I was at the time of the significance of cultural issues, I missed a relevant source of understanding her experiences and her problems. I would now, being more experienced as a counsellor and I hope more culturally aware, be more interested in her experiences as a person who was brought up in a communist totalitarian state where there were (she told me) police guards in her university on the look-out for subversive student behaviour. This and other culture-related factors had connections with problems she was having relating to people she was mixing with in England, including myself in the client–counsellor relationship. She felt 'watched' and criticized, and wanted to run away from responsibilities. While I was at the time sufficiently aware of her abandoning mother as a source of transference, I missed a second potential source, that of counsellor as representing the cold observer of the totalitarian state she had lived under.

The forming and maintenance of a therapeutic relationship depends on finding ways of working together that are mutually agreed. Culturally sensitized counsellors are flexible up to a point, but boundaries need to be clearly outlined at the beginning – for example, timekeeping, location and duration of therapy and ways of working can be agreed. The client from another culture may want to show appreciation of the counsellor by extending an invitation to visit their home or meet outside the counselling setting. Situations like this can be avoided if the client has been given clear guidelines concerning boundaries and the reasons why they exist (e.g. issues of convenience, availability, protection of the client and maintenance of the therapeutic 'role') at the onset of the therapy. A fear of being 'politically incorrect', being unconsciously prejudiced and being regarded as racist can seriously undermine the counsellor and the counselling work. But the discomfort experienced because of being part of a privileged group is to some extent a 'tables turned' situation that can give the counsellor a sense of the client's culturally biased experiences (e.g. of being judged/ stereotyped by race or culture, or on presumptions and assumptions of the other culture). The counsellor needs to explore their own cultural and identity difference. A willing attitude is conveyed when the counsellor acknowledges the client's angry feelings with regard to racist attitudes and discrimination, giving the client permission to express the injustices and their effects, and is prepared to look at issues like stereotyping, power and inequality.

A creative integrative approach

Counselling across race and culture requires an openness, flexibility and spontaneity on the part of the counsellor. The counsellor should be prepared to learn from the client's world and focus on what is important in their life. For example, it may be possible to work with other traditional philosophies or healing methods; acknowledging that beneath the client's cultural identity are beliefs and assumptions that sometimes merge with and sometimes challenge the counsellor's own. Cross-cultural counselling may be delivered through individual or couple therapy, family or group counselling and may employ specific interventions (e.g. relaxation training or empathic reflection). The counsellor must consider the cultural appropriateness of what is being offered and at the same time be prepared to adopt an integrative approach, drawing on ideas and techniques from existing theories or therapies including those which hold meaning for the client.

Concept of self

In white-dominated Western cultures a dualistic view of reality predominates. Western perceptions of reality, dominated by Cartesian thought, assume that there is a sharp distinction between mind and body. Eastern thought, on the other hand, senses reality holistically, generally perceiving body, mind and spirit as being aspects of a single unified reality. The healing process is duly directed towards the whole person – body, mind and spirit. Healing can be a combination of various forms; for instance, yoga, chanting, meditation, relaxation techniques and diet. In contrast, counselling belongs to the individualist view of 'mental' cure in the form of Freud's 'talking cure'.

Differences in outlook are also evident ontologically, in views of selfhood and the sense of self. While Western thought views the person in an individualistic sense – each person is seen as an autonomous separate individual with strong boundaries – non-Western collectivist cultures understand selfhood as being created and re-created through relationship, connectedness and interaction – the self exists in and through these. Individualistic concepts such as 'autonomy' and 'achievement' may appear alien to someone socialized by a collectivist culture where social systems, and religious commitment, drive personal decision. Conversely, virtues such as 'honour' or 'duty' may seem restrictively traditional to the individualist mind-set of modernity.

Past/present orientation

A similar tension sometimes exists between individualist and collectivist notions of time. Western society is generally more 'future and goal orientated'. 'Progress' has become an icon, the past is dismissed as 'archaic' and 'old fashioned' and time is perceived as linear, forward looking and clock orientated, work and leisure being divided into distinct parts of the day or week. Collectivist cultures, on the other hand, are more likely to be 'past orientated', with a sense of continuity pervading the present. Ideas, values and belief systems may be expressed through oral tradition and parents, grandparents and ancestors in general are often honoured and revered. Time is circular with less distinction between work and play. Leisure is a largely individualist secular notion. Muslims, for example, pray six times a day, preceded by washing their hands, feet and other parts of the body. During the festival of Ramadan eating is forbidden between sunrise and sunset. The tension created by these different perceptions of time is sometimes manifest in the way humanistic and psychodynamic counsellors may invite the client to 'shake off the shackles' of past influences and internalized values/roles of past generations – to challenge, confront and even reject authoritarian and parental demands – a process which may seem anathema to a client who has been immersed in a reverential attitude to the past.

Belonging

Just as concepts of time may differ in cultures, so may attitudes of spiritually belonging to a specific place. In the modern, mobile societies of the industrialized world community is no longer at the heart of society. A cultural identity is inextricably affected by past and origins, and an awareness of a homeland or the homeland of the forefathers. Few people in the huge cities where most of the world's population now live interact within the same community – dominated by extended families, clan or tribe – as their grandparents did. For counsellors brought up in this mobile world where pride is taken in being part of a European community or the ability to 'globe hop', the acute sense of place experienced by the collectivist sense of reality – the profound emotional, social and spiritual attachment to a particular place – may be difficult to grasp. Also, counsellors need to be aware of the relationship between personal problems and political socioeconomic realities. It is necessary to embrace the historical perspective when making sense of current experience. The way that someone feels may be not only a response to what is happening now, but in part a reaction to loss or trauma that occurred in earlier generations. A client must be understood as being a participating member of a culture and not perceived purely in psychological terms. The identity, experience and emotions of the client must be set against the backdrop of their cultural milieu. Feelings of loss and expropriation (the taking away of property or state); the legacies of an imperialist or colonialist past need acknowledging. Sometimes it is appropriate that the counsellor helps the client to explore the possibilities of political or social activity as a means of coming to terms with their heritage.

Religion

There is no single concept of 'normal' that applies across all persons, situations and cultures. Mainstream concepts of mental health and illness must be expanded to incorporate the religious and spiritual dimension which influences the lives of those brought up in Hindu, Muslim, Sikh, Jewish and Rastafarian and other cultures. It is important to take a flexible and respectful attitude towards other therapeutic values, beliefs and traditions. Counsellors must assume that their own view of reality is culturally based. Counselling theories have been developed from white Western therapists (mainly European and American), inextricably influenced by Judeo–Christian morality. Ideas of morality formed by religious belief may differ between the majority culture and minority cultures.

Institutionalized racism

One area where good practice in counselling is evident is the willingness to talk about cultural issues and not succumb to race-avoidance or race-neutralizing interventions. It is essential to acknowledge the reality of institutionalized and overt racism and discrimination in the lives of clients. Power imbalances between therapist and client may reflect the imbalance of power between the cultural communities to which they belong. The failure to address the racial context of the client's concerns will restrict or destroy the client's ability to express themselves. Race avoidance may lead to the client concurring with the counsellor's definition, thereby diminishing their rights of autonomy. Counsellors must acknowledge that institutionalized racism permeates many agencies – the police, education and health. To quote the MacPherson Report (1999):

> ... the collective failure of an organisation to provide an appropriate and professional service to people because of their colour, culture, or ethnic origin is institutionalised racism. It can be seen or detected in processes, attitudes and behaviour which amount to discrimination through unwilling prejudice, ignorance, thoughtlessness and racist stereotyping which disadvantages minority ethnic people.

Most counsellors are white. There are relatively few black counsellors or black clients. It is essential for counsellors from all backgrounds to be aware of their own stereotypes, attitudes and feelings in relation to people from other ethnic groups. Many black clients will have experienced institutionalized and overt racism and will carry the scars of these experiences into the therapeutic relationship. As part of any training programme, therefore, counsellors need to confront and challenge their own prejudices and ignorance. This may be a very painful process as trainees may find themselves challenging their own core beliefs and assumptions as well as those of their peer group and families.

In order to meet the needs of ethnic minority clients, counselling agencies must ensure that their services are accessible to all; for instance, by being willing to work in ethnic minority community locations. As well as publicity drives they could employ outreach workers, hire bilingual or bicultural staff and provide crèche facilities. Issues of ethnic representation of staff need to be addressed, as well as the setting up of agencies which are run by and for members of specific groups. It needs to be acknowledged, for example, that Muslim women might be better placed to counsel Muslim women clients; likewise male Rastafari counsellors might be the most appropriate people to counsel Rastafari men.

The following is a first-hand account of experiences in training and working as a counsellor by a black Rastafari woman called Morowa.

At the start of my training I was very sure of wanting to recognize where I stand in my concept of my own identity. I fiercely wanted to protect and retain my identity, which I've struggled to gain through my own awareness and appreciation of the 'Black Consciousness Movement' of the 1960s and the Rastafari movement of which I became part of in the later 1970s.

I was conscious that in the area of counselling, which is so under-represented by Black people – less so Rastafari women – that I didn't want to be a 'token Black' or be considered as 'one of them', as a Black person who becomes part of a profession that is viewed as 'white' (such as counselling) is often perceived to be.

I was also aware of assumptions I had of not wanting the 'white' psychology to 'mess up my brain'. The structure of the course wasn't culturally biased and I was one of only two Black 'counsellors' (the other was a male) out of a number of twenty. This number seems to reflect the percentage of potential Black counsellors entering the area of work.

At times, in isolation within group discussion, when I raised issues around race, it was often met with great feelings of unease; even so there were usually a few members who were willing to engage with it by working with feelings it evoked in them and with the dynamics it created.

Through my experience of working in a women's counselling service I've seen the lack of Black women who use this form of therapy as a healing process. The agency opened twelve years ago to address the issues around inequality, making the 'white middle-class service' available to women who normally would not have been able to make use of this form of therapy. Working psychodynamically, it offers free counselling to women who may be thought of as being 'disadvantaged' by issues such as class, gender, race, sexual orientation and mental illness. When I began working there I was the first and only Black counsellor. This realization came with ambivalent feeling. I also experienced feelings of isolation and it seemed I was expected to be the 'expert', have all the ideas and answers to anything to do with 'recruiting' Black women to the service.

Almost immediately I experienced feelings around my worthiness to be there in the agency; e.g. 'I cannot fail', 'Am I good enough, as good as the white counsellors?' I felt many of these feelings were actually to do with my limited experience of the 'real counselling relationship'.

How much was really internalized racism? I had to struggle with the reality of being a 'novice' and detach it from any negative internalized feelings. I also had a feeling of responsibility around being 'good enough', as a failure on my path would, I assumed, affirm any negative feelings that might be around (from managerial staff) regarding the ability of a Black person within this field of work and therefore influence any future developments.

As a Black counsellor I feel a satisfaction that I can be part of the process of the 'provision of choice' within the service in trying to encourage and accommodate people of my race and culture.

I feel nevertheless that there is no point making a service accessible for ethnic minority groups if the theoretical approach remains rigid and doesn't continue to strive to become flexible to account for cultural needs of such users. Failure to do so would be refusing to acknowledge that there are differences between races due to their strict cultural roots.

Morowa Selassie, 1998

Summary

A summary of the considerations for crosscultural practice:

■ The counsellor's awareness of their own cultural bias and values.

■ The counsellor's willingness to engage with the client's frame of reference/world view.

■ Learning about your client's culture – don't rely on your client to inform you.

■ The possibility of internalized oppression and self-rejection wherein the work would include affirming a positive self/ group identity.

■ The counsellor's ability (and that of the organization or agency providing a service) to be flexible, adaptive and open to self-challenge, e.g. offering a matched counsellor or interpreter.

■ Becoming familiar with specialist literature on working with particular client groups.

■ The acknowledgement of societal inequality and discrimination as well as the subjective reality of the client.

■ Cultural transference – the significance of the counsellor's identity for the client and power inequalities e.g. 'I wonder what it is like for you to be telling this to a white person'.

■ The counsellor's ability to be non-defensive in exploring their own racism, which many regard as an inevitability of those who are members of the majority culture.

RESOURCES

Contact details

Asia

Hong Kong

Hong Kong Professional Counselling Association
c/o Student Development Services, City University of Hong Kong,
83 Tatchee Avenue, Hong Kong

Australasia

Australia

Australian Association of Marriage and Family Counsellors
Mrs Sadie Henschkle, Secretary, 12 Payton Avenue, Dernancourt,
SA 5075, Australia

Australian Institute of Professional Counsellors
Tel. (07) 3857 2277 Fax (07) 3857 2644
Head Office: PO Box 260, Lutwyche, Qld 4030, Australia
Suite 15, Lutwyche City Shopping Centre, 543 Lutwyche Road,
Lutwyche, Qld 4030, Australia

Sydney Counselling Service
http://www.sydney counselling.com.au/home.htm
Sydney Counselling Centre, DRA-Assoc. No. Y16282-24, Level
3, 12 Thomas Street, Chatswood, NSW 2067, Australia

University Counselling Service
Tel. 2 692 3484
University of Sydney, NSW 2006, Australia

New Zealand

New Zealand Association of Counsellors
Tel. 09 267 5973
17 Corokia Place, Manukau City, Auckland, New Zealand

Europe

European Association for Counselling
Tel./Fax 00 353 1661 7279
PO Box 6699, Dublin 2, Eire

Eire

Irish Association for Counselling and Therapy
Tel. +353 (0)1 230 0061
8 Cumberland Street, Dun Laoghaire, Co. Dublin, Ireland;
contact: Grace O'Donnell

France

Valerie Davidson
Tel./Fax +33 (0) 5 53293167
Fournet, 24220 Allas les Mines, France

Great Britain

British Association for Counselling
Info. line 0788 578328 Office Tel. 0788 550899 Fax 0788 562189
1 Regent Place, Rugby CV21 2PJ, Great Britain

Counselling
http://www.counsellingcharity.freeserve.co.uk/
Registered charity supplying counselling information in the UK,
including: free listing of all colleges offering counselling courses,
free listing of all counsellors trained in the UK, database of
counselling courses, counselling vacancies.

North America

Canada

British Columbia Council of Clinical Counsellors
Tel. 0101 604 595 4448

Canadian Guidance and Counselling Association
Tel. 613 230 4236 Fax 613 230 5884
00 220 Laurier Avenue West, Ottawa, Ontario, Canada K1P 5Z9

The Counselling Foundation of Canada
http://www.counselling.net/mainpage
92 Avenue Road, Second Floor, Toronto, ON, M5R 2H2, Canada

United States of America

American Counseling Association
http://www.counseling.org/
Fax 7038230252
The ACA's on-line information includes: ACA News, Employment,
Government Relations, Information for Consumers/Media, ACA
Branches and Divisions. Members of ACA can access information
on expanding skills, ACA World Conference, Student in Counselor
Education, Resources and Books.
ACA Members' Services Tel. 800.347.6647, ext. 222

Council for Accreditation of Counseling and Related Educational
Programs (CAC/REP)
Tel. 703/823-9800, ext. 301 Fax 703/823-1581
e-mail CACREP@aol.com
5999 Stevenson Avenue, Alexandra, VA 22304, USA

American Association of Marriage and Family Counselors
255 Yale Avenue, Claremont, CA 917711, USA

Council for Accreditation of Counseling
Tel. 904 392 0733
University of Florida, 1215 Norman Hall, Gainsville, FA 32605,
USA

Visual aids resources

Concord Video and Film Council

201 Felixstowe Road, Ipswich IP3 9BJ
Tel. 01473 76012 Fax 01473 274531

This company will supply their catalogue, *Counselling and
Psychotherapy*, which details videos available covering a range of
topics; for example, group therapy, grief therapy, counselling the
drug abuser, Carl Rogers in action (conducting encounter groups,
counselling an individual, facilitating a group). Also offers the
'Three Approaches to Psychotherapy' series; Part 1 is a film of
Carl Rogers, Frederic Perls and Albert Ellis individually engaging
in therapy in their different orientations with a client named Gloria.

SUGGESTED FURTHER READING

Chapter 1

Clarkson P. *The Therapeutic Relationship*. London, Whurr: 1995.
Khan, M. *Between Therapist and Client: The New Relationship*. New York, W.H. Freeman & Co.: 1991.

Chapter 3

Rogers, C.R. *Client-centred Therapy*. Boston MA, Houghton Mifflin: 1955.
Rogers, C.R. *On Becoming a Person*. London, Constable: 1974.
Kirchenbaum, H. and Land Henderson, V. (eds) *The Carl Rogers Reader 1*. London, Constable: 1990, pp. 323–5.

Chapter 4

Casement, P. *On Learning from the Patient*. London, Routledge: 1990.
Egan, G. *The Skilled Helper: A Systematic Approach to Effective Helping* (3rd ed.). Belmont CA, Brooks/Cole: 1986.
Kirchenbaum, H. and Land Henderson, V. (eds) *The Carl Rogers Reader 1*. London, Constable: 1990.
Nelson-Jones, R. *Practical Counselling and Helping Skills* (2nd ed.). London, Cassell: 1988.
Rogers, C.R. *A Way of Being*. Boston MA, Houghton Mifflin: 1980.

Chapter 5

Jacobs, M. *Still Small Voice: An Introduction to Pastoral Counselling*. London, SPCK: 1982.
Nelson-Jones, R. *Human Relationship Skills: Training and Self Help*. London, Holt, Rinehart and Winston: 1986.
Nelson-Jones, R. *Practical Counselling and Helping Skills* (2nd ed.). London, Cassell: 1988.

Chapter 6

Assagioli, R. *Transpersonal Development: The Dimension Beyond Psychosynthesis*. London, Harper Collins: 1991.

Dickson, A. *A Woman in Your Own Right – Assertiveness and You*. London, Quartet: 1982.

Jung, C.G. *Man and his Symbols*. New York, Doubleday: 1964.

Luft, J. and Ingham H. *The Johari Window: A Graphic Model for Interpersonal Relations*. Berkeley, University of California Press: 1955.

Ozaniec, N. *Teach Yourself Meditation*. London, Hodder and Stoughton: 1997.

Sheppard, L. *Wake up to your Dreams*. London, Blandford: 1994.

Wilson, P. *The Calm Technique – Simple Meditation Methods that Really Work*. Wellingborough, Thorsons: 1987.

Wills, P. *Teach Yourself Visualisation*. London, Hodder and Stoughton: 1996.

Chapter 7

Bion, W.R. *Experiences in Groups*. London, Tavistock Publications: 1961.

Carkhuff, R.R. *The Art of Helping*. Amherst MA, Human Resource Development Press: 1972.

Clarkson, P. *The Therapeutic Relationship*. London, Whurr: 1995.

Hinshelwood, R.D. *What Happens in Groups*. London, Free Association Books: 1988.

Ivey. A.E. and Galvin, M. 'Microcounseling: a Metamodel for Counseling, Therapy, Business and Medical Interviews', in Larson, D. (ed.) *Teaching Psychological Skills, Models for Giving Psychology Away*. Monterey CA, Brooks/Cole: 1984.

McLeod, J. *An Introduction to Counselling* (2nd ed.). Buckingham, OUP: 1998.

Chapter 8

Section 1: The Psychodynamic Approach

Bowlby, J. *The Making and Breaking of Affectionate Bonds*. Tavistock/Routledge: 1979.

Dryden, W. (ed.) *Individual Therapy: A Handbook*. Buckingham, OUP: 1990.

Erikson, E. *Childhood and Society*. London, Palladin: 1977.

Freud, A. *The Ego and Mechanism of Defence* (rev. ed.). London, Hogarth Press: 1968.

Jacob, M. *Psychodynamic Counselling in Action*. London, Sage: 1988.

Jacob, M. *Still Small Voice*. London, SPCK: 1982.

Jacob, M. *Swift to Hear*. London, SPCK: 1985.

Jacob, M. *The Presenting Past*. London, Harper and Row: 1986.

Jacobi, J. and Hull, R.F.C. (eds) *Psychological Reflections*: Princeton, Bollingen Series; New Jersey, Princeton University Press: 1973.

Jung, C.G. *Memories, Dream, Reflections* (rev. ed.). New York, Pantheon Books: 1973.

Jung, C.G. (Read, H., Fordham, M., Adler, G., eds; Hull, R.F.C., trans.) *The Collected Works of C.G. Jung*. XX Series (Bollingen), New Jersey, Princeton University Press: 1953–71.

Malan, D.H. *Individual Psychotherapy and the Science of Psychodynamics*. Oxford, Butterworths: 1979. (Chapter 10, 'The Dialogue of Psychotherapy and the Two Triangles')

Segal, H. (Masud, M., Khan, R., eds) *Introduction to the Work of Melanie Klein*. London, Hogarth Press: 1973.

Winnicott, D.W. (Winnicott, C., Shepherd, R., Davis, M., eds) *Home is where We Start from: Essays by a Psychoanalyst*. Harmondsworth, Penguin: 1986.

Winnicott, D.W. *Playing and Reality*. Harmondsworth, Pelican: 1974.

Section 2: The Humanistic/Person-centred Approach

Khan, M. *Between Therapist and Client: The New Relationship*. New York, W.H. Freeman & Co. 1991.

Kirschenbaum, H. and Land Henderson, V. (eds.) *The Carl Rogers Reader 1*. London, Constable: 1990.

Mearns, D. *Developing Person Centred Counselling*. London, Sage: 1994.

Mearns, D. and Thorne, B.J. *Person-centred Counselling in Action*. London, Sage: 1988.

Nye, R.D. *Three Psychologies: Perspectives from Freud, Skinner and Rogers* (4th ed.). Belmont CA, Brooks/Cole Counselling: 1992.

Rogers, C.R. *Client-centred Therapy*. London, Constable: 1951.

Rogers, C.R. *Carl Rogers on Encounter Groups*. Harmondsworth, Penguin: 1969.

Rogers, C.R. *On Becoming a Person*. Boston, Houghton Mifflin: 1961.

Section 3: The Behavioural/Cognitive-behavioural Model

Bandura, A. *Social Learning Theory*. Englewood Cliffs, NJ, Prentice Hall: 1977.

Beck, A.T. *Cognitive Therapy and the Emotional Disorders*. Harmondsworth, Penguin: 1976.

Beck, A.T. and Weishaard, M. *Cognitive Therapy*, in Freeman, A., Simon, K. M., Beutler, L.E. and Arkowitz, H. (eds) *Comprehensive Handbook of Cognitive Therapy*. New York, Plenum Press: 1989.

Ellis, A. *Reason and Emotion in Psychotherapy*. New York, Lyle Stuart: 1962.

Hock, R.R. *Forty Studies that Changed Psychology*. Englewood Cliffs, NJ, Prentice Hall: 1992.

Kanfer, A. and Goldstein, A. (eds) *Helping People Change* (3rd ed.). New York, Pergamon: 1986.

Marzillier, R.L. and Hall, J. (eds) *What is Clinical Psychology?* (2nd ed.). OUP: 1992.

Meichenbaum, D. 'Cognitive-behaviour Modification', in Kanfer, A. and Goldstein, A. (eds) op. cit.

Trower, P., Casey, A. and Dryden, W. *Cognitive-behavioural Counselling in Action*. London, Sage.

Wessler, R.L. 'Affect and Nonconscious Processes in Cognitive Psychotherapy', in Dryden, W. and Trower, P. (eds) *Developments in Cognitive Psychotherapy*. London, Sage: 1988.

Chapter 9

Freud, S. *The Essentials of Psychoanalysis. The Definitive Collection of Sigmund Freud's Writing*. London, Hogarth Press: 1986.

Hock, R.R. *Forty Studies that Changed Psychology*. Englewood Cliffs, NJ, Prentice Hall: 1992. (Anna Freud's paper on her father's work on 'defences')

Reber, A.S. *The Penguin Dictionary of Psychology*. Harmondsworth, Penguin: 1985.

Segal, H. (Masud, M., Khan, R., eds) *Introduction to the Work of Melanie Klein*. London, Hogarth Press: 1973.

Chapter 10

Bowlby, J. *Separation: Anxiety and Anger* (vol. 2 of *Attachment and Loss*). New York, Basic Books: 1973.

Novaco, R.W. *Anger Control*. Toronto, Lexington: 1975.

Novaco, R.W. 'Anger and Coping with Stress', in Foreyt, J.P. and Rathjen, D.P. (eds) *Cognitive Behavior Therapy*. New York, Plenum: 1978.

Polster, E. and Polster, M. *Gestalt Therapy Integrated*. New York, Vintage: 1974.

Chapter 11

Grief

Bowlby, J. *Loss, Sadness and Depression* (vol. 3 of *Attachment and Loss*). London, Penguin: 1980.

Kubler-Ross, E. *Death – the Final Stage of Growth*. Englewood Cliffs, NJ, Prentice Hall: 1975.

Levine, S. *Meetings at the Edge – Dialogues with the Grieving and the Dying*. New York, Anchor: 1984.

Worden, W.J. *Grief Counselling and Grief Therapy – a Handbook for the Mental Health Practitioner* (2nd ed.). London, Routledge: 1991.

Suicide

Berent, I. *The Algebra of Suicide*. New York, Human Sciences: 1981.

Lester, G. and Lester, D. *Suicide: The Gamble with Death*. Englewood Cliffs, NJ, Prentice Hall: 1971.

Self-harm

Harrison, D. *Vicious Circles: Good Practices in Mental Health*. London, University of North London: 1996.

Spandler, H. *Who's Hurting who? – Young People, Self Harm and Suicide*. Manchester, England, 42nd Street: 1996.

Johnstone, L. 'Self Harm – Lucy Johnstone Interviews Diane Harrison', *Openmind*, vol. 68: April/May 1994, pp. 20–1.

Abuse

Briere, J. *Child Abuse Trauma: A Theory and Treatment of the Lasting Effects*. London, Sage: 1992.

Dale, P. 'Counselling Adults who Were Abused as Children', in Palmer, S. and McMahon, G. (eds) *Handbook of Counselling* (2nd ed.). London, Routledge: 1997.

Davies, J.M. and Frawley, M.G. *Testing the Adult Survivor of Childhood Sexual Abuse: A Psychoanalytical Perspective*. New York, Basic Books: 1994.

Forward, S. *Toxic Parents: Overcoming the Legacy of Parental Abuse*. London, Bantam Press: 1990.

Masson, J. *Against Therapy: Emotional Tyranny and the Myth of Psychological Healing*. London, Fontana: 1990.

Miller, A. *Banished Knowledge: Facing Childhood Injuries*. New York, Doubleday: 1990.

Chapter 12

d'Ardenne, P. and Mahtani, A. *Transcultural Counselling in Action*. London, Sage: 1989.

Dupont-Joshua, A. 'Working with Issues of Race in Counselling', *Counselling*, vol. 8, no. 4: 1997, pp. 282–4.

Lago, C. and Thomson, J. *Race, Culture and Counselling*. Buckingham, OUP: 1996.

McLeod, J. *An Introduction to Counselling* (2nd ed.). Buckingham, OUP: 1998.

Pedersen, P. 'Multicultural Counseling', in Brislin, R.W. and Yoshida, T. (eds) *Improving Intercultural Interactions: Modules for Cross-cultural Training Programs*. Newbury Park, CA, Sage: 1994.

INDEX

abuse 11, 240–7
  sexual 11, 64, 188, 234, 235, 240, 241, 243–4
acceptance 19, 32, 38–9
acting out 197
active imagination 101
active listening 9, 43
Adler, Alfred 148
adverse stimulus 52
affect 186–7
age of counsellors 22
alternative therapists 24
analytical perspective 1, 99
anger 203–17
  appropriate and inappropriate 209–12
  chart 208
  Gestalt techniques for dealing with 209, 210
  and the psychodynamic perspective 214–16
  and self-harm 235, 236, 237
  and the trainee counsellor 203–6
  and video work 212–14
anima/animus 150–1
anxiety 175, 194
  and negative self-statements 184–5
  and systematic desensitization 173, 176–9
archetypes 149–50
art, sublimation in 196–7
Assagioli, Roberto 88, 99
assertiveness training 92–4, 203, 208
assessment on training courses 116–19
attachment theory 135–6, 190

Bandura's social learning theory 170–1
Beck's cognitive distortion model 180–1
behavioural therapy 1, 124, 167–88
  and child development 170–2
  problems tackled by 172–3

  and self-harm 238–9
  and the therapeutic relationship 179–80
  treatment 173–9
  see also cognitive–behavioural therapy
bio-energetics 196
Black counsellors 263–5
body language 51–4, 67, 92
  client 54–5, 70
  counsellor 51–4
  and practice sessions 77, 81, 83
borderline personality disorder 197–8
Bowlby's attachment theory 135–6, 190
brief counselling work 4–5, 69

Casement, Patrick 62
catharsis 198
challenging the client 65–8, 70–1
Clarkson, Petrushka 122
client-centred therapy see person-centred therapy
codes of ethics/practice 122–3
cognitive distortion model 180–1
cognitive–behavioural therapy 66, 93, 124, 180–8, 195
  dealing with anger 207, 213–14
  and victims of abuse 246
collective unconscious 100, 150
communication skills/problems 27–9, 34–7
complexes 198
conditioning
  classical 167, 169–70, 179
  operant 167, 168–9
confidentiality 9, 11–12, 241–2
confrontation 65–8, 70–1
congruence 19, 31, 53, 77, 81, 154–5, 157–8
  and incongruence 157, 161
Core Conditions Model see Rogers, Carl
counsellor–client relationships 9–12
  and abuse 244–5
  and anger 206

in behavioural therapy 175–80
and cultural issues 253–9
and immediacy 63–5
and optimal frustration 202
person-centred approach to 159–65
psychodynamic approach to 145–6, 202
and supervision 114
and training 120, 122
transference in 62, 63, 137–43, 141, 142
countertransference 63, 138, 139
and self-harm 239
in supervision 114–15
and victims of abuse 245
crisis situations 230–1
CUE (congruence, unconditional positive
regard and empathy) 19
cultural issues 224–5, 227, 248–65

Darwin, Charles 167
death, and grief 218–28
defences 143–4, 146, 163, 189–97, 214
denial 190–1, 214
depression 41–2, 198–9, 225–6, 232
and self-harm 235
developmental psychology 128–37
displacement 191, 214
doctors 41–2
dreams 99–101, 147–8

eclecticism 119–22
Egan, Gerard 17–18
Ego 126, 130, 189–90, 192, 194
elderly people, and self-harm 236
Electra complex 129–30
Ellis, Albert 74–5, 182, 183–4
emotions, and cultural differences 250–1
empathy 9, 19, 31–2, 32, 43–4, 49–51, 156
and grief 224
and suicidal clients 233
in teacher–pupil relations 38
empty chair technique 100, 207, 226–7
Erikson's stages of psychosocial
development 130–4, 191
ethics, code of 122–3
examinations 116

families 28–9, 30–2, 176
fantasies/phantasies 200
feedback 75–8
fifty-minute therapy hour 11
fixation 191–2
free association 144, 199
Freud, S. 4, 17, 33, 90, 121, 124–30, 259

and catharsis 198
on defences 189–90
and developmental stages 128–30
on dreams 99–100
and fantasies 200
and free association 144, 199
and Jung 147, 148
and narcissism 201
and non-conscious states 187
on sublimation 196–7
on transference 137–8
and the unconscious 125–7
friends 12–13, 28, 29, 30–2

gender roles and culture 251–2
genuineness 19, 31, 32, 38, 53, 154–5
Gestalt therapy 100, 103, 124, 207, 210
Gibran, Kahlil 16
grief 218–28
group supervision 113
groupwork 108–11

helper self-sharing 68–9
holistic medicine 24
humanistic approach 1, 3, 9, 151–66, 260
and training 103, 122
see also person-centred therapy
humour 53

Id 125–6, 130, 189, 190, 192, 194, 196–7
idealization 192
immediacy 63–5, 70
impulses 199
incongruence 157, 161
individuation 148–9
integrated or eclectic approach 9, 107, 119–22
and culture 252
and victims of abuse 245–6
intellectualization 193–4
introjection 199–200, 214
intuition 50

Jacobs, Michael 144, 145, 192–3
Jewish way of mourning 224
Johari window 90–2
Jung, C.G. 16, 21, 144, 147–51
and the active imagination 101
and dreams 99, 100, 147–8
and the group matrix 110
on regression 194–5

Khan, Michael 122
Klein, Melanie 135, 136–7, 193, 196, 198
Kohut, Heinz 215, 216

Laing, R.D. 29
learned affective state (LAS) 187
life experience of counsellors 21–2
life transition 8
listening 9, 43, 82–3

McLeod, John 185–6
Malan's triangle of conflict model 139–41
Maslow's hierarchy of needs 151–3
meditation 97–9
Meichenbaum, D. 183, 184
memory, and cognitive distortion 181
metacognition 181–2
minimal responses 59, 70
mirroring 57–8, 215–16

narcissistic personality disorder 201
NATs (negative automatic thoughts) 180
negative reinforcement 168
neuroses 201

object relations theory 136–7, 144, 214
observer role 79–80, 81
    and supervision 111–15
Oedipus complex 128–9
optimal frustration 202

pair work 78–9, 80, 81–5
paranoid-schizoid position 193, 198, 200
paraphrasing 43, 46, 54, 55–7, 58, 60, 70
    practice in 83–5
part object 193, 196, 200
Pavlov's dogs 169–70
Perls, Fritz 100, 103, 245
person-centred therapy 19, 25, 53, 68, 124,
        151–66
    and defences 190
    and grief 224
    and psychodynamic counselling 166
    and the therapeutic relationship 159–65
    training techniques in 103, 121
    and victims of abuse 246
personal background of counsellors 22–3
personal therapy for counsellors 5, 20–1,
        25, 116
    and anger 203–6
phantasies/fantasies 200
phenomenological developmental history
    (PDH) 187
Piaget's cognitive development 130–1, 135
positive reinforcement 168
posture, and body language 52–3
practice 72–85
    code of 122

feedback 75–8
    role play 78–85
    self-exploratory exercises 73–5
    and theory 115–16
presenting problems of clients 7–8, 112, 218
probation officers, and counselling skills 42
professional training for counsellors 4, 6, 7
projection 115, 192–3
projective identification 193
psychodynamic approach 9, 99, 124–51,
        189, 260
    dealing with anger 214–16
    and defences 190
    and the person-centred approach 166
    and training 106–7, 120, 121–2
    and victims of abuse 245–6
psychosomatic disorder 202
psychosynthesis 99
psychotherapy and counselling 2, 3–5

qualities of the counsellor 16–19, 162–3
questions 43, 44–9, 70

race and cultural issues 224–5, 227, 248–65
racism, institutionalized 262–3
rational emotive behaviour therapy (REBT)
        124, 182–3
rationalization 193–4
reaction formation 194
reality testing 226, 231
REBT (rational emotive behaviour therapy)
        124, 182–3
regression 194–5
Reich, Wilhelm 195–6
reinforcement, in behavioural therapy 171
relapse prevention 186
relaxation exercises 88–90, 95–7, 177
religion 261–2
reparative relationship 216
repression 195–6, 214
resistance 65, 143–4, 146, 196, 215
Rogers, Carl 3, 17, 18, 19, 38, 53
    core conditions model 53, 153–6
    on empathy 51, 156
    on intuition 50
    person-centred view 156–8
    and teacher–pupil relations 38, 39
    on the therapeutic relationship 159–62,
        163
    and training 103, 106–7
role play 35, 72, 78–85, 87
roles of counselling 5–7, 16–26, 145–6

selection procedures for counsellors 18–19
self-development 86–101, 108–11
self-disclosure 68–9, 145, 222, 233
self-exploratory exercises 73–5
self-harm 233–9
sexual abuse 64, 188, 234, 235, 240, 241, 243–4
    and confidentiality 11
sexuality, and immediacy 63, 64
shadow side 147, 149, 150
silences 59, 60–2
skilled helper, view of the 17–18
skills used in counselling 43–71
    acquiring 15, 27–42
    and cultural issues 252–3
    training 72, 106–7
Skinner, B.F. 167–9
social learning theory 170–1
splitting 196, 198
stress management 94–7, 203, 208
sublimation 196–7
suicidal clients 228–33
summarizing 43, 58–9, 60, 62, 70
Superego 126, 189, 190, 192, 197
supervision during training 111–15
sympathy, and empathy 51
synchronicity 150
systematic desensitization 95, 173, 176–9, 185–6

teachers 33–41, 71
therapeutic relationship *see* counsellor–client relationships
Thorndike, E.L. 167–8

time, cultural differences in attitudes to 260
training as a counsellor 4, 5, 23–4, 24–6, 72
    courses 103–23
transactional analysis 93, 124
transference 62, 63, 137–43, 141, 142
    and cultural issues 255–6
    and the psychodynamic approach 145, 146, 214
    in supervision 114–15
transmuting internalizations 216
triads, practising skills in 79–80, 81, 107
triangle of conflict model 139–41
triangle of insight model 141–3

unconditional positive regard 19, 25, 30–1, 32, 38, 53, 155–6
unconscious 124, 125–7, 149
    collective 100, 150

video work 212–14
visualization 87–92, 121
vivas 117–18

Watson, J.B. 167, 179
Winnicott, D.W. 97, 136, 137
Wolpe, Joseph 95, 176–9
words
    and body language 53–4
    list of evocative/feeling words 61
    used by clients 60
work situations, applying counselling skills to 32–42, 70–1
working alliance 10–11
workshops 86–7